KOREA
Canada's Forgotten War

For my sons –
    Paul, Mark, and Tim –
with love and respect

Macmillan Paperback 34

KOREA
Canada's Forgotten War
John Melady

MACMILLAN OF CANADA
A Division of Canada Publishing Corporation
Toronto, Ontario, Canada

Excerpts from *Korea: The Untold Story* copyright © 1982 by Joseph
C. Goulden, reprinted by permission TIMES BOOKS/The New York
Times Book Company, Inc.

Excerpts from *The Dark Broad Seas* by Jeffry V. Brock used by
permission of The Canadian Publishers, McClelland and Stewart
Limited, Toronto.

Canadian Cataloguing in Publication Data

Melady, John, date.
    Korea: Canada's forgotten war

(Macmillan paperbacks ; 34)
Bibliography: p.
Includes index.
ISBN 0-7715-9278-7

1. Korean War, 1950–1953 – Canada.   2. Korean War, 1950–1953 –
Personal narratives, Canadian.
I. Title.

DS919.2.M44   1988   951.9′042   C87-095271-4

Originally published 1983 by Macmillan of Canada under
ISBN 0-7715-9780-0
First Macmillan Paperbacks edition 1988

Macmillan of Canada
A Division of Canada Publishing Corporation
Toronto, Ontario, Canada

Printed and bound in Canada

CONTENTS

FOREWORD

The Korean War was the first time since World War II that Canadian troops had been in action against an enemy. It is therefore an important part of Canadian history. It is appropriate to have such a distinguished author write about it.

Unfortunately, many of the stories of the Korean conflict written by non-Canadians don't mention Canadian troops at all, and one rather gains the impression from such books that our troops were not there, or that they played a very minor role. This book should set the record straight on that matter and be of great interest to Canadians and others.

Although in numbers our force was smaller than some, the Canadian reputation was most impressive and the fine soldiering record was very hard to beat. Volunteering from all across the country and from all walks of life, the force was truly representative of Canada.

John M. Rockingham, CB, CBE, DSO, ED, CD, LLD
Major-General
First Commander
25 Canadian Infantry
Brigade Group

PREFACE

A few years ago I attended the Remembrance Day ceremonies at the National War Memorial in Ottawa. What I saw impressed me: the veterans, the diplomats, the bands, the wreath-laying, the last post. Unfortunately, the prayer for fallen comrades was incomplete. The men who lost their lives in two world wars were eulogized at length, yet the young Canadians who died during the Korean campaign were barely mentioned. It is my hope that this book will help to rectify that oversight. I believe that all of us who enjoy the freedom and the bounty of this land owe them, and all the men and women who fought with them, our apologies for having forgotten them, and our gratitude for what they did for us.

While this book may not be as complete as some would wish, and may not mention every battle and every unit, I hope what I have written leaves the reader with a greater understanding of what happened in Korea, and an increased awareness of why Canadians went there. Even though I have tried to tell the story as clearly and as accurately as possible, I realize that some inaccuracies are probably inevitable, and I take full responsibility for them. Because I have never been in the armed forces, I realize that my point of view may differ somewhat from that held by the person in uniform. On the other hand, because I am not torn by loyalties to any one branch of the services, I have tried to make this account as objective as possible. I realize, however, that I could not have told the story, objective or otherwise, without a great deal of help from a number of people. Whatever merit this book may have is due in large measure to their interest and their assistance.

In addition to those men and women who are actually named in the text, I would like to extend my sincere thanks to the following: May Askew, Doug Astels, Bill and Lana Barnicke, Gord Bates, Marg Begg, Harry Birkenshaw, Dave Boyd, Jim Breckonridge, Albert Campbell, Bob Chamberlain, Frank Chapman, Lloyd Cox, Frank Donnelly, Cliff Fielding, Andy Foulds, Harris Fulford, Vance Glendinning, Jin Soo Han, Harold Holland, Al Hollett, Rod Howitt, Roy Ingram, Ross Jeffries, Doug Johnson, Frank Jones, Dick Kenzie, Joe Kim, Stan Kopinski, Ambassador Kyoo Hyun Lee, Charles Magne, Alberta McNairn, Doug Miller, Craig Mills, Herbert Norris, Stan Obodiac, Ontario Arts Council, Claude Plumpton, Mary Poechman, Bob Post, Mac Powell, Art Prince, Cyril Sharp, Colonel K. Simonson, William Smart, Gord Smith, Jack Wells, and Susan White.

I am especially grateful to Doug Gibson and Anne Holloway of Macmillan of Canada. Without their encouragement, advice, and direction, this book might never have been written.

Two other individuals contributed far more than even they may realize: Esther Parry, who not only transcribed hundreds of hours of interview tapes and typed the manuscript, but acted as an invaluable resource during the entire project; and my wife Mary, who through her love, support, and patient direction enabled me to finish what I set out to do.

John Melady
Trenton, Ontario
April 1983

PROLOGUE

The Canadian patrol moved out at dusk. Along the low ridge, then slowly down the slope and on through a narrow gap in the mine-field. One officer and fifteen men in single file — silent, cautious, their faces blackened in the gloom, their eyes and ears straining to detect the presence of an enemy who was as elusive as he was deadly.

Once outside the wire, the patrol veered slightly left and crept softly forward towards a little stream called the Nabu-ri. Somewhere near it, they spread out and settled silently, waiting in ambush for the Chinese in no-man's-land.

Several minutes passed, without a sound, without even the whisper of a mournful wind. There was no moon, and only an occasional star pierced the layers of stringy cloud, far above this war-torn land called Korea. The time was 10:30 p.m. The date: May 2, 1953.

The patrol waited, motionless, hardly daring to breathe, each man trying to ignore his racing heart and his feeling of being utterly alone.

Then, from somewhere to one side, the sense of a presence. Silence. Nothing. Yet several young Canadians turned, waited, and finally saw a dozen darkened shapes against the murky sky. But just as quickly as they appeared, the shapes vanished into nothingness. Then, some forty feet to the rear, a muffled cough.

The men in the patrol spun around and scrambled for the partial safety of a rice-paddy wall. As they did so, the deadly stutter of a burp gun shredded the silence of the Asian night. By the time the sound of the shots echoed back from the scrubby hills, a boy who was hardly a man folded into a crumpled heap and rasped his final breath into the dust of an alien land.

The patrol leader, Lieutenant G. B. Maynell, immediately called for a flare over the area. This order would be his last. As the flare arched into the warm spring night, some sixty Chinese surged towards the small Royal Canadian Regiment patrol, shot Maynell in the head, and enveloped his men in a blistering hail of fire from point-blank range. Almost half the patrol died on the spot, one or two were captured, and a tattered handful were still alive when the firefight ceased. These began groping their way towards safety. Corporal J. C. McNeil, who had assumed command after Lieutenant Maynell's death, led them.

The journey was not easy. Locating the gap in the minefield was tricky at the best of times, as one misstep could easily become one's last. Yet slowly, laboriously, and with a kind of desperate courage he perhaps did not know he had, Corporal McNeil brought the remnants of his band to the Canadian wire.

Some would get no further.

A large contingent of Chinese lay in ambush just in front of the minefield gap. A vicious skirmish followed and the unfortunate young Canadians who had just extricated themselves from one debacle were forced to flee in disarray from a second. Miraculously, a few survived and made their way through both wire and land-mines to safety.

A second RCR patrol under Lieutenant D. W. Banton went to assist McNeil and his men but stumbled into the same ambush and was also scattered. Banton himself was shot, almost before he had gone a hundred paces. Corporal W. D. Pero replaced him.

By this time, waves of Chinese were crossing no-man's-land and surging towards the Canadian lines on Hills 97 and 123. While the first of the attackers cut through the coils of barbed wire on the approaches to the slopes, Chinese artillery opened up on the Canadian defenders. As the shelling lifted, the assault troops pressed forward, tossed concussion grenades, and stormed the trenches while the young RCRs desperately tried to stand their ground.

The evening of the attack, the Canadian senior officer in Korea at the time, Brigadier Jean V. Allard, had been invited to dinner with U.S. Commander Lieutenant-General Maxwell Taylor, at Eighth Army Headquarters, some seventy-five miles south of the front.. "General Taylor had asked me to join him for dinner and then stay and return after breakfast the next morning," recalls Allard. "But I had a feeling that an attack was imminent so I excused myself and started back. I had my jeep with me and my staff car and all my communications, so I was able to listen to what was happening as I went along. As we were passing Uijongbu we heard that there was some shelling to both the left and right of the Canadian position, so I told my driver to step on it.

"It was about eleven-thirty when I got back. For about fifteen minutes after that, there was dead silence on the radio. Then suddenly the Chinese artillery opened up and the attack was on."

As the Chinese stormed over the Canadians, the defenders fought back with rifle fire, grenades, and ultimately with bayonets and gun butts. Cursing, screaming, shouted warnings, and cries of agony, all added to the horror of those terrible moments. Choking dust, smoke, the sickly-sweet odour of blood, and the stench of excrement and nausea wafted over the trenches. Finally, the Canadians retreated into their own bunkers and called for fire on their own positions.

Within seconds, mortar, tank, and artillery shelling blanketed the Canadian lines. Just as quickly, the Chinese started to fall back. Second Lieutenant E. H. Hollyer, who was there that night, recalls the scene. "At one point during the shelling, I asked for it to be lifted to investigate the situation. The enemy had sustained heavy casualties, the trenches being literally filled with them. The Chinese were rolling their dead and wounded over the lip of the hill where litter-bearers were hauling them away."

Even though the shelling continued for some time, the attackers had ended their drive. By 1:00 a.m. the Canadians started to reoccupy their former positions, while those who had to do so bandaged broken men and counted corpses. There were many of both.

1

LAND OF THE
MORNING CALM

The warm breeze blows in off the Yellow Sea, sweeps across the harbour, and seems to die among the scrubby pines along the shore. Far above, on the headland, maples shimmer in the haze of the Asian sun. The muted sound of a ship hangs in the air while dusty roses droop in the drought of a Korean summer.

At the rear of the park, clusters of people in holiday clothes gaze at the statue of American General Douglas MacArthur and stoically read the inscription below it. Then they turn to look out over the harbour to Wolmi Island, to the sparkling sea beyond. Finally, having paid homage, they trudge back to their buses and depart. The General is alone again.

Today, the massive bronze and granite MacArthur memorial dominates this park, high on a rocky promontory overlooking the bustling port of Inchon, on the west coast of the Republic of South Korea. The inscription on the memorial, in both Korean and English, tells of a wartime landing made here, a landing that had a profound effect on the course of the long and terrible holocaust that devastated this beautiful land over thirty years ago.

The landing at Inchon, conceived and planned by the five-star general some still call a genius, was an operation largely carried out by military forces of the United States of America, along with representation from other countries, all of whom were acting under the auspices of the United Nations. One of those nations was Canada.

This is the story not only of Canada's participation at Inchon, where our presence was decidedly minimal, but of our role in this conflagration on the other side of the world — in Korea, the scene of Canada's forgotten war.

What has been called the "Korean conflict" began on June 25, 1950, and ended, after months of interminable negotiations, in an armistice signed on July 27, 1953. Before peace was restored, thousands of young Canadians, some of whom had never heard of this Asian nation, and had certainly not dreamed of visiting it, would fight on the blood-soaked soil of this unfortunate land.

When the hostilities began in Korea that June morning in 1950, Canada was still recovering from the far more cataclysmic Second World War, which had ended on Tokyo Bay less than five years earlier. Not only in the larger cities such as Toronto, Montreal, and Vancouver, but in scores of smaller centres like Estevan, Corner Brook, and Camrose, men and women who had recently worn uniforms were still trying to obtain jobs, build homes, and buy cars amid a post-war shortage as severe as it was widespread.

The peacetime economy, which had so recently been geared to heavy industry and the needs of the military, faced acute transitional pains in the change from arms production. Rationing, the unpopular but necessary war measure, was not immediately suspended when the hostilities overseas ceased. This in itself led to protests by several groups, such as western ranchers and Montreal butchers. The former wanted to sell more beef to eastern outlets, while the latter grew tired of telling customers that only so much meat could be purchased. Both agitated for better prices. When rationing was finally abandoned in mid-August 1947, no one was sorry.

By 1950 the trade union movement had grown considerably. And whether he had come back to build cars or to drive trucks, the ex-soldier not only wanted to work but wanted to be paid a fair salary for his efforts. In 1942 slightly more than half a million Canadians were unionized. By 1949 the figure had doubled. In almost every union, the push for increased salaries was a first priority. Then, as more and more people found themselves with money to spend, the dream of owning a home became a reality. In virtually every city and town across the country, new "sub-divisions" were created, where houses were built in a manner not unrelated to the assembly-line type of construction used in manufacturing.

Large tracts of land were staked out and belching bulldozers carved streets, crescents, and winding avenues out of what had often been prime farmland. Sewers, water pipes, and electrical conduits were installed as the developments progressed. Then, when they were finished, places with pretentious names such as Maple Glen, Orchard View Estates, and Parkwood Luxury Village became part of the urban geography of Canada.

These idyllic settings were supposed to provide the ultimate "good life" for the people who populated them. But even though the housing lots might have been bigger, the taxes lower, and the air fresher than downtown, few suburban developments were Utopian. Generally, the houses not only were designed in much the same way, they *looked* the same. Most were dull, painted in muted colours and fronted by manicured grass. Each home housed a single family. Most had one or two children, a car, a dog, and lots of crabgrass — a weed whose eradication often supplanted the weather in the daily conversation over the back fence. Few wives worked out of the home. Instead, they formed coffee clubs, joined Parent-Teacher associations, and ran car pools for kids.

In addition to a passion for conformity in housing, Canadians embraced conservative clothing trends of the era. Young men sported "drapes" or "strides", trousers with baggy knees and narrow cuffs. Generally, a white T-shirt under a V-necked outer sweater was also part of the style. Young women greeted their dates in straight or pleated skirts and sweaters or white blouses. Both sexes wore white bobbysocks and penny loafers, shoes with a little pocket on the instep for a coin. Many males had brush cuts or, for the more adventurous, a *de rigueur* combination of both long and short hair: brush cut on top and long, greasy hair combed back on the sides. Many girls wore ponytails.

Because television broadcasting did not begin in Canada until September 1952, radio was still the primary form of home entertainment at the outset of the decade. Hit-parade songs such as "Goodnight Irene", "Mule Train", "Tennessee Waltz", and "On Top of Old Smoky" enjoyed wide popularity. Outside the home, young people — and a few who were not so young — necked through grade-D horror film; at neighbourhood drive-in theatres, or "passion pits", which were springing up outside of towns from Halifax to Nanaimo. But when teenagers were not groping in the back seat of Dad's '47 Chevy, they were bouncing around gymnasium floors, doing such wild gyrations as the Mexican Hat Dance or the Bunny Hop. Their older brothers and sisters who could prove they were over twenty-one could drink Crystal Lager out of clear bottles in foul-smelling hotel beverage rooms painted bread-mould green. There was generally no entertainment, and strippers were fallen women who might get down to pasties and a G-string. Sex was too discreet to be discussed. Even though *Playboy* magazine was first published in 1953, it was judged too scandalous for Canada and was banned here until 1957.

Perhaps that was why newspaper articles judged to be somewhat erotic were allocated far more space than they merited. For instance, young journalist Knowlton Nash, who would go on to far greater things, wrote an article on women's underclothing that the *Vancouver Sun* spread across three columns on May 5, 1951. Entitled "Built-Up Bras or Falsies Worn by Most Canadian Women Now", its contents were less than memorable.

In the world of sports, pro teams enjoyed large followings. The Toronto Maple Leafs were the most popular team in hockey, largely because of Foster Hewitt's Saturday night radio broadcasts of their games. On the gridiron, the future lacklustre Toronto Argonauts won the Grey Cup in 1950, the trophy awarded to the best football team in the country.

In the Maritimes, Newfoundland had been Canada's tenth province for one year. In Alberta, Imperial Oil was starting to reap the rewards of discovery following their oil strike at Leduc four years earlier. In Quebec, an obscure French-Canadian intellectual, who in years to come would have a profound effect on the same industry, helped edit a French-language journal. But even though he would be better known in the future, when the first issue of *Cité libre* came out in June 1950 Pierre Elliott Trudeau was not exactly a household name.

Several things which are well established today did not even exist when Canada went to war in 1950. There was no Stratford Festival, there was no subway anywhere in the country, and there were no universal old age pensions. We had never had a Canadian-born governor general, Jean Drapeau as mayor of Montreal, or a Nobel Prize-winning prime minister.

We did have a $2.50 licence fee on radios, liquor permits in some provinces, the Toronto *Telegram* and several other now-defunct newspapers, and gasoline prices of 30¢ for something called a gallon. We were building highways, welcoming immigrants, and electing Liberal governments in Ottawa. Louis St. Laurent was Prime Minister.

This then was the optimistic, affluent country that Canadians left when they went to fight in Korea.

On the other side of the world, a divided nation called Korea was enjoying the last vestiges of calm before the outbreak of a bloody war that would threaten to engulf humanity.

Korea is a 1000 km-long, comma-shaped peninsula tacked onto the Asian mainland immediately south of both China and Russia. This nation of mountains and rice paddies is bordered on the west by the Yellow Sea, on the east by the Sea of Japan, and on the south by the Korea Strait. Two hundred and six kilometres across this strait is Japan.

Because of its strategic position between Japan and the Asian mainland, Korea has had a history of upheaval, subjugation, and strife almost unequalled anywhere else. In centuries past, invading armies from the north used the peninsula as a land bridge in order to invade Japan. For its part, Japan also used Korea, in the worst sense of the word, for plunder and for journeys of conquest into

China and what is today the southeastern USSR. With every conquest, Korea and its people suffered, but in their agony they grew stronger, more individualistic, and more determined never to lose their pride.

In times of peace, Korea developed its own unique and rich artistic culture. Ancient murals, jade jewellery, celadon pottery, and the exquisite golden crowns of the Silla dynasty displayed today in climate-controlled museums all attest to the glory of the past. Koreans have also been inventive, often more so than we in the Western world realize. A type of central heating where not only the smoke but the heat from the cooking fire passes under the floor in order to provide warmth has been a feature of Korean homes for centuries. Movable metal printing type was invented and used in Korea in 1234, more than 150 years before Johann Gutenberg was born.

But it is the Japanese who perhaps did as much as any outside nation, albeit for their own purposes, to bring Korea to the attention of the outside world. In 1910, through annexation, Japan began an unpopular and bloody rule in Korea that was to last for thirty-five years. While the struggles and trials of this period are far beyond the scope of this book, one incident in particular is of interest to Canadians.

During the spring of 1919, a widespread though initially covert independence movement grew in Korea. Its leaders decided that the struggle would be totally non-violent, but the Japanese overlords who ran the country reacted differently. In the village of Suwon, on April 15,

> a squad of Japanese troops ordered about 30 villagers to assem- ble in a Christian church, closed all the windows and doors, then set the building afire. While the church was ablaze for five hours, the Japanese soldiers aimed a concentrated barrage at the confined civilians, killing all, including women and infants. The Japanese soldiers also burned 31 houses in the village, then set fire to 317 houses in 15 villages in the vicinity.

The independence movement itself was never truly crushed, and its existence became better known elsewhere because of the massacre. A Canadian missionary named Frank Schofield, who had been doing church work in the area, went to Suwon and, after witnessing the nightmarish effects of the tragedy, informed the outside world. He also continued to speak out in Korea about the oppressive measures used by the Japanese overlords. Because of the humanitarian position he took and his condemnation of the evils he saw, Dr. Schofield has long been revered by the Korean people. When he died at eighty-one, on April 12, 1970, he was buried in the select

Graveyard for Patriots section of the National Cemetery in Seoul. The inscription on his headstone reads: "Meritorious Service for Independence of Korea".

Another Canadian who lived in Korea for a number of years during the Japanese rule was 51-year-old Don Newman, now a Toronto-based commercial pilot. "I was just a youngster when I was there," Mr. Newman recalls, "but that country certainly had an effect on me. My parents were in the Salvation Army and we lived in Seoul for about seven years in the mid-1930s. We were desperately poor and had to rely on packages from Canada in order to stay alive. My sister and brother were there as well, so five people had to be fed and clothed.

"We often had to take my parents' wedding silverware and pawn it for food. Then, when the package came, we would traipse down and get the stuff out of hock. My older brother, who was dark and rather slight, spoke Korean, so he did the haggling.

"I also remember one time my sister Ruth needed a dress for something or other that was going on at school. Because there was no money to buy her anything, my mother had to take the kitchen curtains down and make the dress out of them. Mother also made her own soap because it was too expensive to buy."

When it came time for the Newmans to leave Korea shortly before the Second World War broke out, they faced another problem. "We didn't have much, so there was not much to move," recalls Don today. "But we had a lovable little dog named Peter. As kids, we were quite attached to that little mutt, so when my parents told us Peter could not leave with us, we were quite upset. The Japanese were eating dog, of course, so we knew they would eat our Peter. We couldn't face that. Finally my father had to kill poor Peter and we all gave him a decent burial before we left Seoul."

Even before the terror that was the Second World War erupted across the world, Korea had already become a ruthlessly exploited backwater of Asia. This "Land of the Morning Calm", so named because of the softness of the Korean mornings, which is due in part to the mists that cover its mountains at that time of day, endured ever harsher treatment by the ruling Japanese. "As a boy in school I was forced to learn everything about Japan," a middle-aged Seoul businessman recalls. "We were forbidden to study our own history or read about our own country. We were forced to learn Japanese — even to take Japanese names. For reasons such as this, we Koreans find it hard today to turn the other cheek when dealing with some Japanese."

Mr. Kim Su Doc, Director General of the Korean Overseas Information Service, when asked what his countrymen think today of the Japanese, replies tersely with a smile, "Outwardly we are quite cordial."

The Japanese stranglehold on Korea ended when the Second World War ended, but the particular position that Korea was in at the end of the war was a direct result of negotiations held at the Yalta Conference in February 1945. There, Winston Churchill, Joseph Stalin, and a very ill Franklin Roosevelt discussed, among other things, the Soviet leader's demand that Russia be given a "buffer zone", a series of satellite states in Europe and Asia, all of which she could control, and all of which would be answerable to her.

In addition to other requests, Russia demanded that she be "pre-eminent" in Manchuria. In order to make such a request palatable to the Americans, however, Stalin assured Roosevelt that the Soviet Union would enter the war against Japan soon after Germany surrendered in Europe. Roosevelt agreed. At this point no decision was made as to the fate of Korea.

Two days after the first atomic bomb devastated the city of Hiroshima on the morning of August 6, 1945, Russia went to war against Japan. By this time Soviet assistance was not needed, and in the United States the Russian presence was looked upon with great reservation. After Japan surrendered, the reservation became alarm when it was learned that Soviet troops were moving down through Manchuria into Korea.

At the Pentagon in Washington, what was called the State-War-Navy Coordinating Committee rushed into emergency session and in their wisdom decided that a divided Korea, occupied in the north by the Russians and in the south by the Americans, would be the best method of determining what to do with the Land of the Morning Calm. After all, as far as the Americans were concerned, a divided country was preferable to the loss of a whole peninsula to the Soviets, something that was becoming increasingly predictable as Russian troops continued to move southward.

As the Pentagon committee continued its harried discussions, the question of exactly where to place the dividing line in Korea became paramount. Finally, two young army colonels, Dean Rusk and C. H. Bonesteel III, were directed to "go into an anteroom and see if they could decide on a line compromising State's [the U.S. State Department] political desires with military reality." They chose to divide the Korean nation, from coast to coast, along the 38th parallel of latitude. This was accepted by the Russians.

Now that the war was over, and the line separating the two Koreas settled, the Japanese troops north of the 38th parallel in Korea were ordered to surrender to the Russians, while those in the south would turn themselves in to the Americans. While we know little of the capitulation as far as the north is concerned, there is plenty of documentation regarding the Japanese capitulation south of the parallel.

Six days after the war ended, the first U.S. soldiers landed at Inchon and from there moved inland to Seoul.

"I was only seventeen when I lied my way into the U.S. Army and the unit I was with spent a year and a half at Kimpo airport, near Seoul," recalls former Corporal John Fenaughty. This businessman, who now operates out of Toronto, also remembers his feelings about the time.

"The Koreans were desperately poor; they were living in shacks and virtually starving. Their lives were not made any easier — nor were ours for that matter — because a lot of the Japanese had not heard that the war was over so they were in no hurry to surrender. Every day more and more of them were rounded up, however, and we gradually gained control of the situation.

"The Koreans looked at us as saviours of their country, because at the time they hoped that all of Korea was going to be free. As we know, this never happened. I used to wonder what kind of saviours we were, though. I was just a kid with a gun. Most of the time I was more scared than the Japanese I was guarding. One night I remember holding a gun on this guy we had just brought in. He was in one corner of a room and I was in the other. If he had moved at all, I would have shot him. He looked mean and I was terrified. My hands were sweaty, shaking, and my throat was so dry that if the guy had moved, I don't think I could have ordered him to stop before I shot. I know that it was experiences like this that made me glad to get out of Korea.

"When I finally got the order to leave, I got roaring drunk, grabbed a jeep and went screaming around the compound. As a parting gesture, I drove out to the airstrip, revved up that old jeep, and raced wide open down the main runway. Unfortunately, I apparently had some trouble after that. I drove to the terminal building, bounced up the three or four steps, and crashed through the double doors before I stalled. Some guys grabbed me and the next thing I knew I was delivering a long, logical explanation about the affair to the C.O. He wasn't too impressed, I guess, but because I was leaving the next day, let me off."

Retired Canadian Forces Colonel Bentley MacLeod was also in Korea in the period following the Second World War.

"Even though I was always a Canadian," he explains, "I went to high school in Buxton, Maine, and joined the American army after graduation. That was why I ended up landing at Inchon in

October 1946 with the U.S. Seventh Division during the occupation. By the time I got there, however, the Korean police had things pretty well under control, but we were still running down Japanese soldiers who were hiding out. These were guys who had been in Korea so long they had married Korean girls and settled there. However, under the terms of the surrender, we had to find these soldiers and send them back to Japan. No one seemed to care what happened to their families.

"I was only an eighteen-year-old private in the infantry when I was there but I learned a lot from the experience. We were on duty along the parallel, but we also guarded bridges, railyards, and so on. We also used to see the Korean police in action. If they yelled at a guy to stop and he hesitated, he was dead. They never bothered to argue or give an order the second time. They just shot."

As time went on, the two halves of Korea evolved in distinctly separate ways. In the north, the Russians began building both an army and a government they could control. Thousands of Koreans who had fled the Japanese into Siberia and Manchuria were relocated in their homeland. Many of these people not only had fought guerrilla operations against the Japanese, but had lived with Communist influences so long that they were especially useful to the Soviets. Once these Koreans were re-established at home, they were moulded into the hard-core nucleus of both an army and a North Korean puppet regime answerable to Moscow.

With these in place, and an iron curtain lowered around half the peninsula, "Russia subjected the north Korean populace to five solid years of [anti-American] propaganda," mostly to the effect that the Americans were to blame because they were blocking the re-unification of Korea. The Soviets went on to charge that the United States was opposed to a unified country because she needed Korea for military bases in that part of the world.

In the south, the situation was much more fluid. The Americans wanted to see Korea unified, but they were able to make little progress towards this end. Nor were they able to make great strides in developing a stable form of government in the section of the peninsula under their control. One of the reasons for this failure lay in the man chosen to head the U.S. occupation there — Major General John R. Hodge.

Even though General Hodge was an effective soldier, his skills as a politician were sadly lacking. While some historians refer to him as "a cultured gentleman, without affectations, basically friendly in nature and well-disposed toward the Korean people", he is mentioned by others as the man who is supposed to have said, on his arrival in Seoul, "Koreans are the same breed of cats as Japanese." If

he indeed did make such a remark, it is highly unlikely that it en-
hanced his popularity. After he was ensconced in the Japanese Governor General's palace, an act that in itself irritated many Koreans,
he continued to have real difficulty gaining a firm hand in the
country. At the beginning of his tenure he even gave permission for
the Japanese police in Korea to retain their arms as a means of
quelling possible insurrections. This order in itself was so conten-
tious as far as the Koreans were concerned that Washington had to
order Hodge to rescind it.

His greatest difficulty lay in his failure to understand the political
aspirations of the Korean people and to somehow help them devise
a workable system of self-government. Various politicians came
forward, each claiming support from certain segments of the populace. But because Hodge was unsure of whom he could trust, and
because he never fully understood any of them, he refused to hand
the mantle of power to any faction. Finally, General Douglas Mac-
Arthur, his superior in Tokyo, did the job for him. MacArthur wanted
a Korean leader, and despite objections in Washington and in Korea
itself that he had picked the wrong man, he sent Dr. Syngman Rhee
to Seoul.

The sixty-nine-year-old Rhee held a master's degree from
Harvard and a Ph.D. in international law from Princeton, and had
lived in continental United States and Hawaii for the previous thirty
years. During his entire career he had been a staunch advocate of
Korean independence, so much so that he had been imprisoned,
then exiled from his homeland, by the Japanese because of his
opposition to their rule. In 1919 his supporters in the independence
movement elected him High Commissioner for Korea in what they
called the government in exile. In that position he had badgered the
United States, China, Switzerland, and even Russia for help in making
Korea independent. His rebuff by Russia was so pointed that the old
man became as anti-Communist as he was patriotic. This combination was just what MacArthur wanted.

Acting on MacArthur's orders, Hodge welcomed Rhee and his
Austrian wife, the former Francesca Donner, to Seoul and set them
up in a suite in the best hotel in the city. The General hoped his
troubles were over. At last a leader for the Koreans had been located
who was, in his own view at least, "the embodiment of his country's
cause".

However, Hodge's troubles were far from over. The various fac-
tions within the country continued to bicker among themselves over
who should be pre-eminent. On top of this, the United States was
involved in on-going negotiations with the Russians over what to do
— ultimately — with Korea. At various times, suggestions for an

independent country were raised, and just as quickly vetoed by the Communists. Meanwhile, the United States was drastically cutting her standing army at home and abroad. The Second World War had been over for two years and across the country congressmen and senators were under pressure to reduce military spending and let as many service personnel as possible return to civilian life. Most who spoke out against the size of the defence budget agreed that U.S. troops would still be needed in Europe as a buffer against the Soviets, but as far as the Orient was concerned, they regarded the threat there as figuratively and literally more remote. Finally, on September 25, 1947, General Dwight Eisenhower, Chairman of the Joint Chiefs of Staff, sent a memo to Secretary of Defense James Forrestal stating that the U.S. had "'little strategic interest' in keeping bases and troops in Korea". President Truman and the U.S. National Security Council agreed.

The United States then asked the United Nations to oversee national elections for all of Korea. Predictably, the Russians refused to go along with the idea. Accordingly, an election was held in the south only, and over ninety per cent of all eligible voters turned out for it. Syngman Rhee won his seat in Seoul and ultimately went on to become the President of the Republic of Korea, three days after a new constitution was promulgated on July 17, 1948.

During the balance of that year and after, large numbers of U.S. troops came home, until by the spring of 1950 only a token force remained. By that time the United States had decided that their Far East defence perimeter would bypass Korea. In a speech to the National Press Club in Washington on January 12, 1950, Secretary of State Dean Acheson informed his listeners — and through them the world — that America would continue to defend such places as the Philippines and Japan, both of which were too important to risk losing to the Russians. Korea was not included, and by implication at least, was forgotten.

While all this was happening, a massive 135,000-man, well-equipped army of North Koreans was involved in manoeuvres along the 38th parallel, less than an hour's drive from downtown Seoul.

2

ATTACK ON THE 38TH

The war began in the rain. At 4 a.m., June 25, 1950, the roar of artillery shredded the silence over the ancient hills of Korea. Along the 38th parallel, from west to east, belches of flame cut the darkness, and the thud of mortar shells, the cries of the wounded and dying, and the curses of fighting men signalled the North Korean attack on the south, the start of the Korean War. And even though it was still too dark to notice, the monsoon-swollen streams ran red with human blood.

An estimated 90,000 North Koreans charged across the parallel that night. There were seven infantry divisions in all, as well as a small amphibious force on the east coast, a motorcycle regiment, border constabulary, and 150 T-34 tanks. These monsters, each weighing thirty-five tons, were armed with 85 mm cannon and two 7.62 mm machine-guns. In the initial stages of the war they would prove to be unstoppable — largely because they would face no such vehicles in the south. It had always been the considered opinion of the Americans that the use of tanks in Korea was impossible. No tank could operate in the bottomless ooze of a rice paddy, and what passed for roads barely supported a truck. None the less, the T-34s rumbled on.

Because the war started when it did, thousands of Republic of Korea soldiers who ordinarily would have been thrown into the border battle were nowhere near the parallel when the fight for their homeland began. In theory there could have been upwards of 38,000 South Koreans defending the frontier — but in the pre-dawn darkness that Sunday, probably no more than 15,000 faced the Communist attack. One-third of the ROK soldiers were on leave. Several thousand more were in reserve twenty or more miles to the south. Most of their officers were in Seoul attending the official opening of a new officers' club. Nor were there many American advisers at the front. They had also decided to spend this early summer weekend enjoying the amenities offered in the capital. It was little wonder, then, that the Communist attack was so successful. In some places they outnumbered the South Koreans by as much as five to one. In addition, they had a decided advantage in fire-power.

While all this was happening in Korea, life on the other side of the world was rather tranquil. In Ottawa it was still early afternoon of the previous day. The stores along Bank Street were crowded as civil servants did their weekly shopping. On Wellington, the House of Commons was quiet, except for the Saturday tourists who looked into the chamber and listened as guides drew attention to points of interest. After the weekend, the twenty-first session of Parliament would resume sitting.

In British Columbia, grounds-keepers at the Capilano and Shaughnessy golf courses were doing last-minute checks on the fairways and greens in preparation for the Pacific Northwest Golf tournament scheduled to get under way on Monday morning. In Nelson, the jury in Doukhobor leader John Lebedoff's arson trial was stalemated in its attempt to decide whether or not the man had conspired to burn a local community hall.

In New Brunswick, few people were swimming at the Northumberland Strait beaches. The water was still too cold to be comfortable. In Ontario, haying season was in full stride and many of the same farm lads who were spending this day building hay from a hay-loader would be building bunkers near a river called Imjin a year hence. Across the prairies, the wheat, barley, and oat fields waved in the wind, while the men who planted them watched the skies and prayed for favourable weather. In Toronto, the swimming pools were open and the shrieks of children mingled with those of the gulls at Sunnyside.

Those who followed international events may well have been listening to their radios that afternoon, but would as yet hear nothing from Korea. The first dispatch did not come for several hours after the attack from the north began, but when it did come an American reporter would score a world scoop for his efforts.

Jack James of United Press had been in Korea for almost a year, long enough to have several reliable contacts in both Korean and U.S. army and government circles. The latter proved especially useful to him in obtaining the biggest story of his career. A few minutes after eight, James drove his jeep through the dreary Sunday morning rain to the offices of the U.S. Embassy, located at the time atop a nondescript hotel near downtown Seoul. Later, he would tell anyone who asked that he had gone there to pick up a raincoat he had forgotten a day or so earlier. In all probability the visit resulted from a tip from a friend at the Embassy concerning the outbreak of hostilities along the parallel, and James presumably concocted the raincoat story in order to protect his informant's identity. The practice by Embassy personnel of leaking stories to the press was officially discouraged.

As soon as he got to the Embassy press room, James started phoning everyone he knew who might have information from the front. Gradually he obtained enough snippets of news that, by the time U.S. Ambassador John Muccio arrived at the chancery, James had his story almost written. By 9:30 he was told that the Ambassador was ready to alert Washington. That was all James needed. He raced to his jeep and drove to the cable office, almost two kilometres away. From there, at 9:50 a.m., Seoul time, he filed for the world the news that war had broken out in Korea. The dispatch arrived in San Francisco almost as James filed it in Seoul. The message was relayed to New York, rewritten there, and sped to Tangier, Manila, and then back to Seoul. Before noon it had been translated into Korean and "appeared on the streets as a UP bulletin in Seoul's Sunday morning newspapers." By this time it had also been picked up by radio stations across Canada, and thousands of listeners heard that there was war in a country they knew nothing about. To them, Korea was as remote as the moon.

Even though Washington first learned of events in Korea from the UP bulletin, Muccio's cable arrived moments later. It was followed by other dispatches from Seoul as the situation there became clearer. Because the war began on a weekend, many of the senior government officials were out of town, so scores of aides were kept busy alerting those who had to know. In several instances, however, radio bulletins provided the first information.

One of the men who had left Washington was Harry Truman. The President had officiated at the opening of an airport in Baltimore that Saturday and then had flown on to Kansas City. From there he went by car to his home in Independence, Missouri, for a rest. Shortly after a family dinner that evening, his restful holiday ended.

"It was about ten thirty on Saturday night," he recalled, "and I was sitting in the living room reading. The phone rang and it was Dean Acheson calling from his home in Maryland. He said, 'Mr. President, I have serious news. The North Koreans are attacking across the thirty-eighth parallel.'"

Truman discussed the situation with his Secretary of State, and wondered if he should return to Washington that evening. Acheson dissuaded him until more clarification on the news from Korea was received. It was decided, however, that Acheson should request an emergency meeting of the United Nations Security Council to look into the events in the Far East.

The President put down the phone and prepared for bed. His daughter, Margaret, who was there with her parents, noticed her father's reaction to the call he had just received and told of its effect on the family. "None of us got much sleep that night. My father made it clear, from the moment he heard the news, that he feared this was the opening round in World War III."

In Canada, the news from Korea was given more and more prominence in radio bulletins during the day on Sunday. By nightfall, the first clamourings were heard in Ottawa as to where this country stood relative to the North Korean invasion. George Drew, Leader of the Conservative Opposition, began formulating questions about Korea which he would air in the House of Commons the next day. Howard Green, the P.C. member for Vancouver Quadra, prepared to ask Defence Minister Brooke Claxton about Canada's defence preparedness, particularly in the Pacific. Gordon Graydon, the Tory member from Peel, was concerned about the safety of five Canadian women who had been working for a United Nations commission in Korea.

On the government side, Claxton, Prime Minister Louis St. Laurent, External Affairs Minister Lester Pearson, and other senior officials conferred, both in person and by telephone. Conversations were held with their counterparts in Washington, London, and Paris, and with diplomats at Lake Success, the temporary home of the United Nations, a few miles outside of New York City.

It was at Lake Success during the Sunday afternoon that the North Korean invasion was discussed by the U.N. Security Council. While the debate was lively as to just where the U.N. should stand, the decision-making was easier because of an accident of history six months earlier. At that time, the Soviet Union had become incensed because it had been unable to convince the world body to seat Communist China as a U.N member in place of the Nationalist Chinese. The Soviet delegate, Yakov Malik, had walked out of the Security Council in disgust, and on June 26 had still not returned. Because of his absence, a U.N. resolution condemning the North Korean attack and calling for the withdrawal of North Korean forces to the thirty-eighth parallel passed by a 9–0 vote. It was now almost 6 p.m., Sunday, New York time.

In the interim, the situation in Korea had grown steadily worse.

Despite heroic efforts by the ROK forces, the Communist onslaught continued in most areas along the front, but in particular in a two-pronged attack leading southward toward Seoul. Later on, and with the perfect 20/20 hindsight of critical American servicemen, South Korean troops were faulted because of their failure to hold the line in the first days of the war. While such disparagements are perhaps true in part, any blanket condemnation of ROK fighting spirit is grossly unfair. In some instances, these soldiers were up against odds of five to one, attempting to stop tanks with pistols.

There were countless examples of selfless bravery in this war, but none more unsung than the deeds of South Korean soldiers in the first couple of days after hostilities erupted. Near Kaesong, soldiers in the 1st ROK Division were up against the dreaded T-34 tanks but lacked the fire-power to deter the enemy. In utter desperation, the defenders finally "swarmed over the enemy tanks and tried to open the turrets to drop grenades inside." In another instance, "South Korean forces tried to fight the tanks with 2.36 inch rocket guns, but in vain, and then organized a suicide team and had it destroy four enemy tanks with rockets and hand grenades." Nevertheless, most of the tanks rumbled on and the fall of Seoul became more and more probable.

While reports of their early success in the invasion were followed with delight by the Communists in Pyongyang, the capital of North Korea, and presumably in Peking and Moscow as well, they tried to shift the blame for the invasion. In a broadcast early Sunday, Radio Pyongyang warned South Korea to "suspend its military adventure near the 38th parallel" or else North Korea would have to resort to "decisive measures". In effect, the radio broadcast accused the South of starting the war.

This same theme was continued in a national radio address at 9:30 a.m. when the North Korean leader, Kim Il Sung, spoke to his people:

> The South Korean puppet clique has rejected all methods for peaceful reunification proposed by the Democratic People's Republic of Korea, and dared to commit armed aggression . . . north of the 38th parallel. The Democratic People's Republic of Korea ordered a counterattack to repel the invading troops. The South Korean puppet clique will be held responsible for whatever results may be brought about by this development.

While Kim was spouting this rubbish, his armies were cutting deep into the South. Nevertheless, his words and leadership had a profound effect on his people, who regarded him as an almost godlike figure who would lead them and their country to untold heights of glory. This man, like some of the other deified mortals of history, had rather commonplace origins.

Born Kim Song-joo in northwestern Korea in 1912, he is credited with having fought in guerrilla operations against the Japanese during their occupation of his homeland. Other aspects of his past are rather obscure, and what has been written about him has come largely from the Communist propaganda mills, so its veracity is questionable. His father was poor but supposedly very brave. It's doubtful that the father was highly educated, yet we are told that he used his natural gifts for healing to open a hospital for the poor. The father is said to have died a patriot's death at the age of thirty-two.

When he was twenty, Kim Song-joo changed his name to Kim Il Sung, because that had been the name of a courageous freedom fighter who had led uprisings against the Japanese some three decades earlier. The name change worked wonders. The new Kim was revered as the original seems to have been — and indeed many North Koreans thought he was the genuine article. His following grew as his reputation as a fearless guerrilla leader spread. Some time in the late 1930s and early 1940s he is known to have lived in Russia, where he fell under Soviet influence. Finally, in 1945, he turned up in Pyongyang, as the Moscow-chosen leader of the North Korean people.

Somewhere along the line Kim acquired virtues, skills, and miraculous leadership abilities that no mere mortal could ever emulate. In a tongue-in-cheek article about the man in the *Toronto Star* on June 9, 1982, writer Gwynne Dyer refers to Kim as an author whose books contain "some of the most preposterous self-glorification ever published: you can read any three paragraphs at random and reduce any Western audience to hysterics. Kim Il Sung apparently not only created the world, but he also built all the mountains and fertilized all the flowers. . . . [He] has . . . shot the biggest bear, solved the women's question, discovered the rarest orchid, and defeated both Japanese and U.S. imperialism single-handed."

Dyer also quotes from an article published in a North Korean Communist newspaper early in 1982: "People of the world, if you are looking for miracles, come to Korea. If you are looking for successes, come to Korea. Christians, do not go to Jerusalem, come to Korea. Do not believe in God, believe in the great man." The great man of course is Kim Il Sung.

But regardless of whether or not his claims to greatness rested on fabricated foundations, Kim's charisma affected many. Nora Rodd, now a Canadian Communist and in 1950 a member of an organization which called itself the Women's International Democratic Federation, visited North Korea during the war. When she was there, she met Kim. During an interview in late May 1982, she called him "a man who is greatly respected, a great fighter, [a] great and beloved leader. He definitely loves his people and is greatly loved by them. They nearly worship him." Even though many years have passed since Mrs. Rodd was in Korea and talked with him, she still refers to Kim Il Sung as "a great man".

Back in the United States, fears spread that this war was more than just a border battle. At his Missouri home, President Truman attempted to maintain a business-as-usual attitude on the Sunday morning. While his wife and daughter Margaret went to church, he drove to his brother Vivian's farm outside of Independence but returned shortly before noon. At 12:35 Acheson called to report that the situation in the Far East was deteriorating. The President decided to return to Washington immediately. By this time he seems to have made up his own mind to send assistance to Korea, but the decision was not finalized until later that day. Nevertheless, his parting words to Acheson, "Dean, we've got to stop the sons of bitches no matter what," leave little doubt as to where Truman stood.

That evening the President met with thirteen of his top military and civilian advisers in order to discuss the Korean situation. The advice he was given as to what response the United States should make varied, depending on the individual who gave it. Some wanted the army to go in. Others disagreed. One or two believed the navy and the air force would be enough. All wondered where Russia stood in the whole affair — and what, if any, response Russia would make if the United States did in fact commit troops to this fight in the Land of the Morning Calm. All assumed that Russia was ultimately responsible for the fact that the invasion had come about.

Finally, it was decided that (1) General MacArthur would send ammunition and supplies from Japan to help the beleaguered ROK forces; (2) MacArthur would begin the immediate evacuation of American citizens from Korea; (3) the U.S. Seventh Fleet would leave the Philippines and proceed north to the Formosa Strait in order to prevent the Korean conflagration from spreading. At this point Truman insisted that these actions were to be taken "under authority of the U.N. resolution passed earlier that day".

While this meeting was being held, Canadian External Affairs Minister Lester B. Pearson was talking to reporters in Ottawa about what he believed was happening in Korea. The ever-present Soviet menace was mentioned, and everyone wondered what role the Russians were playing in the events along the 38th parallel. Because no one really knew, the talk shifted to what response the United States might make in Korea. Pearson speculated, in an off-the-record comment, that he "did not expect a U.S. military response to the invasion." When in fact the exact opposite occurred, he admitted that he had been caught by surprise — first by the invasion by North Korea itself, but as much so by the U.S. stand which grew out of the aggression.

When the House of Commons resumed sitting on Monday, June 26, Korea was uppermost in the minds of most members of Parliament. Lester Pearson addressed the problem. He told Tory leader George Drew and the rest of the Commons that the North Korean attack was "unprovoked aggression and a breach of the peace", and went on to say that he hoped some action on the part of the U.N. would be successful in ending the hostilities. He also stated that Canada would give full support to the United Nations in its efforts to restore the peace in Korea.

Later in the sitting, Defence Minister Brooke Claxton told the House that a previously proposed visit by Canadian naval units to European waters might have to be cancelled if the situation in Korea got worse. The three destroyers *Cayuga*, *Athabaskan*, and *Sioux*, which were stationed at Esquimalt in British Columbia, had been scheduled to join their sister ships *Huron* and *Micmac*, as well as the aircraft carrier *Magnificent*, for anti-submarine exercises with the British in late August.

Questions from George Drew and Howard Green prompted Claxton to point out that even though Canada had intended to send Royal Canadian Air Force squadrons to Europe for training purposes, the main purpose of the RCAF would still be the defence of Canada.

Gordon Graydon (P.C., Peel) asked the Minister of External Affairs about the safety of Canadians known to be in Korea. In his reply, Lester Pearson said that as far as could be determined, no Canadians were in danger, but if any were, Ottawa would take whatever action it could to protect them. A day or so later the *Toronto Star* reported that five Canadian women who had been in Korea were now safe, as were ten diamond drillers from northern Ontario and Quebec. Both groups had reached Japan by ship.

While no one in the Western world really knew what the North Korean invasion actually portended, the spectre of International Communism and its spread across the world were always alarming. The Red menace had been the ominous threat for years, but in the late 1940s and early 1950s this fear was acute. As soon as news of the invasion in Korea broke, the question in most minds in the West was: What are the Communists up to now? And even if the attack might have been made by their Korean puppets, most observers in the West assumed that Russia was pulling the strings.

Since September 5, 1945, the day Igor Gouzenko walked out of the Russian Embassy in Ottawa carrying 109 documents that revealed the existence of a massive Soviet spy network in North America, Russian espionage activity had been of serious concern in Canada. Six months to the day later, Winston Churchill told the world in a speech at Fulton, Missouri, that an "iron curtain" had descended across much of Europe. By the time the Korean War broke out, estimates of those in Moscow's control in Eastern and Central Europe *alone* were in excess of ninety million people. Despite the formation of the North Atlantic Treaty Organization on April 4, 1949, there was still no completely effective response to Soviet policy.

In the United States, from January 1947, federal government employees, and afterwards most state and local governments, had to swear oaths of loyalty in order to obtain jobs. These loyalty procedures were further tightened in 1950 when the Communist Party and other organizations connected with it had to register their members with the Attorney General's department. People from outside the country who had ever been Communists were not allowed into the United States at all. Finally, under the leadership of Wisconsin Senator Joseph McCarthy, the "Red Scare" reached its peak. But by the time McCarthy became pre-eminent, the war was well under way in Korea.

3

THE FALL
OF SEOUL

At 9:00 p.m., Monday, June 26, 1950, United States President Harry S. Truman met with several of his key advisers at Blair House in Washington for the second top-level strategy conference over Korea. As these men arrived at this temporary home of the first family (the White House was being renovated), their looks and manner betrayed the seriousness of the moment. During most of the day, one report after another, each more disturbing than the one before, had come in concerning the advance of the North Koreans, the problems in evacuating American nationals, and the virtual certainty of the fall of Seoul. Now, as each man hurried past reporters, and collected his thoughts prior to the commencement of the meeting, a sense of expectancy and urgency seemed to settle over the gathering.

Further bulletins from Ambassador Muccio told of battles being fought as close as seventeen miles from the South Korean capital. Muccio himself was worried but as yet not about to abandon his post. He had, however, given the order for the evacuation of American civilians and their dependants. While many of these people would be flown out of Kimpo, some seven hundred were taken in almost every type of conveyance to Inchon, where they were jammed into a Norwegian fertilizer ship that in normal times had facilities for her crew and a maximum of six passengers. Plans had called for half the crowd to leave on a Chinese ship, but the thoughts of embarking on a vessel run by Orientals was too much for the frightened Americans. They simply did not trust the Chinese and refused to board the second ship.

During the same day the South Korean National Assembly met and drafted a message to Truman and his government asking for "increasing support and . . . effective and timely aid". Korean Ambassador John Chang had met with Truman and asked for military

Princess Patricia's Canadian Light Infantry (Princess Pats) troops boarding the American naval ship Private Joe P. Martinez in Seattle, Washington, November 1950, en route to Korea.

1

Canadian troops maintained a high standard of fitness during the eighteen-day voyage to Korea. Here men of the 2nd Battalion, PPCLI, exercise on board the Joe P. Martinez, November 1950.

2

Crowded shipboard conditions were part of their first taste of military life for Canadian recruits. Shown here are members of the Royal 22nd Regiment (the Vandoos).

Captain F. Lebel, padre of the 2nd Battalion, Royal 22nd Regiment, celebrates the regiment's first mass in the lines near the Han River, May 1951.

adier John Rockingham briefs platoon and company commanders of the 1st Battalion, PPCLI, on
al in Korea, October 1951.

adier Rockingham today with the author.

Lieutenant-Colonel Jacques Dextraze, Commanding Officer, Royal 22nd Regiment, Korea, November 1951.

Lieutenant-Colonel J. R. Stone, Commanding Officer, 2nd Battalion, PPCLI, Korea, November 1951.

The war displaced thousands of Koreans, who were forced to flee as refugees, like this family, photographed as they were moving south, June 1951.

The bombed bridges across the Han River were replaced by pontoon bridges for troop movement. Crossing are armoured vehicles of "C" Squadron, Lord Strathcona Horse, May 1951.

Twenty-five-pounder gun of the 2nd Battalion, Royal Canadian Horse Artillery, in action, May 1951.

Combat scene with Royal 22nd Regiment riflemen and Bren-gunner.

Personnel of the 1st Battalion, R22R, digging a battlefield trench, which would be used for sleeping, taking cover, and moving along.

assistance. The meeting was an emotional one for Dr. Chang, who argued his country's case with a direct and passionate vehemence. The President tried his best to reassure the diplomat, telling him that help was on the way but that the Koreans would have to defend themselves until that help arrived.

The fact that they were unable to put up a fight strong enough to deter the Communist advance was rather graphically illustrated not only at the front but as far south as Seoul. Shortly after noon on the first day of the war, two North Korean Yak-9 fighter planes had flown over Seoul as well as the airport at Kimpo. Later it was assumed that the two had been on a reconnaissance mission, because at three o'clock the same afternoon and later at seven in the evening, both Kimpo and Seoul airfields were strafed with cannon and machine-gun fire. In both instances, some of the few planes South Korea had — and these only trainers at that — were damaged. During the first raid, glass was blasted out of the control tower at Kimpo and a nearby fuel dump was set ablaze. The dump was still burning when an American C-54 air transport plane was destroyed in the second attack. At the time, neither the South Koreans nor the Americans were able to fight back. The former lacked the aircraft to do so and the latter the necessary permission from Washington. The following day, however, when the column of trucks, buses, and cars of fleeing American civilians snaked its way eastward from Seoul towards the harbour at Inchon, U.S. aircraft were in the skies protecting the evacuation.

The second conference at Blair House was in a way more decisive than the first had been. Now the participants had a better idea of just what was happening in Korea and had their first experience of coping with this new threat. The meeting was brief, businesslike, and decisive. When it was over, the United States navy and air force were given permission to "support the Republic of South Korea . . . but only south of the 38th parallel".

By this time, President Syngman Rhee, his family, and members of his staff had fled from Seoul — without even telling John Muccio.

Almost as soon as he had received the go-ahead to take the offensive in the air war, General MacArthur directed Air Force General Earle Partridge to have his planes attack military targets north of Seoul: supply dumps, bridges, tanks, artillery, and moving columns of troops and trucks. Initially, bad weather over North Asia grounded the planes, but by the morning of June 28, skies had cleared across the Korean peninsula and twelve B-26s left Ashiya, Japan, for bombing runs on the railyards of Munsan, near the 38th parallel. The raids themselves were reasonably successful, but the planes had trouble returning to base. As they flew over the target area, all were damaged by anti-aircraft fire from the ground, one so badly that even though it returned safely, it had to be scrapped. Ten others were repairable but one crashed on approach to Ashiya, killing the entire crew. Other sorties involved F-80 fighter planes and four B-29 bombers.

During the day on Tuesday in Seoul, more and more staff from the U.S. Embassy were departing. These people made their way to Kimpo, some ten miles from downtown, boarded any aircraft available, and headed for Japan and safety. Late in the forenoon, Dean Acheson ordered John Muccio to get out as well. Reluctantly, the Ambassador packed his bags, scooped up a handful of cigars and a case of Scotch, and headed out of Seoul. As his jeep bounced along the highway leading south, he passed hundreds of Koreans walking in the same direction.

The exodus from the capital had originally been a rivulet. As long as the general populace thought the ROKs were holding the line to the north, few moved out. However, as the news from the front grew more ominous, more and more people decided to flee. Finally, when the ROK 2nd and 7th divisions defending the northern outskirts of Seoul collapsed and columns of soldiers headed for the Han River bridges and safety, panic swept the city. In the early evening, North Korean planes dropped leaflets demanding that everyone in the capital surrender. This only added to the confusion.

The rivulet swelled to a torrent. Thousands and thousands of terrified men, women, and children left their homes and surged out of the city. The streets leading to the four bridges over the Han River — one three-lane-highway overpass and three railway trestles — were packed with a jostling, crying, barely moving sea of humanity. Most of these people carried bundles of belongings, the pathetic treasures of a lifetime spent in the humid, teeming metropolis of Seoul. Many women balanced hastily tied parcels of clothing on their heads while they carried one and sometimes two crying children in their arms. Men stooped under A-frames — individual carry-alls shaped like a large capital A and strapped on the back — packed high with cooking pots, scraps of food, and often tools of the bearer's trade. Old men in white pyjamas and boot-shaped slippers, and ancient women bent double from years in rice paddies, were shuffled and shoved forward in the dust.

While this ocean of people inched southward from Seoul, the last planes that dared do so landed at Kimpo, paused only long enough to allow new batches of passengers to scramble on board, and then roared into the air and headed for Japan.

The last of these planes that came in on a rescue flight brought with it four American correspondents — from *Time*, the *Chicago Daily*

News, and both the *New York Times* and the *Herald Tribune.* Even though the pilot who brought them thought they were crazy to stay, the stories they dispatched in those first few calamitous days after their arrival showed the Western world the chaos and pain that was South Korea in late June and early July 1950.

The correspondents saw American soldiers burning piles of documents on the shell-shattered tarmac at Kimpo, South Korean soldiers tossing aside their weapons and fleeing blindly to the south, civilians abandoning their homes and leaving, often forever, and harassed American military advisers and Korean officers trying to remain calm amid the upheaval around them. Finally, they saw the bridges of the Han destroyed, along with hundreds of people who were crossing them at the time.

Even today, thirty years after the war, these bridges are the lifelines of Seoul. There are fourteen spans over the great river now, and, out of necessity, more are planned. In places, the river is almost one kilometre wide and is the greatest natural obstacle in the area. On the night of Tuesday, June 27, 1950, however, the four bridges were the only way across that obstacle.

The chaotic jumble of massed humanity shuffled from dozens of streets in downtown Seoul onto the bridges, and in particular the large highway artery. The numbers of people crossing continued to increase as time went on, until by midnight there were so many pedestrians on the bridges that no one seemed to be going anywhere.

At 2:15 a.m., the four American correspondents found themselves stalled halfway over the river. Their jeep had been following a truckload of ROK soldiers which itself was not moving. Frank Gibney of *Time* magazine recalled what happened at this point: "Without warning the sky was lighted by a huge sheet of sickly orange flame. There was a tremendous explosion immediately in front of us. Our jeep was picked up and hurled fifteen feet by the blast."

None of the newspeople were seriously injured, but the soldiers in the truck died on the spot, as did almost eight hundred others in the blast itself, from the fall into the river forty feet below, or from drowning. Later, an investigation into the reason for the debacle would fix blame on the Korean army's chief engineer for the "manner" in which the bridges were blown. In all probability, however, he was a scapegoat for an order that originated with a civilian authority. At any rate, the engineer's attempts to prove that he was innocent were of no avail. He was shot.

The idea of blowing the bridges before the arrival of the enemy was probably a good one — if the civilian refugees and the ROK soldiers had been given time to cross. But because the bridges were destroyed prematurely, the bulk of the ROK forces were stranded on the north side of the river just as the Communist armies were moving into the fringes of Seoul. From this point, the virtual disintegration of the ROK army accelerated.

As the situation on the war front grew more hopeless as each hour passed, the U.N. Security Council convened at Lake Success. After several hours of debate, and still without the presence of the Soviets, the Council made a decision.

In the early hours of Wednesday morning they voted to endorse the action already taken by the United States. In addition, other members of the U.N. were asked to "furnish such assistance to the Republic of Korea as may be necessary to repel the attack and restore international peace and security in the area."

These words took Canada to war.

Later that same day Lester Pearson was asked in the House of Commons to state what Canada's position would be, in the light of the new resolution at Lake Success. He replied that Canada intended to confer with other U.N. members in order to decide what action might be taken. Both he and Prime Minister Louis St. Laurent wanted to be certain "that the restraint of North Korean aggression was . . . a United Nations operation and not merely an endorsement by the United Nations of unilateral action by the United States."

The following day Pearson told the House that the U.N. had asked Canada to supply one or two people who would act as military observers in Korea. The two, Lieutenant-Colonel Frank White and Wing Commander Harry Malkin, would work with the U.N. Commission. Twenty-five days later the pair became the first Canadian servicemen to reach Korea during the war.

Even though Pearson had clearly indicated that only one or two observers had been requested, the message that seems to have filtered down to many Canadians was that this country would soon be in a war and therefore more men would be needed in the army. This situation was particularly true in Toronto, where local recruiting offices were swamped with men wanting to join the army and go off to Korea to fight. On June 29, the *Toronto Star* reported that the number of inquiries was "the highest since the Second World War". The same day, Canada placed an embargo on goods being shipped to North Korea. The United States had done the same thing a day or so earlier.

In the United States, politicians of every stripe had debated the action their country had taken, or was about to take, in Korea. It was Senator William F. Knowland, a prominent Republican from California, who first used the phrase "police action" as it came to be applied to the Korean War. Knowland felt that because North Korea had broken international law by the invasion of the South, the actions of the United States were akin to the actions of a police officer who might follow a criminal after a crime had been committed.

The same week, President Truman used the phrase, as did Prime Minister Louis St. Laurent in his June 30 statement in the House of Commons in Ottawa. Canada's role in Korea, according to St. Laurent, would be a "police action under the control and authority of the United Nations for the purpose of restoring peace to an area where aggression has occurred." In the same speech, St. Laurent offered the services of three Royal Canadian Navy destroyers for service in Korea.

That was the same day that Harry Truman sent U.S. ground forces to fight in the Land of the Morning Calm.

Across Canada support for both the U.S. and the U.N. action was strong. In Ottawa, all Opposition parties supported the government, while old soldiers and would-be soldiers throughout the country dreamed of donning uniforms and going off to war.

One of these was Vancouver-born Jeffry Brock, who would soon assume the duties of Commander Canadian Destroyers Pacific. Brock was holidaying near Kenora, Ontario, when he heard of the news from Korea. He and a partner had been fishing in the Lake of the Woods, but because they were catching nothing, they switched on a portable radio in the boat and settled back with a couple of beers. "Our idle chatter was interrupted by a news bulletin," recalled Brock, "about a seemingly serious invasion of South Korea by forces from the North."

Sensing that Canada might somehow become involved in the matter through our membership in the U.N., Brock headed for the nearest telephone in order to contact Ottawa. The Director of Naval Plans and Operations suggested that Brock report to the naval base at Esquimalt, British Columbia, as soon as possible.

Another Canadian, whose name would soon become a household word across the country, was already in British Columbia. John Ròckingham, who, as a brigadier, would lead our troops in Korea, was a civilian when the Korean War broke out, working as Superintendent of Pacific Stage Lines, a bus company.

George Griffiths was a nineteen-year-old kid pumping gas in Brighton, Ontario. Ferdinand Demara, a footloose, likeable braggart, was looking for fame and glory in New England. Keith Aiken, now of Lethbridge, had actually joined the army shortly before Korea and would see others who signed up after him get to the Far East first. Jacques Dextraze was employed by a sewing-machine company in Quebec. Ed Haslip worked for a chemical company in Sarnia. Pierre Berton wrote stories for a magazine called *Maclean's*, and a youngster from Simcoe named Red Kelly played hockey in Detroit.

Before many months would pass, all of them would spend time in Korea.

While the armies of Kim Il Sung were consolidating their hold on the fallen city of Seoul, Canada's most westerly naval establishment was rapidly achieving war readiness. The base at Esquimalt is located on the southern tip of Vancouver Island, little more than a stone's throw from downtown Victoria. Here, amid some of the most beautiful scenery in the country, naval ratings hustled to and fro, preparing three Tribal Class destroyers for action. Decks were swabbed, stores taken on board, and fuel supplies topped off. On July 5, in scenes similar to the televised departure of British vessels to the Falkland Islands in 1982, wives and sweethearts gathered to bid tearful farewells to the men of the *Cayuga*, the *Athabaskan*, and the *Sioux* as the ships slipped from their moorings and sailed away to war.

In Korea the situation was desperate. For days, fires burned in almost every town and village and palls of acrid smoke hung over the hulks of blasted buildings and deserted streets. Those among the population who remained scavenged for food and water, mourned murdered relatives, and in many cases tried to recover from the savagery of shellfire, gang rape, and torture. With the North Korean advance, atrocities became commonplace as hundreds of men, women, and children were executed before they could flee, or were shot because they too readily supported the wrong side. And still the Communists swept south.

It was into this inferno that General MacArthur was ordered to send untrained, ill-prepared, soft, and immature young Americans. For years, MacArthur had called the shots in Japan. He ruled like a god, a benevolent yet authoritarian one. By most accounts this humourless, proud, hypersensitive son of a war hero and grandson of a judge did a reasonably good job in Japan, yet in spite of his claims of understanding the "Oriental mind", he had little first-hand contact with ordinary Japanese and virtually none with Koreans. When the Korean War broke out, he had been away from the United States for over thirteen years.

MacArthur resided in the American Embassy in Tokyo but had his office in the Dai Ichi insurance building, a ten-minute drive away. As his chauffeured black 1941 Cadillac taking him to work purred through the streets, all traffic lights were switched to green for his convenience. Each day curious Japanese watched him and bowed deeply as he passed.

During his time in Japan, MacArthur received visitors in much the same way that a great king might grant an audience. Grant McConachie, the colourful ex-bush pilot who rose to the presidency of Canadian Pacific Airlines at the age of thirty-eight, admitted that he had been impressed by MacArthur when he met him in the Dai Ichi in January 1949. McConachie had gone to Japan to obtain operating permits for his airline to fly into Tokyo on a regular schedule. He spent almost a month doing the necessary legwork in the capital, but at each step along the way he was told to "see MacArthur". Finally the Canadian Ambassador, Herbert Norman, arranged a fifteen-minute meeting with the General. When McConachie got to MacArthur's office, the Great Man puffed on his pipe and talked about shipping, good tobacco, the Hudson's Bay Company, the Banff–Lake Louise Area of Alberta, and backfiring problems on his DC-4 aircraft. The fifteen minutes flew by and a now desperate McConachie thought his month-long wait for this precious interview had been wasted. As he was about to leave the office, he finally had a chance to blurt out his reason for being there.

"I don't think you have a problem," MacArthur replied. "Be downstairs at nine tomorrow morning and it will be all fixed up. Don't worry about the permits." McConachie did what he was told and showed up the following morning. The permits were waiting, and CP still flies to Japan.

One year later, Lester Pearson met MacArthur. He, like McConachie, had been impressed by the General and called him "the most arresting and magnetic personality . . . I have ever been exposed to . . . the most imperial, proconsular figure I have ever seen."

> I recall a luncheon he gave for my wife and me. There was more ceremony than . . . in Buckingham Palace or in the Vatican. Mrs. MacArthur was already there with all the aides in attendance. As we waited we started to get fifteen-second bulletins: the General has left his office; the General is on his way; the General will be here shortly. We were lined up. There was a hush. The doors were thrown open and there was General of the Army and Field Marshal of the Philippines Douglas MacArthur. I felt that I ought to fall down and worship.

When the three destroyers *Cayuga*, *Athabaskan*, and *Sioux* arrived at the Japanese port of Sasebo on July 30, MacArthur sent an aircraft to bring Captain Jeffry Brock to Tokyo for a meeting. Brock experienced the carefully orchestrated entrance but admitted that the General "was a man of great personal magnetism." Captain Brock added: "He was one of the very few persons I have met in my life who seemed surrounded by an aura of greatness." Brock had other encounters with MacArthur, and even though he admits admiration for the General, he never believed MacArthur was particularly profound, or even an exceptionally great commander.

"He became one of the world's most famous captains of war partly by luck and by being in the right place at the right time . . . but his handling of the Korean conflict did nothing to enhance his military prestige."

Canadian Brigadier John Rockingham spent about forty-five minutes with MacArthur. The meeting did not go well. "They had orchestrated my arrival, right down to the second," Rockingham recalls. "Then when I finally got into his office he sat on his big chair, his throne as it were, and talked at me. All the while I could hardly see his face because of the bright light from the Tokyo sun streaming into the room through a window right behind him.

"Then when my visit was over, I went downstairs and they wouldn't let me out of the building. MacArthur was about to leave and the honour guard was all around. When he did leave, there were thousands of Japanese lined up on both sides of the steps and on the road down to his car and he paused and looked around from right to left and all the Japanese sucked in their breath in amazement. He took advantage of every bit of this show. I thought he was a self-satisfied show-off."

In order to further enhance his presence in Japan, MacArthur went to some lengths to surround himself with sycophantic lackeys who catered to his every whim and agreed with everything he did or said. He also screened servicemen who were posted to Japan in order to keep the brightest and the best close to him. The others, the ones who in his opinion did not measure up, were never near the Embassy or the Dai Ichi. These, when the opportunity came, were sent to Korea.

Many of them were clerks, drivers, cooks, office assistants, and so on. Most of them had joined the army, not to fight, but to obtain a job that promised security, travel, a uniform, and a chance to learn a trade. Very few had combat training. Most enjoyed Japan and the amenities it offered: regular hours, lots of recreation, cheap booze, and live-in love. Hundreds of U.S. occupation servicemen had Japanese girls residing with them.

And while the prospect of going to Korea to actually *fight* was anathema to most of the young Americans in Japan, the attitude had been nourished by MacArthur's office, and in fact by the General himself. Even though his sphere of command included Korea, in the years between the end of the Second World War and the outbreak of the Korean War he had been to Korea only once — and then for just a few hours. He hated the place and used assignment there as a kind of punishment for mistakes. In fact "one young soldier was offered his choice of court-martial or Korea."

As the North Koreans consolidated their hold on Seoul, MacArthur decided he would fly to Korea and see for himself what was happening. He landed at the badly damaged airfield at Suwon and then drove the twenty miles north to Seoul in a beaten-up old Dodge sedan. Just south of the Han, the General climbed the ridge which overlooks Seoul and watched as the capital burned, refugees fled, and mortar shells exploded in the distance. After an hour or so observing the panorama of destruction below him, he climbed back into the car and retraced his journey. Later he claimed to have formulated his strategy for the coming weeks while standing on the ridge that afternoon. Prior to leaving Suwon, MacArthur conferred for an hour with President Rhee, who had come to the airfield to meet him. After assuring the old Korean leader of all the support possible, MacArthur strode across the pot-holed tarmac, climbed into his plane, and returned to Tokyo. The next day he asked Washington for more help.

As June became July and July faded into August, more and more American soldiers found themselves in Korea. Unfortunately most of them had become boxed into a small area in the southeastern part of the country inside what came to be called the Pusan Perimeter, after Pusan, the second-largest city. Here three U.S. divisions, along with five South Korean, attempted to hold out against fifteen North Korean divisions and one armoured brigade. The U.N. forces had been steadily pushed down the peninsula by the advancing North Koreans, and were now in danger of being driven into the sea.

As the gravity of the situation in Korea increased, United Nations Secretary General Trygve Lie asked for more help from member countries. Several responded, including Britain, New Zealand, Australia, and South Africa. As far as Canada was concerned, her three destroyers were already in the Far East. And, in addition, No. 426 RCAF Squadron had begun ferrying supplies to Japan from McChord Air Force Base in Washington. Now, however, the time had come to send in ground troops.

4

CANADA SIGNS UP

At 6:30 p.m., Thursday, August 7, 1950, the phone rang in the Vancouver office of the Superintendent of Pacific Stage Lines. The tall, dark, burly man who answered shouted into the instrument and rebuked the secretary who had allowed the call to come through. The Superintendent was in the middle of a meeting and the interruption was an annoyance he did not need. His company, a subsidiary of British Columbia Electric, operated a fleet of buses in the province and was involved in a union dispute with the drivers. Relations with the union executive were not always amicable at the best of times, but today the Superintendent had been dealing with something he thought was ridiculous — the request by the union for all drivers to have the same 12:00–1:00 lunch hour.

"You can't expect me to close the whole damn system at noon just because you want to eat together," he shouted at the union representatives in his office. "And your suggestions that I could hire extra men to drive over lunch hour is crazy. The shift system and the layovers look after that," he roared.

Then the Superintendent grabbed the phone.

The man on the line was Brooke Claxton, Minister of National Defence. He was making an urgent call from Ottawa to tell John Meredith Rockingham that Canadian ground forces would fight in Korea and to ask Rockingham to lead them. After five years as a civilian, Rockingham would be going back into uniform.

Probably no better choice of commander could have been made. John Rockingham was a soldier's soldier — six feet four inches tall, and darkly handsome, with wide shoulders, a trim waist, and a parade-square bellow that could be heard a dozen blocks away. The 195-pound Australian-born Rockingham came to Canada in 1930 and enlisted in the Canadian Scottish Regiment. When the Second World War started he was a lieutenant. When hostilities ceased in 1945 he was a brigadier with a CBE and a DSO and Bar. He had never shirked his duty or backed down from a challenge. Once, when a

German sniper grazed his nose with a bullet, Rockingham was so angry he took off after the man, cornered him, and shot him on the spot. On another occasion a German gun crew jumped him in a forest on the Scheldt. Even though he was alone at the time, Rockingham recovered his composure, took three of the enemy prisoner, and dropped two others with a couple of bursts from his machine-gun. Later, on VE-day, Rockingham accepted the surrender of a large submarine base at the port city of Emden, Germany. After the capitulation ceremony he intended to ride in his scout car through long lines of armed Germans, who would easily be able to shoot him. The German commander was afraid something might happen and advised the big Canadian to carry a white flag. Rockingham exploded in fury.

"Go to hell," he told the German. "You just get into that jeep up there and drive straight ahead. If any of your men try something, I'll empty my whole Bren mag into your goddamned head. Now *move*!"

Rockingham always refused to order any man to do what he would not do himself. His men knew this and respected him for it. They also gave him their complete loyalty in return.

"He was hard on his men, but a lot harder on himself," recalls Jacques Dextraze, the ascetic general who would later become Canada's Chief of Staff. "Rockingham drove his men until they dropped, but he was a magnificent soldier."

"I remember seeing him chew a man out until the guy cried," says Brigadier-General Joe Cardy. "He was hard on his men but he always backed them. If he had a major fault, it was his tendency to get too close to the lines, to put himself in danger. He was too valuable to lose. He was a first-class leader of men."

Another officer who served under Rockingham told me: "He was tough, but tough on himself as well as on the rest of us. He worked hard and played hard. I've seen him drink Scotch with ice, Scotch with water, and if there was none of the first two, Scotch with Scotch. He never spared himself, but the next morning he was the first man on the job."

Now John Rockingham was about to tackle the biggest job of his career.

The debate as to exactly what Canada's contribution in Korea might be had been heating up for some days. The departure of the three destroyers for the Far East had eased the discontent for a while, but there was still a large cross-section of vocal Canadians who thought we were not doing enough. The protests again softened when the RCAF began ferrying supplies to Japan, but there was always the insistence by some that the army would have to go in.

On July 12, the U.N. Secretary General was informed that

Canada's three destroyers, which had departed Esquimalt on July 5, would be placed under U.N. operational control as soon as they arrived in Japan. This was acknowledged, but two days later the Secretary General asked for more help — particularly ground troops. The request was carefully considered, both by the Cabinet Defence Committee and by Lieutenant-General Charles Foulkes, Chief of the General Staff, and his senior officers. After a great deal of serious study, neither group felt that Canada could spare any troops from her existing strength. Foulkes in particular felt that if Canada sent a modest regular-force contribution to the Korean campaign, it would require "almost every trained soldier in the army". Foulkes, as it turned out, had given a lot of thought to recruiting a special force. He felt that if such an outfit were established, it could be made available for U.N. use and the regular force could be kept in Canada for requirements at home. In essence, however, no Canadian ground troops could be sent to Korea because "no ground forces of any significant size were ready."

But still the clamour continued.

Newspapers across the country urged the government to do *something* and soon. As early as July 1, following the proroguing of the House of Commons, the *Globe and Mail* expressed its dissatisfaction with the way this country had faced the situation in Korea: "Canada, to the dismay of her citizens, is once again fumbling an opportunity in . . . international affairs." A week later, on July 7, the *Vancouver Province* argued that every member of Parliament had a responsibility "to this country to face the problems", particularly in Korea.

By the end of the same month, others had taken up the cry. In a column in the *Vancouver Sun* on July 31, 1950, Roy W. Brown maintained that "as a symbol of unity and a declaration of complete support of the program of the United Nations to fight for peace in the world, a force of 1,500 or 2,000 Canadians would . . . have a value far in excess of that number of individuals." In the August 1950 issue of the *Canadian Forum*, in an article written some time before publication, historian Frank Underhill chided Canadians for their criticism of American unpreparedness, particularly when this country was "able to send only three destroyers to the Korean War." The *Ottawa Evening Citizen*, on July 28, pointed out that "Canadian co-operation with American troops [would be] . . . the best prospect of effective Canadian help." By July 31, the *Globe and Mail* reported that "the Canadian Government is considering the recruitment of a special volunteer contingent for active service in Korea. It will be gratifying if the Cabinet at last acknowledge this country's duty to send ground forces. . . ."

About the same time that Canadian newspapers were making the case for our increased participation in Korea, murmurings in the United States indicated that Americans were not terribly impressed by our lack of commitment either. *Time* magazine on July 31 stated that "Washington insiders" were of the opinion that our initial failure to contribute ground troops was "disappointing". Ottawa was certainly aware of this undercurrent of dissatisfaction, and by mid-July the matter had been simmering too long to be ignored.

Lester Pearson went on a secret visit to Washington to see Dean Acheson and from there to the U.N. for talks with Trygve Lie. To Pearson, the Washington meeting seems to have been the more important. He expressed satisfaction with his discussions there and later summarized what had been covered. Dean Acheson outlined the significance of Korea as far as the United States was concerned, but he stressed that any actions in the Far East should be part of a concerted U.N. effort. Pearson later wrote that Acheson emphasized "the tremendous importance of contributions to the Korean operations from United Nations countries. . . . He strongly hoped that Canada could join others in offering such forces."

Mackenzie King, the tenth prime minister of Canada, who left office in 1948 and was succeeded by Louis St. Laurent, died on July 22, 1950. King had always tried to keep Canada out of Korean affairs, particularly following a U.S. request late in 1947 that we assist in supervising elections there. He felt at the time that the Russians would oppose free elections in the north anyway, so our supervision would be useless. Nor did he want to be seen by Russia as helping to push the U.S. aggressive policy towards the Soviets.

But now King was dead. The St. Laurent Cabinet went by train to Toronto for the funeral. Then, in a somewhat ironic twist of history, the politicians devoted much of the trip back to Ottawa to a discussion of Korea. As one of those present told a reporter later: "This was the first time since the Korean crisis began that the ministers had been together for a period of hours without the tyranny of an agenda, free to talk the subject out." And even though it would not be announced to the public for some days, by the time the special train carrying the Cabinet pulled into Ottawa that night, the decision to send ground troops to the Far East had been made.

Finally, on August 7, St. Laurent went on the national CBC radio network and told the nation that an expeditionary brigade of five thousand men would be recruited for Korea. The day after the Prime Minister's speech, recruiting offices were busier than they had been in years. Long lines of would-be soldiers stood in the streets for hours, waiting to be processed, waiting to go away to war. In order to enlist, men had to be physically and mentally fit, and between the ages of nineteen and thirty-five, although tradesmen and married men could be as old as forty-five. Once accepted, most of the new recruits were to be sent to one of three places: Wainwright, Alberta, to the Princess Patricia's Canadian Light Infantry (PPCLI); Petawawa, Ontario, where the Royal Canadian Regiment (RCR) would train; or Valcartier, Quebec, where they would join the Royal 22nd ("Vandoos") Regiment. The circumstances of their enlistment varied.

Often groups of men who had been drinking draft and telling war stories piled out of local pubs and went *en masse* to recruiting stations. If they seemed sober enough they were sometimes accepted right away. Generally, however, the lot were sent packing and advised to return the next day. Rarely did as many come back. Others who arrived alone were often hustled through, occasionally with rather rudimentary physical examinations. Many more were weeded out as soon as they got inside the door.

There were boys of fourteen who wanted to look older and men of sixty who claimed to be forty-three. Many were running from debts, their wives, or the law. Others came because they needed work. Many who turned up wanted to relive their imagined glory days of the Second World War. Some came because their buddies came. Hundreds showed up because they wanted excitement, a break in what were otherwise humdrum lives. Many signed up on the spur of the moment, with no more thought than they would give to which coat they might wear to a corner store.

George Henderson, of Stratford, Ontario, was on a walking tour across Canada when he heard Lester Pearson talking on the radio about Korea. "I was walking for something to do," he says now. "I thought walking around Korea would be the same as walking in Canada, so I joined the army the day I heard Pearson's speech. I later found out that walking in Korea was not so great."

In British Columbia, a veteran by the name of Stone was running a summer resort when the Korean War started. A friend in the army suggested that he return to uniform. Stone did so — and within weeks led Canada's first contingent to the Far East. Today "Big Jim" Stone is revered by many in the PPCLI as the greatest Canadian soldier who ever fought.

After he had obtained his discharge from an infantry battalion at the end of the Second World War, Ed Haslip had gone to work for the Dow Chemical Company in Sarnia. When Korea started, he got his severance from Dow, packed his things, and drove the sixty miles to London to join the RCRs.

Andy MacKenzie of Montreal was involved in forming the Royal Canadian Air Force No. 441 Fighter Squadron at St. Hubert, Quebec, when the Korean War began. He immediately began hoping the entire squadron would be sent to the Far East. When that did not come to pass, he managed to persuade his superiors to let him fly a slot position with the Americans. In the years since Korea, he has often had second thoughts about his eagerness. "Korea was a devastating theatre for me," he recalls. "I am a different man today because of that war."

But not only were fellows like Stone, Haslip, and MacKenzie all veterans, they were also physically fit. Many of those who arrived at recruiting posts, and many who actually got into uniform, were something less than perfect specimens.

John Beswick was a young army intern who did medicals at Chorley Park in Toronto. "We had all kinds of characters who showed up," Beswick recalls. "Originally we were supposed to take veterans, because we had all the medical records on these guys. They were not supposed to be accepted, however, until their medical records were assessed. But then we found out that the whole thing was a bit of a political game.

"There was a competition between Montreal and Toronto to see who could get the most recruits. All kinds of people arrived. One day Toronto was ahead, the next day Montreal, and so on. We got terrible people mixed in with the good ones. One guy showed up with a big bloody scar from his neck to his belly. When I asked him what it was, he said, 'Appendectomy.'

"We had one lad later, just before he was thrown out, who told the psychiatrist that when he was a teenager at home on the farm he used to get up at night and go out and strangle sheep. This guy had been in the goddamned Medical Corps.

"Many of us went to Fort Lewis in Washington for training before we went to Korea. I remember riding on a bus one day with one of our guys, a chap who had been a Hong Kong prisoner [in the Second World War]. He had all sorts of dietary deficiencies, beriberi, visual loss, middle-ear disease. As we rode along on that bus, the sky, which had been heavily overcast for days, suddenly cleared and you could see the brilliance of Mount Rainier some miles away. I said to the guy, 'Isn't the mountain beautiful?' He didn't hear me. I shouted the question. This time he heard me but asked, 'What mountain?' He was not only half deaf, he was half blind as well. He was sent home.

"One guy who made it to Korea with the first contingent was sent back soon because he was schizophrenic. This fellow had been free from all the communicable diseases all right, but he started talking about his friend who was running around inside his hat. When he came back from Korea, he was in a strait-jacket. The psychiatrist who went out to meet his plane asked the guy if he was going to be good. 'Oh yes,' he answered. 'I'll be good tonight, but I ain't promising nothin' for tomorrow.'"

In all, there were twelve recruiting depots across Canada, from Halifax to Vancouver. Because of the rush to enlist, undesirables appeared everywhere. Two of the most obvious were a man of seventy-two who actually got into the army — for a time — and a man with an artificial leg. "There is at least one recorded case of a civilian who on impulse got on board a troop train in Ottawa with a newly enlisted friend and was found weeks later in Calgary, drilling with the PPCLI."

Years later, Colonel Jim Stone commented on the enlistment. "They were recruiting anybody who could breathe or walk. Brooke Claxton pushed the enlistment along because he was a politician at heart and didn't really give a damn about what else was happening. He was recruiting an army in order to fight. We had to show some of the first guys how to put their shoes on."

The actual departure from home for the men and later the women going to Korea was traumatic in some cases, boisterous in others, and quiet in many. But whether he or she was leaving for the first time or for the third, with the first group to go or with the last, most Canadians who went to Korea recall the circumstances of their leaving.

Don Eager of Consecon, Ontario, caught the train at nearby Trenton. "Dad and a friend of his drove me into town. Because we were early we decided to go to the Queensway for a beer. After a few minutes, my dad excused himself and left for a while. When he returned, he handed me a package and then we gulped another drink and raced to the train. I was a pretty lonely boy but I had Dad's package for comfort. It turned out to be three bottles of Black and White Scotch. I opened one to ease my pains. Then by the time I got to Toronto the Trans-Continental for the west was ready to go. I found my berth, had another couple of drinks, and didn't wake up until we pulled into Sudbury the next morning. I wasn't lonely any more."

Jean Mickle went to Korea with the Royal Canadian Army Medical Corps. The young physiotherapist had been stationed at Shilo, Manitoba, when she received the posting. She was both surprised and somewhat annoyed at the news: surprised because she did not realize physiotherapists would be sent to Korea, and annoyed because she had just bought her first car, a new Ford coupe. Shortly after the transfer notice arrived, she wrote to a nursing-sister friend who was already in Korea and asked her advice. The answer was rather blunt: "Forget the car. You'll never get another chance like this." She accepted both the advice and the posting.

Bud Scriver was a twenty-year-old private stationed at Kingston. "One morning they lined us up on the parade square," he recalled. "They told us that we were all going to Korea, unless we had a damned good reason why we couldn't go. I couldn't come up with any reason fast enough, so away I went. It was as simple as that."

Frank Cassidy of Montreal was in Korea long before Canadian soldiers were sent there. One weekend he had driven to Plattsburg, New York, joined the American army, and one year later found himself with the U.S. occupation troops in Japan. When war broke out in Korea he was part of the Eighth Army in the fighting at Taegu. Shortly after he learned that Canadians were going to be sent to Korea, he returned to the United States as a sergeant and obtained his American discharge. While still on leave, he went back to Montreal, enlisted in the Canadian army, did his basic training all over again, and left for Korea the second time — as a lance-corporal.

Lorne Barton was a stoker in the Royal Canadian Navy at Halifax when he learned that he was to go to war. "I was in the drafting office at the Engineers' School, working under the Chief Stoker, helping him to make up drafts for some of the chaps going to Korea," he says. "I happened to come in one morning and I was typing up drafts and my name appeared. I asked the Chief if it was a joke and he said, 'No, I'm quite serious. A stoker on the *Nootka* broke his leg last night and you're taking his place. You have to be out of here by 3 p.m. Have a good trip.' I only had time to send home for fifty dollars and say goodbye to my wife. She wasn't too happy about my leaving so quickly. We had only been married three weeks."

The man affectionately known to many troops as "Padre Joe" was stationed in the Maritimes when he received his posting to Korea. Major, and much later Brigadier-General, Joe Cardy had been living in Fredericton, New Brunswick, when he was told he had been selected for duty in the Far East. "I just had time to pack up my house, put my wife and our two-year-old boy on a ship for England where her parents lived. Then I went off in the opposite direction," recalls Cardy.

Stu Meeks was a kid in Kingston just before the Korean War broke out. Because his father was in the service, young Stu decided he should follow the tradition. When he was still just fourteen, he was tall and muscular and looked eighteen, so he decided to capitalize on his looks. He bought some ink erdicator and changed the date of birth on his baptismal certificate. Then, with the help of a city policeman, he got a sheet of the Chief's stationery, typed up a character reference that mentioned the new birthdate, and then went to join the army.

Seventeen-year-old Don Muir of Seaforth, Ontario, was partying with some friends one night and they all decided to join the army. The next morning the friends had second thoughts about the idea, but Muir decided to go ahead. His job as an apprentice mechanic at a local garage was not exciting enough anyway. Because he expected his mother to object to his plans, he pulled coveralls over his good clothes and pretended he was leaving for work. Instead of going to his job, he went to a trucking firm, stashed the coveralls in a garbage can, and hitched a ride to a recruiting office. There, he lied about his age, passed his physical, and became a soldier. "The first that Mother knew that I'd gone was when the guys from the garage called to see if I was coming to work," he says.

As the number of enlistments grew, so did the feeling that additional recruits should be accepted, over and above the five-thousand-man army originally intended. By August 18, the Chief of the General Staff told the Cabinet that recruitment had reached the five thousand mark and at the same time asked for more men so that the Special Force, as it was called, would have replacement personnel, should the need arise. The recommendation was accepted and recruiting depots were told they could take up to ten thousand men.

While the enlistment of recruits was going ahead, the officers of the Special Force were also being selected.

As soon as the Minister of National Defence finished asking the Superintendent of Pacific Stage Lines if he would accept an appointment as Brigade Commander for Korea, John Rockingham put down the phone and turned to face the transit union representatives in his Vancouver office. They had been waiting for the conversation with Ottawa to end and were shuffling in their chairs, impatient at the delay. One of them asked, "What are you going to do about our demands?"

Rockingham jumped up, strode to the door, and opened it with the words: "Nothing. You can go to hell as far as I'm concerned."

The negotiators trooped out.

"I was really more concerned about how I would tell my wife about the phone call than I was about handling those ridiculous union demands," Rockingham says today. "As I drove home, I was rehearsing what I was going to say, but it turned out she already knew. Claxton had called my home first and my wife had given him my office number. Then she had heard a radio bulletin about the possibility of a brigade going to Korea. She put the two together and anticipated what I would be telling her.

"Then I interrupted a dinner party my boss was giving and broke the news to him. He was good about it though. Even told me I could have my old job back.

"Very soon after my return call to the Minister accepting the appointment, it was announced by the media. That same evening my personal batman from the Second World War appeared at our front door with a brush sticking out of his pocket. He didn't even say hello, just looked at my scruffy shoes and muttered, 'Well, here we go again.'"

The next day Brigadier Rockingham flew to Ottawa to work on specific details concerning the formation of the fighting force, but in particular to oversee the selection of the officers for the Brigade. Wartime experience was important, indeed was "the over-riding consideration . . . if the brigade was to be ready to fight in the shortest possible time." By the time the selection of officers was completed, training for Korea was commencing.

For the first weeks, the training was being done in several places across the country as units of the Special Force received their introduction to army life from their active-force, or regular-force, counterparts. In the first days after the call-up, this training continued virtually non-stop except for interruptions to distribute supplies as these arrived. Gradually, as each unit became more professional, regular-force personnel became less and less necessary. Because of a nation-wide rail strike that began on August 22, however, difficulties ensued relative to the transporting of troops. By the time Parliament met on August 29 and ordered the railway workers back to their jobs, hundreds of volunteers for Korea were stranded all over Canada. As it took a few days to round them up and send them to the camps where they belonged, more valuable training time was lost.

As fall approached and the weather became cooler, Defence Headquarters in Ottawa started looking for alternative sites where the new army could complete its preparations for war, because winter training facilities were judged to be inadequate in Canada. A suggestion that some of the training be done in Japan was rejected by General MacArthur as "politically unwise", as Canada had not been part of the post-Second World War occupation force there. The General suggested the island of Okinawa, but it was rejected as unsuitable by Canadian Brigadier F. J. Fleury, who inspected the place. Finally, Fort Lewis, a large American military camp in Washington State, was chosen.

During October, advance units of the groups who would be training in Fort Lewis went there to make the necessary arrangements for those who were to follow. On November 11, the first train to Fort Lewis left Valcartier, Quebec. The journey took five days. By November 21, the last of twenty-two trains had pulled into the American camp. In all, 286 officers and 5,773 other ranks had been transported.

But some never arrived.

At ten thirty-five on the last morning of the operation, a seventeen-car westbound troop train carrying 340 soldiers crossed a long trestle over a 500-foot mountain gorge, 312 miles west of Edmonton. Just east of a hamlet called Canoe River, British Columbia, the train entered a long, sweeping uphill curve. At that moment, a speeding transcontinental express from the opposite direction banked into the same curve. Forty-five seconds later, the mountains echoed as the two great engines crashed headlong into each other.

The tremendous impact heaved the engine of the army train into the air and tossed it backwards and down on the coaches immediately behind it. Several cars were thrown from the rails and wood coaches buckled like cordword as steel cars slammed into them. The baggage car and sections of the express left the rails. Shattered steel, broken glass, and broken men were hurled into the air like tenpins in a bowling alley in hell. The roar of escaping steam blotted out the cries of the injured, but at the same time scalded many where they lay.

Soldiers and civilians poured from both trains and began to assist those who were crying for help. Their work was slow and often futile as the temperature outside was fifteen degrees below zero Fahrenheit and they had to tramp through half a foot and more of snow to reach those who were trapped.

Rescuers told tales of horror. Sergeant Michael Knopp of Vancouver saw a boot protruding from the wreckage. When the boot was finally extricated, a shattered foot was still inside it. Elsewhere he saw a severed head and part of a torso. One soldier was cut in two. Only the hand of another was found. The leg of a crew member was retrieved.

Lieutenant Paul Cullen of Montreal stood shaking at railside and considered himself lucky to be alive. He had been riding in the third coach from the front of the military train when the car ahead of his telescoped and landed on the front of the one in which he rode. Almost all of the dead and injured had been at the front of the train.

"Most of them never knew what hit them," Cullen told a reporter later. "Our coaches, all of wooden construction, just disintegrated. The wreckage was piled a good fifty feet high. It wasn't recognizable as anything but a jumble of twisted steel and splintered wood."

In all, twenty-one men died that morning, including four who were never found. Close to seventy were injured, some of them severely — from the impact and from the scalding steam, which, as soon as it burned into exposed flesh, froze in the bitter cold, turning its victims into grotesque, pain-wracked hulks. Most of the dead and injured were soldiers and train crew, the soldiers part of the 2nd Regiment of the Royal Canadian Horse Artillery.

The following spring, on May 9, 1951, a well-publicized manslaughter trial opened in Prince George, British Columbia. There, a 22-year-old Canadian National Railways telegrapher named Alfred John Atherton was accused of causing the wreck and the deaths which resulted from it because he had supposedly sent an incomplete message to the westbound train. Atherton's transmission informed the conductor of the troop train that he was to move onto a siding called Cedarside in order to let an approaching express pass. Unfortunately, though Atherton was certain the location was included in the message he sent, the conductor of the military train swore that the two words "at Cedarside" were not present in the transmission he received.

The Crown was represented in the trial by a former First World War officer, Colonel Pepler, Deputy Attorney General of British Columbia. Atherton's lawyer was John Diefenbaker. The trial itself was lively, and Diefenbaker won an acquittal for his client by convincing the jury that snow on the telegraph wires could have been responsible for the incomplete message which resulted in the tragedy. In so far as the soldiers on the train and the railwaymen were concerned, however, a heated exchange between Colonel Pepler and Diefenbaker would be remembered long after the outcome of the trial was known.

On the afternoon of the first day of the trial, a senior executive from Canadian National Railways was in the witness-box. The fact that CN had steadfastly refused to accept responsibility for the Canoe River crash, and seemed to be using young Atherton as a scapegoat, irritated the man who would become our thirteenth prime minister. He shuffled some papers, drew himself to his full height, jabbed an accusing finger at the official from CN, and said: "I suppose the reason you put these soldiers in wooden cars with steel cars on either end was so that no matter what they might subsequently find in Korea, they'd always be able to say, 'Well, we had worse than that in Canada.'"

Pandemonium broke out in the courtroom. The Crown Attorney sputtered an objection and said he was shocked and pointed out that such inflammatory procedure was unacceptable in a court in British Columbia. Then, because the trial technically concerned the deaths of railwaymen rather than soldiers, he inadvertently blurted out the comment: "I want to make it clear that in this case we're not concerned about the deaths of a few privates going to Korea."

Diefenbaker jumped to his feet and roared, "You're not concerned about the killing of a few privates?'' Then he added with icy sarcasm, ''Oh, Colonel!''

From then on, Atherton was out of danger.

Long before the Canoe River trial took place, thousands of soldiers from every Canadian province had undergone training at Fort Lewis. Men who were there regard the place with mixed memories. Dr. John Beswick recalls a party in the officers' mess where the orchestra was conducted by a fellow named Lawrence Welk. Sudbury native Ken McOrmond tells of making movies and of guys shaving their heads. Others recall the immense size of the Fort Lewis property — ninety thousand acres. Jim Brown, a native of Egmondville, Ontario, and later a dispatch rider in Korea, remembers the rain. ''It rained harder there than I thought possible,'' he says. ''Sheets of rain that turned every damned low spot into a lake.''

The incessant rains softened open areas that tanks churned into gumbo. The rains fell on the troops as they trained, ran down their necks and drenched their clothes, so that even though uniforms were dry in the morning, they were clammy after five minutes out of doors.

The Canadians noticed other things at Fort Lewis. The casual, often sloppy dress of the Americans. The profusion of U.S. flags. The amusement of American soldiers at the speech patterns of these men from the north, and their utter bewilderment when elements of the Royal 22nd Regiment conversed in French.

But most of all they remember Rocky.

No soldier who trained at Fort Lewis can forget Rockingham. The big brigadier seemed to be everywhere at once. Driving his own jeep around the compound, sitting on the edge of the turret of his armoured scout car, wearing a crash helmet and roaring down a hillside on a motorcycle as he observed the training of the Field Ambulance Corps, clambering onto an M-10 tank during manoeuvres, or taking the salute on the parade square as a bitter wind whipped ice particles out of the northern Washington sky.

The men loved him. They would have followed him anywhere and they composed a song about him that became the theme song of the Brigade. There were several versions of the song, but the most printable is as follows:

Why don't you join up?
Why don't you join up?
Why don't you join old Rocky's army?
Two bucks a week. Nothing to eat.
Great big boots and blisters on your feet.
Why don't you join up?

Why don't you join up?
Why don't you join old Rocky's army?
If it wasn't for the war, we'd have pushed off before —
Rocky, you're balmy!

While the units which together formed the 25th Canadian Infantry Brigade were training in Washington, United Nations forces were having more and more success in Korea. The terrible retreats of the summer and the near-disasters as the Communists came close to sweeping everything before them into the sea had halted. The brilliant landing at Inchon described in the following chapter prepared the way for U.N. troops to advance again. So rapid was the new U.N. offensive that for a time it looked as if Canadian ground forces would not get to Korea before the war ended.

For this reason it was decided that one battalion should be sent immediately to the Far East, so that the Canadians would at least be on the ground in Korea before hostilities ceased. The unit chosen to go was the 2nd Princess Patricia's Canadian Light Infantry under the command of Colonel Jim Stone. They were preceded by an advance party of 350 all ranks who left in late October, and on November 25, Stone and his men boarded the American troopship *Private Joe P. Martinez* for the journey from Seattle to Pusan, Korea.

This departure, like the departure of so many armies to so many wars, was a festive occasion. "All ranks of the unit embarked in high spirits," reported the *Calgary Herald*. Colonel Stone said his troops were "in great shape, and happy. They have absorbed training faster than any unit I have ever known. They are also more enthusiastic than any I have ever known," he added.

The troops were transported from Fort Lewis at dawn in buses and taken directly to the ship. A U.S. navy band played as the Canadians boarded. Finally, the embarkation procedures over, the *Martinez* weighed anchor, slid out from the pier, and headed into the Pacific. The sounds of music fell farther and farther behind.

5

THE VOYAGE
TO KOREA

Whether they travelled on the *Private Joe P. Martinez*, or on one of the other ships that carried troops to Korea, Canadian soldiers all remember how they went to war. They remember the ship, the crowding, the food, the length of the voyage, and the sea — the boundless, heaving sea.

"I didn't think it was possible to be sick for two weeks straight," recalls one man. "My stomach turned so many times, I thought I was inside out. I had never been on a ship before, so the whole thing was a new experience. But after being seasick, I know ship life is not so great. In a way, I even dreaded the trip home. I knew I'd upchuck for five thousand miles or whatever it was, and I did. Now I stick to my car if I want to go anywhere."

Others remember the food on the ship.

"It was not so bad, really, although on the *Martinez* we ran short of potatoes, so they started restricting them to one meal. Then I recall guys swiping cases of tinned pineapples that were supposed to be for dessert. They sold the tins below decks and we all had to do without at mealtime. Colonel Stone found out what had happened and rubbed it in. I can't recall any more food being stolen."

"Everybody had some money when we boarded in Seattle," says George Henderson. "But then we started playing Crown and Anchor and a handful of guys ended up with the money. The rest of us were soon broke. There were times, though, that we found it hard to find space for even a card game. Our bunks were piled four or five high and there sure wasn't a lot of privacy."

Colonel Jim Stone also remembers the crowding. "There were about two thousand men on the *Martinez*, roughly a thousand Americans and the same number of Canadians. My stateroom was a closet in the doctor's office, just room for a seven-foot bunk, two and a half feet wide. We fed in a continuous line, twenty-four hours a day, two meals a day, walking past the kitchen. There were the usual crap games going on. Guys would win some money and then bribe the cooks to give them a big steak."

Captain H. C. (Bud) Taylor went to Korea on the *Marine Adder*. "It was dreary and miserable transportation," he says. "We shared the ship with Americans whose approach to shipboard life was somewhat different than ours. They stayed in the holds and became terribly seasick and miserable throughout the trip. We thought the way to combat the problem was to pretend there wasn't one, so we got our troops out on deck and did exercises. But then when P.T. was over, everyone trooped down into the stinking holds again.

"Because I was in the Royal Canadian Regiment, I was used to the formality of the evening meal. We took our best uniforms with us. However, because the weather was warm, and we were on a non-airconditioned ship, that uniform could hardly be described as comfortable. Yet the RCR officers religiously wore it every night, much to the absolute stupefaction of our American neighbours, who could only assume we were doing so as some form of punishment."

Don Eager enjoyed his trip to Korea. "I was on the *Marine Adder*. Just before we were to leave, I developed an ulcerated tooth and there were no dentists on board, so they sent me to sick bay. Then the tooth stopped aching but I didn't let on. I just rested all the way across. I'd read, look out the porthole, or take a stroll around the deck occasionally. I had a ball.

"When I got to Korea, things weren't so good, though. The tooth started aching again and I was sent to the dentist, who was working in the back of an old truck. I had a small plate but the guy grabbed it and threw it into the garbage. Then he pulled five teeth. Guess he wanted to make sure he got the bad one."

Each day during the voyage of the *Martinez*, a group of men compiled a small newspaper for the troops. Lance-Corporal John Dalrymple, who had previous newspaper experience, co-edited the *Eagle-Leaf* along with American John Jacobs. The newspaper began "without even a spot to set its typewriter". When the *Eagle-Leaf* ended publication, it died without improving its lot. Nevertheless, eighteen issues came out — more or less when they should have. The paper covered the day-to-day events on board ship, and when they were available, it included news stories from Canada, the States, Korea, and elsewhere.

One of the most popular items was a regular piece called "Benny Rites Home", a tongue-in-cheek semi-literate "letter" written by Corporal Kerry Dunphy to his "Pop" back in Canada. While parts of Dunphy's letters were prompted by long-forgotten shipboard activities, much of what he had to say is still amusing thirty years later, like his description of the food on board: "a supper of boiled carp, raw turnips, and luke warm milk. Pop, wot are the reel *poor* people eatin?" His comments on an inspection: "Yesterday we had an inspeckshun of our guns. A guy by the name of Armerer tole me mine was the most corroaded gun he evur saw. I said thanx and tole him how I cleaned it to make it so good. He jest sed sumpin about bells ringing and then thur wuz some froth on his lips and he lay down on the deck. He shure is a funny guy — coarse he's a sarjint." On sports: "In the tabul tennus tournement when my fren beet me, I jumped ovur the net too shake his hand. What does 'disqualified fer evur' mean?" And, following an indoctrination film: "We saw a pitcher all about them there Communists. We gotta be careful cuz they look sew much like ordunary peepul."

Each day a short lost-and-found column appeared in the *Eagle-Leaf*. Most of the items that went missing were trivial but of sentimental value to their owners. There were several watches, wallets, lighters, a book or two, St. Christopher medals, rosaries, personal letters, and even a pair of boots. When the *Martinez* crossed the International Date Line on December 6, the newspaper mentioned that the most important missing item was "one day — brand new, never been used. No initials but considerable sentimental value." Soldiers who had birthdays that day missed them. The paper also reported a pair of "found" items the same day: a bayonet that turned up in the Chaplain's office and a set of dentures. In the latter case, the owner was told to "redeem teeth at the orderly room upon properly fitting same".

The *Eagle-Leaf* notwithstanding, it was in the pursuit of booze that real Canadian creativity came to the fore. When the ship stopped at Pearl Harbor on the way across the Pacific, the troops were taken on a disciplined route march but were not allowed liberty. Nevertheless, a handful of men obtained alcohol. One chap scrounged a bottle of bourbon and hid it in his beret as he returned to the *Martinez*. The sergeant-major at the gangplank was searching everyone and "while he went over my battledress blouse and trousers and everything else, he completely missed the beret I held out to him," recalls the soldier. Another man befriended the cooks, borrowed some of their civilian clothes, and bought three bottles of Scotch, one of which he turned over to his benefactors.

But a correspondent for the Canadian Press who accompanied the battalion on the journey was allowed to go wherever he wished in Hawaii. "I took off for the American Officers' Club," recalls veteran reporter Bill Boss. "While I was there I bought three duffel-bags and two cases of whiskey to put in each. I brought the whole thing back to the dry *Martinez*. The booze supply became known as Tiger Mess, and it came in handy later for Christmas dinner and certain other occasions."

As the ship eased out of Pearl Harbor, some Canadians remember seeing a young U.S. private looking back on what would later become America's fiftieth state. The Canadians couldn't decide whether the chap was homesick, blasphemous, or both. "Our Father, who art in Washington, Harry is thy name," the man was saying.

At least two operations were performed on the way to Korea. Both were appendectomies and both were performed by the ship's medical officer, Dr. Mark Nolte of the U.S. Navy. He was assisted by Dr. Ed Karpetz of Spiritwood, Saskatchewan. The unlucky privates who were operated on were Orval Campbell, an Ontario native, and Ralph Clattenburg from Halifax. During Clattenburg's forty-five-minute surgery, the ship encountered some of the worst swells of the trip. On a couple of occasions she listed to thirty degrees, when crockery was smashed and medical instruments were thrown around. Captain K. A. McCann was eventually forced to hold the ship into the wind until the operation was completed.

Finally, the last movie was shown, the last bingo game was played, and the *Private Joe P. Martinez* steamed into harbour at Yokohama, Japan, on December 13, 1950. The ship had not even anchored when the troops were pleading to be allowed ashore. They' had been cooped up for most of nineteen days and were decidedly restless. The argument that the officers heard, however, was to the effect that this would be the last chance for Christmas shopping before the ship went on to Korea. Colonel Stone knew what would happen as soon as the men left the ship, so at first he was reluctant to let them go.

"Much as it was against my better judgement," he says today, "there were so many cries from the soldiers about presents for their loved ones and that kind of thing that I finally relented. I told the platoon commanders to take their men ashore by platoon, to keep them together, supervise them, and get them back to the ship in plenty of time for our departure the next day." Colonel Stone then went to see Brigadier Frank Fleury, the Canadian Military Liaison Officer, at his quarters in the Imperial Hotel in Tokyo. It was from Fleury that the PPCLI Commanding Officer received the order to take his regiment on to Korea as scheduled, and it was with Fleury that Stone was able to relax for the first time since leaving Seattle. "After almost twenty days on a dry American ship, I had to admit that a bottle of Scotch was something marvellous," he recalls.

His men found the same thing to be true.

"When I got back to the ship," says Stone, "it was the biggest shambles you ever saw. These fellows had come back all right, but they had traded off their shirts and God knows what else for women and booze. Much as I was absolutely disgusted with the whole thing, there was only one man who didn't turn up, but he managed to join us by the time we got to Kobe, our other stopover. He had somehow travelled across Japan on his own."

One of the men who enjoyed himself in Yokohama was Stu Meeks. "We had a great time there," admits Meeks. "I even got arrested in Japan. The charge read that 'the accused SC6722, Corporal Meeks, S.A., is charged with having committed the following offences: in that he walked aboard USNS *General W. M. Black*, ship of a friendly nation, did put his King's uniform in a pouch and jump off the fantail into Yokohama harbour.'

"We came back to the ship carrying big tall jugs of sake and we sold almost all of our uniforms except our dog tags. We gathered the guys together and we marched down to the docks and somehow doors and gates kept opening before us because we were pretty boisterous. Then I remember standing at the foot of our gangplank and all the guys up on the deck cheering their asses off at us. We had one quart of sake left and we were drinking it and passing it down the ranks. All the while, the MPs were standing there, tapping their clubs in their hands. When our bottle was empty I took it and smashed it against the side of this ship of a friendly nation. That was also a charge. Finally, we got on board and they put us down in a hold and turned fire hoses on us. I was locked up for a couple of days."

Jim Stone continues: "In my mind I was threatening them with the direst punishments I could dream up — but when I thought it over, I said, 'So what.' There was no harm done really. We had more shirts and all the other things they traded. No one had any Christmas presents, and when we arrived at Kobe a day or so later, damned if I didn't get the same request for shopping. This time I wouldn't let them leave the ship."

Corporal Tom McKay arrived in Yokohama on the *Marine Phoenix* a few months later. The men on that ship were also happy to reach port. "Because it had been such a long trip, it was decided that we could go ashore for four hours, but the deal was that every five or six guys had to go with an NCO — who in turn was responsible for getting them all back. Needless to say, nobody made it back on time. I didn't return until next morning. I was in this little bar and they told me there was a 10 p.m. curfew and I couldn't go out on the street. The bartender offered me his daughter for ten thousand yen or something, so I decided that no matter who she was, this was better than being picked up by the MPs.

"The next morning I took a cab back to the quay, but they had moved the ship overnight. When I did locate it, there were two gang-planks down, with an MP at the end of each. I kept looking around a corner at these guys, and when one of them went for a leak or something, I raced across the clearing, up the plank, and onto the ship. The Sergeant later bawled me out because I had not been present at roll-call and he couldn't figure out how I got on board."

Private John McIntyre, 3rd RCR, recalls his arrival at Kure in February 1953. "We were given two hundred dollars in American money and Colonel K. L. Campbell gave us all a forty-eight-hour pass. He was a terrific chap. After about thirty hours had passed, however, and Campbell had gone on to Korea, a major under him decided to call a parade.

"Well, you can guess what happened. They got the guys back early and some of them were in pretty rough shape. Of course, we were all mad at the major because he cut the leave short. The whole battalion was on parade, over nine hundred of us. Then the major got up in front of us and yelled, 'You are going into Korea tomorrow. I hope to hell you die better than you live.'

"None of us liked that, and at first there was a stunned silence. Then a little guy who had had a few drinks did what the rest of us who were there will never forget. At the top of his voice, he shouted to the major: 'You go to hell.' Then the little guy turned and walked off the parade square and every man followed him. The major was left standing alone. Later on, when we got to Korea, the major went ashore first and accepted a bouquet of flowers as part of the welcoming ceremonies. The guys all booed him."

As the ships moved across the strait between Japan and South Korea, the men who were being taken to war often had diverse explanations both for their actions and for what they expected to find. "I thought the people who lived there would be big guys," one ex-soldier recalls, "like Amazons or something. Of course," he added, "I always did get Africa mixed up with Asia."

"I wondered about the women," said another man. "We had been told that Korean women aged fast, so we used to hope we'd get there before it would be too late."

Many soldiers had never heard of the Land of the Morning Calm. "All I knew was that it was somewhere near China," admits a former officer. "And all I knew about China was won ton soup."

"There was a reporter with us," says Stu Meeks. "His name was [Bill] Boss. We were expressly forbidden to talk to him, and if we did we were to say we were 'professional soldiers going to fight for freedom against Communist tyranny'. Hell, we were kids. We had no idea what Communism was. We were playing cowboys and Indians. We were to hunt Chinamen, and if we caught one we were to kill the sonofabitch."

"Many of the men had no idea why they were there," says Larry Henderson, the former CBC national news announcer and a radio reporter in Korea. "I interviewed fellows there who admitted that. When I was in Viet Nam later on, I heard the same answer. During the Second World War, men knew why they were fighting but Korea was not the same."

Art Johnson of Toronto looked upon the whole thing as an adventure. "I don't think it was really a sense of duty. I do know a lot of guys joined just to get away from their wives. I remember when I was at Chorley Park signing up, a woman came in looking for her husband. She started chasing him, screaming that if he wanted a fight, he didn't need to go anywhere. She said she'd take him on right there and then. I don't imagine he had given much thought to patriotism."

Bentley MacLeod believes that many of the men who went to Korea didn't give a lot of thought to why they were going. "They were just scared the whole thing would be over before they got there. That happens in every war, I suppose. Being in the army is almost like being in a perpetual boys' camp. You have a good time for a year or so and then you do something else. A lot of fellows went to Korea for the good time."

Gordon Young of Hamilton went to Korea for the adventure. He was really "a goddamned lovable rogue", explains a relative today. "He was a true soldier of fortune and he thought Korea was the place to be. He also found civilian life terribly dull."

"I only knew what I read about Korea in books," says Lorne Barton, "and there wasn't much about the place in any book in Canada. I went because I believed it was necessary to go — to support the United Nations. Korea helped me grow up a bit — as World War II did for the men who were in it."

Pierre Berton went to Korea as a correspondent for *Maclean's*. "I had never been there before but I read some books on Korea to get some background on the country," he recalls. "Some of our guys who went there just didn't give a goddam, though. It bothered me to see our soldiers marching over rice paddies which are very useful, which had taken centuries to perfect. But on the whole, the Canadians were better behaved than the Americans. The Americans I saw were awful; they were just conquerors."

Dr. John Beswick: "I had been through war in hot, dusty places, but I was still not really prepared for Pusan. The heat from truck motors, the dust over everything, hot dust."

"I knew where Korea was because I read and enjoyed history," says Gary Gurney, "but a lot of the guys didn't have a clue. I recall telling two or three fellows it was a little appendage that hung down from Manchuria. They asked, 'Man who?' I suppose they thought I was telling a dirty joke."

Jim Stone says his first impressions of Korea will never leave him. "We arrived in Pusan, and there was an American band, all blacks, playing the tune 'If I Knew You Were Coming, I'd Have Baked a Cake'. Then we all got off into what was then a filthy port, and they led us to a tented encampment on one of the islands that was part of the Pusan area. At that time there was no fence or anything, so as soon as my men had their tents up, some of them took off for the nearest red-light district.

"I had a tent next to the medical officer's tent — and I must say we lectured the troops enough about V.D., but all night long they filed past my tent to the M.O.'s to get anti-V.D. shots. I can't recall any of them getting it then, although we had guys in every brothel in town."

Brigadier John Rockingham remembers arriving in Korea. "I was terribly impressed by the hundreds and hundreds of people I saw there. There were people everywhere, in the towns, up on the hills, in the countryside. In Canada we can go for miles without seeing anybody, but that was never the case in Korea.

"My second impression was of the backwardness of the country. I know the Japanese occupation sure didn't help, and it has taken many years to recover from it. I returned to Korea a couple of years ago, and I was truly amazed at the transformation. The country has changed so much."

During the course of my research for this book, most of the Canadian soldiers with whom I spoke mentioned the smell of human excrement used to fertilize Korean rice paddies. More than a few told me they could "smell Pusan before they could see it", because of the stench carried in the offshore breeze. These same soldiers recall the crowding, the filth, and the poverty of Pusan. For that reason, many feel that their first impressions of Korea are impressions they will never forget. It is unfortunate that they all cannot return to see Pusan and the area around it as it is today — with its modern buildings, new subways and world-class hotels. Those who have returned share Rockingham's sense of amazement.

But even if their first impressions of Korea were not too favourable, Canadians who went there in the late fall of 1950 were lucky not to be part of the bitter fighting around the Pusan Perimeter that took place during that summer and early autumn. After the fall of Seoul, the North Korea Communist forces swept down the peninsula and crushed any opposition that stood in their path. As this was happening, the U.S. forces desperately tried to regroup, but without much success. Hundreds of virtually untrained kids were dumped into the Pusan area and rushed northward, often to almost certain death. For example, the third battalion of the 29th Infantry was made up of men who were clerks, electricians, drivers, and the like involved in occupation duty in Japan. They had been through basic training and nothing more — and when ordered to Korea were told they would be given three days of battle training before being asked to fight.

They did not get the three days.

On July 26 the battalion was dumped into battle near the Korean town of Chinju, where they were immediately ambushed by the enemy. These U.S. soldiers, who carried mortars that had not even been test-fired, machine-guns still coated with packing grease, and radios without batteries, were virtually annihilated. At one point, many of them tried to swim a river in order to get away. In the process they dropped their rifles, tossed away heavy gear, and took off their boots. The North Koreans simply stood on the shore and shot everyone in front of them. Of the 757 men in the battalion that had gone into battle, 313 were killed outright, scores were wounded, some so severely that they died later, and over 100 were taken prisoner. Many were never seen again.

There is no doubt that the Joint Chiefs of Staff in Washington knew that such a tragedy was imminent, but because they yielded to MacArthur's insistence that he needed men, any men, and *now*, hundreds of American lives were tossed away. To MacArthur, however, this massacre "was so insignificant in the grand scale of the war that . . . [he] did not even mention it in his memoirs."

There were other tragedies. Reporters on the scene during the retreat towards Pusan filed stories of men who would not live out their teens cut to pieces on hillsides and river banks, and in the stinking filth of rice paddies; men without battle training caring for wounded buddies until surrounded and slaughtered like sheep in an abattoir; men breaking down and weeping bitter tears from frustration, terror, or pain so numbing that death was a blessed peace.

These reporters, many of them Americans, saw a kind of war they did not expect, a war much different from the wars of the past. In this war, they saw Americans run away.

"I saw young Americans turn and bolt in battle," wrote Maggie Higgins of the New York *Herald Tribune*, "or throw down their arms cursing their government for what they thought was embroilment in a hopeless cause."

But the young GIs were not the only ones who were at times

reluctant to hold the line. Lieutenant General Walton Walker, Commanding Officer of the U.S. Eighth Army in Korea, occasionally made himself unpopular with his officers when he insisted that they move forward, show leadership, and *fight*. In one instance he told a general who had come back from the front once too often that he did not want to see the man in a rear area again "unless it was in a coffin". One presumes the laggard general got the message.

While there were many instances of men fleeing the battlefield, sometimes long before they were ever attacked, there were just as many, and probably far more, cases of incredible bravery. Two men whose deeds were examples of courage that was far above the ordinary were General William F. Dean and Father Hermann Feldhoelter.

One night near Taejon, Dean fell down a cliff face as he attempted to get water to some beleaguered troops in the 24th U.S. Division. He was knocked unconscious by the fall, and when he wakened some time later he realized he had torn his head open and smashed one shoulder. "He wandered for thirty-six days in the mountains, trying to elude capture, shrinking from 190 to 130 [pounds], until he was finally betrayed by a pair of South Korean civilians who led him into a North Korean trap. . . ." General Dean was captured and spent the rest of the war in a POW camp.

Late one afternoon, just south of Taejon, some two dozen U.S. soldiers were wounded. Litter-bearers moved in to get the men out, but they too came under the same withering fire that cut the first of the group down. Finally, when all but the priest, Father Feldhoelter, were wounded, he urged those who could walk to place the litters in a circle and then try to get out themselves. To the last two who could walk, the priest said, "You two must leave. You have families and responsibilities. Mine is the duty to stay." The man who related the story continued: "I started crawling away. . . . The Reds — young kids sixteen to eighteen, they looked — were closing in. The litter patients screamed and screamed, 'No, no!' but the Reds shot them anyway. Father Feldhoelter was kneeling by one of the stretchers. He made no sound as he fell."

As the Communists tightened their grip around the Pusan Perimeter, the possibility that the U.N. forces would be driven out of Korea became more and more probable. Hundreds of Americans poured into Pusan and were immediately dispatched northward. But even with the reinforcements, a pull-out seemed imminent.

It was at this juncture of the war that MacArthur attained his finest hour. Almost singlehandedly he convinced those under him, as well as his superiors in Washington, that a major strike behind the Communist lines would be the only way to avert another Dunkirk and prevent the U.N. armies from being pushed into the sea. The place chosen for this killer strike would be the port of Inchon, half-way up the west coast of the Korean peninsula and less than twenty-five miles from Seoul. If the U.N. could launch a major assault there, reasoned MacArthur, then the North Koreans would be divided, and hopefully beaten.

The landings at Inchon were carried out on September 15, 1950 — and were a complete success. While it is not the purpose of this book to dwell on the assault — it is exhaustively treated elsewhere — the fact that it did involve support from our destroyers meant that Canada played a role in the venture.

Within hours of the Inchon landing, the U.N. strike force moved inland towards the capital. At almost the same time the troops under General Walker launched attacks on the encircling North Koreans in the Pusan Perimeter. Finally, with the supply lines to his armies in the south in danger of being completely severed, Kim Il Sung's forces began to fall back in disarray. They would continue to retreat and retreat — followed all the while by rejuvenated U.N. troops. Within days the war seemed to be over, and perhaps it would have been if a major new development had not come to pass. Just when MacArthur thought he had won his war, half a million Chinese soldiers massing along the Manchurian border prepared to disappoint him.

6

A WILDERNESS
OF HILLS

On the morning of Friday, September 29, 1950, a military aircraft carrying General of the Army Douglas MacArthur touched down at Kimpo airport and stopped in front of the partly wrecked terminal building. Two minutes later a second plane with President Syngman Rhee on board landed, taxied into position a short distance from the first, and cut its engines. The two leaders emerged, shook hands for photographers, and climbed into the rear seat of a highly polished black Chevrolet sedan. The car then moved slowly out onto the pock-marked roadway leading towards Seoul. Following the Chev were five other cars and a long line of jeeps. The victorious General was bringing the President of South Korea back to his capital city.

Today the drive from Kimpo to downtown Seoul takes about three-quarters of an hour, on a wide four-lane expressway. The day MacArthur and Rhee returned in triumph, the journey took much longer. For one thing, the road was in poor shape, and the closer the two got to Seoul, the worse it became. Every few yards the official cars had to detour around debris or slow down as they bumped through ruts and over bits of broken masonry. At the south bank of the Han, they eased down onto a long pontoon bridge, dubbed "MacArthur's Bridge" by the overworked marine engineers who had hastily completed the thing eleven hours earlier so that the General could cross there and enter the capital in style. Earlier suggestions that he arrive by helicopter had been turned down as much less dramatic. And, as no bridge existed over the Han in the period immediately after Inchon, the construction had to be rushed, and men were taken from more vital assignments so that it could be ready on time.

The procession passed slowly over the Han, inched up the steep north bank, and entered downtown Seoul past the Namdaemun Gate, the principal entrance to the old city, in existence since the summer of 1398. On every side the burnt and blasted buildings, the smouldering rubble of a town that had suffered but was too proud to die. On past the half-destroyed Seoul City Plaza, then slightly left and northward along what is today the ten-lane, tree-lined Kwang-hwanum-Sejongro Boulevard. Finally, up the twenty steps into the Japanese-built grey stone capital building. There, in front of the mulberry-coloured velvet drapes and a short distance from the falling glass of the shattered rotunda dome, the General re-installed Rhee as President, then bowed and "disregarding the fact that here Christianity was a minority religion . . . invited the assemblage to follow him in recital of the Our Father." MacArthur then said good-bye to Rhee, returned to Kimpo, and five minutes later was airborne for Tokyo.

By the end of the first week of October, virtually all the North Korean troops had been pushed north of the 38th parallel, the dividing line between the North and the South, where the war had begun one hundred days before. At this point, bitter debates raged in Tokyo and Washington and at the U.N. over whether MacArthur should or should not be given the authority to advance into North Korea. Already elements of the ROK army had crossed the parallel, and indeed some had advanced as much as sixty miles into North Korean territory.

MacArthur, of course, wanted to move — and in the end it would appear that his persuasiveness contributed in no small measure to influencing Washington in this regard. In the words of historian Joseph C. Goulden: "President Truman and the Joint Chiefs of Staff watched MacArthur prepare for his march to the north, and they had at least a month in which to countermand his orders if they chose to do so. They did not."

While Truman and other high officials in Washington were attempting to decide whether to let MacArthur continue northward, Chou En-lai, the Chinese Communist Foreign Minister in Peking, informed the world by way of the Indian Ambassador to China that "if United Nations forces crossed the 38th parallel, China would send in troops to help the North Koreans." MacArthur was given this message but discounted it.

But there were others who were not so brazen.

Lester Pearson in his memoirs points out that the view of the Canadian government at the time was that the U.N. troops had gone into this police action in order to drive the North Koreans back to the 38th parallel. Once that objective had been reached, writes Pearson, Canada felt the U.N. "should be very cautious in extending . . . [its] mandate to include a march into northern territory." Prime Minister Louis St. Laurent urged "that the North Koreans be given the opportunity of entering into a ceasefire." Washington ignored the suggestion.

Finally, the United Nations General Assembly would have what in effect was the final word. The Soviet Union had been urging that all foreign troops leave Korea, but Britain proposed that "all appropriate steps be taken to ensure conditions of stability throughout Korea." The nations who had supported going to Korea in the first place now aligned themselves in favour of the British resolution. It passed on October 7. Two days later, American troops crossed the 38th parallel.

Once the parallel had been breached, the U.N. soldiers made good progress. Opposition melted as the advance continued, and after less than seventy-five hours the North Korean capital of Pyongyang fell to MacArthur's forces. On the eastern coast the port of Wonsan was taken by a division of ROK troops. General MacArthur predicted that many of his soldiers would be home for Christmas.

MacArthur's optimistic prediction was revised two weeks later, when China entered the war. The massive Chinese assault began in the west and quickly spread across the entire peninsula. U.N. troops that had driven northward to the Yalu, the river between North Korea and Manchuria, were forced to make a hasty retreat. They pulled back, first to the new positions along the Imjin River, and then, after surrendering Seoul itself, to a position some sixty kilometres south of the capital. The war that MacArthur said was over had started anew.

By this time Colonel Stone and his Patricias were in Pusan. "We had barely got used to being on land when I was contacted by the Americans," says Stone. "A man from Eighth Army Headquarters showed up and told me he was glad we were there. Then he went on to say that they had trucks already to move us, and that we were expected to be at Suwon in three days.

"I objected, of course. My men had not completed their training and I wasn't going to throw them into the line before they knew what to do once they got there. This gentleman expected us to join the 29th British Independent Infantry Brigade. At the time they were still north of Seoul, but the Chinese were moving down. The more I objected, the more obstinate the man became. I told him my men were not trained and he replied that we had come to fight, not to train."

The argument continued for some moments with neither side backing down. Finally, an exasperated Stone asked the American if there was a plane in the area that he could use. He was told there was.

"Since I wasn't getting anywhere with this fellow," says Stone,

"I decided to fly up to Seoul to see General Walker, the man who was commanding the American army in Korea at the time. This was on December 20. I hated to refuse to fight the very first time I was asked, but my troops came first. I had also been instructed by the Minister of National Defence not to fight, except in self-defence, until I was sure my men were ready to go into the line. At that point they were not."

An aide then drove Stone to the crowded Pusan airport, where he caught his flight to see Walker, the colourful little general who envisioned himself another Patton and tried to emulate the illustrious general who was killed in a traffic accident at the end of the Second World War. At this time Lieutenant General Walton H. (Johnnie) Walker had been in Korea for several months and had gained fame and a certain amount of notoriety when, trying to rally his troops during the fighting at Taegu, he forbade them to retreat, ordering them to either "stand or die". They stood, and in due course broke out of the Pusan Perimeter.

"I think General Walker was a fine man," says Colonel Stone today. "I really know nothing about his military capabilities, but as an individual he was very understanding of my position. He had his own opinions, of course, but he didn't try to bully me in any way. His Chief of Staff was a rather snarky individual, though, and he kept talking, telling me that our troops were trained as well as theirs, and so on.

"I was with General Walker for about thirty minutes, in a large office, flanked with all the flags of the nations taking part in the war. He was cordial and the meeting was businesslike. There was nothing social involved. I had not intended to produce my command instructions, but because the Chief of Staff kept getting into the act, I finally had enough. I pulled out the Cabinet order and said, 'Well, sir, I have this piece of paper.' Walker read it and said he didn't want to cause any political trouble. He told me he understood my position and then offered any assistance I needed to complete the training. I then went back to Pusan."

Three days later, General Walker was killed when the jeep he was riding in collided with a pickup truck.

The PPCLI contingent spent December 25 at Pusan, the first Christmas for Canadians in Korea. For most of them, the day was a happy one. A large shipment of mail had already arrived, and packages and letters from home helped to ease the loneliness some of the men were feeling. They were given a beer ration and all the turkey they could eat. The officers had plenty of whiskey, much of it scrounged by reporter Bill Boss in Hawaii and later in Taegu at the Navy-Army-Air Force Institute there. After the dinner was over, several of the more rowdy diners started a singsong, accompanied by someone on the organ borrowed from Father J. J. Vallely, the Roman Catholic padre.

Two days after Christmas the Patricias packed up their gear at Pusan and moved twenty-seven miles to the north, where they began intensive training near the town of Miryang, in an apple orchard on the banks of the river of the same name. The site had been selected by Colonel Stone's second in command, Major Pat Tighe, and was a popular choice because there were no rice paddies, with their accompanying smell, in the area.

The training was, according to those who were there, both thorough and tough — and in the end was completed in six weeks rather than the eight originally anticipated. Colonel Stone had the reputation of being a harsh task-master, and he proved it at Miryang. The troops alternately cursed him and feared him, but when they saw themselves as part of a well-functioning, disciplined unit, they ended up praising him.

But for some the discipline did not come easy.

"Because there were problems," recalls Jim Stone today, "I had to make my own field punishment camp. We had nothing at Miryang and I wanted to teach a few guys a lesson. We put up a large tent with sixteen strands of barbed wire around it and I decided it would be the toughest field punishment camp since Admiral Nelson.

"If any guy got in trouble, we cut his hair off, put him in fatigues, and put a big yellow mark on his back. I made it so damned tough that if a man lasted two days in there he pleaded to get out. After two days I would interview him personally and if he seemed to have learned his lesson I would let him go, with the warning that he still had time hanging over his head. If there was more trouble, then he would go back in — for a long time. Then he would not get out early. The thing worked. We started out with sixteen men in there and we ended up with none. When we went into action, there wasn't a soul in the detention tent. The whole thing wasn't really brutal, but it was terribly demanding physically."

"No one ever actually touched me when I was in there," recalls a former private. "Maybe they weren't cruel, but they sure worked the ass off me. It seemed as if we did everything with a full pack on, and it was always on the run. Did you ever try to eat while running on the spot, with some guy screaming at you to 'hurry up', 'hurry up'? I thought having a leak that way was impossible but I found out that it wasn't.

"We would be told to do fifty push-ups and then they would tell us that was the warm-up. 'Now do two hundred,' or something like that. I lost twenty pounds in two days."

"One day we had a beer ration come up," says Stone, "and some guys swiped a lot of it. I paraded that group in front of the whole battalion and gave them hell. 'These men stole *your* beer,' I told them. '*Your* beer. Not mine. The same kind of guy who steals your beer back here will steal your water at the front line.' Then I gave them each fourteen days.

"There were other kinds of infractions — insolence, refusing an order, sneaking out of camp, breach of duty, that sort of thing."

"One night I was on guard duty," says a man who spent time in a similar detention camp later on. "I knew I was about fifteen minutes before getting off, but as I wasn't sure, I ducked inside a bunker to check the time. As I did so, I saw a *Police Gazette* magazine lying on a guy's bunk. I picked it up and had just begun to leaf through it when an officer came out and realized no one was on guard in the vicinity.

"When they found me, they hauled me up on the carpet and gave me thirty days. I'll never forget the detention barracks. I recall my first few seconds inside the door. There was a rough stucco wall with a spot on it. The Sarge told you to touch your nose to the spot and do 180 to the minute. That was tough but it was just the beginning.

"We slept on the floor, of course, and in the morning we shaved. All the dirty water ran into one place — a pit outside. We then had to run an obstacle course and part of it led up to this pit with all the soapy water in it. There we had to grab a rope and swing across. The only thing was, you'd have to be really running in order to get across. But even if you didn't fall in, they would make you do it again and again until you got so tired you fell in.

"Another part of the course had barbed wire stretched just above the ground. You had to crawl as fast as you could under this with a full pack. Half the time you ripped your rear end open. We also had to run uphill in sand, with full packs — until we dropped. Yes, I sure remember being in detention."

Whether by a sojourn in "Stone's Stockade" or in the Canadian detention barracks that were located later on in Seoul, going AWOL was always punishable.

While the Pats were at Miryang, one of those who took off was a chap who thought the training was going too slowly. The soldier left on his own, hitched a ride north, and joined an American outfit north of Seoul. While he was there, the Chinese attacked and the Canadian distinguished himself by winning a Silver Star. When he turned up at Miryang again, Colonel Stone is said to have congratulated him and then sentenced him to thirty days.

The combination of hard training, effective discipline, and the development of unit cohesiveness all contributed towards either making or breaking the men who would go into battle under Jim Stone. "There's no doubt that the 2nd Battalion of the Patricias was the finest bunch of men I ever commanded," says Stone today. "They were all together in everything. They believed in the unit and they believed in their NCOs and their officers and they believed in me. We got rid of the ones that didn't fit in. Those were the dispirited apes who couldn't take it; the cold and the hunger and that kind of thing got to them."

Shortly before they went into battle, the Patricias were able to pick up valuable experience guerrilla-hunting in the nearby hills. One night two New Zealand soldiers were killed when their jeep was ambushed on the road between Pusan and Miryang. A day or so later a Canadian was wounded by a sniper. It was after the second incident that Colonel Stone had his men, in the company of Korean police, scour the area villages and ridges for the elusive enemy. The search was reasonably successful; two guerrillas were killed and, from traces of blood found in more than one location, others were wounded.

Finally, on February 15, 1951, seven months and twenty-one days after the North Korean armies launched their invasion of the south, Canadian troops were ready go to to war.

Now, instead of joining the British 29th Brigade, the PPCLI contingent was ordered to marry up with the 27th Commonwealth Brigade, then composed of English and Scottish troops, Australians, New Zealanders, and Indians, the latter a field ambulance unit. With the addition of the Canadians, the brigade was representative of more of the Commonwealth.

The move to the front was not easy. The Canadians travelled most of the way by truck, in terrible weather and along worse roads. In all, the distance between Miryang and the front was about 150 miles, but the journey took over two days. Because almost eighty per cent of Korea is mountainous, the long motorized column was forever gearing up or gearing down, rounding blind corners or crossing makeshift bridges over gorges that were jagged indentations in every mile of roadway. Often the visibility in the low, scrub-covered mountains was nil. Blowing snow and sleet bothered the drivers and slowed the procession to a crawl and often to a virtual halt. Finally the trucks could go no further, so the troops clambered off, stretched their aching muscles, and formed up for the five-mile march across country to the front lines.

The going was difficult. Uphill, downhill, through scrub brush, over half-frozen creeks, marsh, brambles, and slippery, jagged rock. The Canadians carried full packs, and Korean porters, stooped under

A-frames, brought most of the supplies. One or two jeeps were rammed through as well. Slowly, laboriously, the contingent advanced to within a quarter of a mile of the front, when they stumbled onto something none of them ever forgot.

Littered along the side of the makeshift trail were the broken, bloody, grotesque-looking, half-frozen bodies of sixty-eight black Americans. These were some of the ill-trained, ill-prepared, desk-bound troops MacArthur had dumped into Korea and then left to fend for themselves. Most of the dead were clothed in pyjamas or long underwear and almost all were in sleeping bags. Because they had lacked proper field training they hadn't dug in for the night and the Chinese had descended silently and slaughtered the entire lot. One or two who had obviously tried to get away were face down in the underbrush, their bodies contorted in death, with dark brown splotches of dried blood across the torso. All had been shot, bayoneted, or both.

"This was the greatest lesson my troops ever had," says Jim Stone. "They saw the bodies and the sight sure made an impression. After that you couldn't *get* one of my men into a sleeping bag at the front. They would lie on it and pull a blanket over themselves but they wouldn't get inside. The fact that there were just as many British troops near by who had also been attacked that night taught another lesson. The British had dug in before going to sleep and they didn't lose a man."

Once the Canadians found themselves in the line, they began to understand the unpleasantness of war. Going away to fight for one's country was romantic when the bands were playing and people were cheering, but living twenty-four hours a day, seven days a week, in hastily dug trenches, sloshing around in soggy snow, with the cold rains of winter pouring down your neck, was far from pleasant. At this time the static war was still in the future, when bunkers could be constructed and made somewhat comfortable. For the Patricias near Changhowon, forty-six miles southeast of Seoul, the Korean winter was a bitter winter.

"I was always cold," recalls one man. "Rain was running down my neck, my hands were numb, and I never seemed to be dry. Kneeling in the snow, or advancing in the rain, my knees and the front of my legs became wet. Then the dampness soaked right through and the skin underneath became tender and raw."

Pierre Berton described the scene in an article for *Maclean's* on June 1, 1951: "The trenches, waist high, two and a half feet wide, were dug in deep snow and frozen soil. The section was hardly dug in before rain mixed with sleet began to fall. . . . The men's parkas, battledress, and underwear became soaked and then frozen. They crouched in a foot of ice water. . . . Blankets turned to sopping rags."

"I could never understand why anyone would want to live in parts of Korea," says Gary Gurney today. "Windy, cold, barren, rocky, poor. Nevertheless, I think we were better equipped for winter than any of the other troops there. We had wind suits, good boots for cold weather, gloves. Compared to the poor New Zealanders who were on artillery, or the Australians and English, we were super-equipped."

Anyone who has ever been in Korea, or has flown over that country, remembers the hills. Jagged, with scrub trees and rocky outcrops. Steep, convoluted ridges — hundreds of them — fanning out every which way, stretching to the horizon. To the officers and men of the PPCLI, and to all the Canadians who came after them, much of this war was a war in the hills, against an enemy that was both ruthless and elusive, skilful and persistent, often silent and always deadly.

The hills themselves became a foe. Monotonous, endless, nameless; generally identified only by their height in metres. One ridge looked like every other ridge, and beyond each ridge was another, and another, and another. The first battalion objectives for the Pats were Hills 404, 444, and 419, while Australian and British troops fought for Hills 523, 614, 484, and 450. If ever soldiers bled and died for apparently pathetic objectives, it was in Korea. "C" Company, commanded by Major J. H. B. George, lost four men in an attack on Hill 444, but it is doubtful if those who were there would recognize the objective a week later — all the terrain was so similar.

It was in this area that Canadians first saw napalm used against an enemy. This substance, later to gain so much notoriety in Viet Nam, is gasoline that is chemically thickened, or jellied, causing it to spread over the ground while burning. The thickener is a combination of aluminum naphthenate and fatty material from coconuts. The "na" of the name comes from naphthenate, while "palm" refers to the tree of the same name.

The substance was dropped in containers of 100 or 150 gallons that had been slung under the wings of attacking aircraft. In Korea, one canister of the substance would smother half an acre of ground, and would burn at 3000 degrees Fahrenheit. Its effects were horrendous, and according to *Time* magazine on February 12, 1951, it terrified the opposing Chinese "more than any other weapon".

It was also controversial.

British Broadcasting Corporation reporter René Cutforth tried to tell his listeners just what this jellied gasoline would do. Cutforth "described the lazy fall of the canister, the roaring flame on impact, and the rush of heat so intense . . . he felt as if his eyebrows had been singed. 'Then over this scene of silent desolation . . . the smell of roast pork, for that's what a napalmed human being smells like.'"

The BBC refused to carry Cutforth's dispatch.

As February 1951 became March, the Commonwealth troops gradually moved northward. The advance — "slow, remorseless plodding from ridge to ridge . . . clearing mud huts . . . firing round after round into apparently empty hills . . . long patrols by day and longer watches by night" — went on, regardless of weather, casualties, or an elusive, fleeting enemy.

American General Matthew B. Ridgway, the Eighth Army Commander following General Walker's death, was determined to drive the Chinese and North Koreans to the 38th parallel and beyond. Slowly, almost imperceptibly at times, he seemed to be succeeding in his efforts. The Commonwealth Brigade advanced some sixteen miles between the middle of February and the first week of March, but still the Red troops holding what has been called a "wilderness of hills" seemed as numerous as ever.

And for good reason.

Even when General MacArthur was claiming that the Chinese would not enter the war, they were in fact doing just that. From the frigid wastes of Manchuria they came, crossing the bridges over the Yalu, generally hiding in railway tunnels and caves during the day and travelling by night. They came by the thousands. They travelled quickly. They travelled lightly. But most of all they travelled without being seen. If ever an enemy could be called stealthy, it was the Chinese in Korea. In the first days after their arrival in the Land of the Morning Calm, they were indeed the invisible enemy.

This unseen enemy wore a quilted dusty-brown cotton uniform that afforded barely adequate protection against the elements but was highly effective as camouflage. Instead of the heavy combat boots worn by the Canadians and others, the Chinese wore a kind of slip-on running shoe with rubber soles. These troops rarely carried any identification that could be called official. Each soldier had his own food with him, enough rice or other ground grains to last four or five days — and longer in emergencies.

On occasions when the Chinese had to move in the daytime, they did so in such a highly disciplined fashion that it bordered on the unbelievable. On the afternoon of November 26, 1950, an American pilot named Harry Henneberger was returning to base after a reconnaissance sweep near the Yalu River. With him were three other aircraft, all F4U Corsairs out of Hungnam. During the flight, Henneberger "glanced down at the ground ten thousand feet below, and was startled to see a solid mass of Chinese infantry come to a complete halt in full marching order on the snow-covered wastes beneath his wing tips." The American could hardly believe what he saw.

But there were other times when whatever it was that pilots saw was not what was there. Even though the Communists hid trains and trucks in tunnels during the day, trucks were also left outside, disguised as native huts. In addition, "straw aircraft were put on dummy airfields and good airfields were camouflaged to appear riddled with craters and completely unusable." Sections of railway bridges were lifted out by cranes during the day and hidden until nightfall, when they were replaced. Straw or brambles were spread on tracks to simulate breaks. Construction equipment was deliberately left along railways so that pilots would think the lines were under repair. Often several rails were removed and hidden until dark. Truckers carried oil-soaked rags which were lit during attacks to give the appearance of destruction. Truck hoods were opened and even wheels removed to simulate repairs.

It was with stratagems such as these that the Chinese were able to move, undetected, for so long and so far. This was the enemy the Canadians were fighting in Korea, an enemy whose skills, daring, stealth, and ruthlessness were on a par with any foe our soldiers ever faced. These Chinese attacked in massive numbers, swiftly inflicted whatever damage they could, and then melted into the myriad of hills, often taking their dead and wounded, and sometimes even Canadian dead, with them.

On February 28 the Patricias overran Hill 419, finding as they did so the bodies of four Canadians who had been killed during an earlier engagement. All four had had their clothing and guns taken by the Chinese. Finding that some of their friends had been treated this way in death bothered many Canadians, and from time to time individuals had to be removed from the front. One chap who had downed a couple of snipers during earlier fighting apparently realized what it was that he had just done. He dropped his rifle, and turned and raced screaming back to his commanding officer. The soldier was sent home. His actions had an impact on those around him, but they were able to put the incident in perspective and managed to carry on. Those who saw what had happened, and so many others who heard about the occurrence, never forgot it.

On March 7 the PPCLI were involved in another fierce engagement as they attempted to take Hill 532 from a stubborn and hidden enemy. The attack on the hill began at 6 a.m. and involved two companies of Canadians, supported by mortar fire, bombardment from the New Zealand Field Regiment, U.S. tanks, and air strikes near the summit.

The terrain was steep and treacherous, and the advance was slow. Canadians moved in crouched positions, slithered on their bellies, or tried to dart from one overhang to the next. At times they succeeded. At other times, Chinese machine-guns opened up from camouflaged dugouts and ripped into the attackers, sending them bleeding and in pain down the face of the slopes to where the medics toiled to save lives.

In the early afternoon, snow began to fall, in big, sloppy flakes, and had it not been for the deadliness of their business, the soldiers of two armies would have seen the transformation of the slopes into vistas of beauty. But these fighting men were too busy, too intent on doing what they had been ordered to do, too intent on staying alive.

And while we may never know how many Chinese died that day, although somebody counted almost fifty bodies, six young Canadians breathed their last in the bloody snow halfway up that Korean hill that wasn't even important enough to have a name.

For Private L. Barton of "D" Company, the afternoon was both tumultuous and terrible. Shortly after the snowfall began, the young batman to a platoon commander was hit by a shot fired from somewhere above. At almost the same time his commanding officer was shot, along with several others in the platoon. At first Barton flattened himself into a gully in order to have a look at his wound and to try to decide what to do next. When he realized that almost everyone else had been hit, he stood up, yelled at those who were uninjured, and told them to follow him. Ten feet higher and he was hit again, and again. Then, in a direct response to his courageous leadership, the walking wounded on the ridge plunged forward toward their objective. Finally, half dead from loss of blood, spent adrenalin, and fatigue, the young soldier could go no further. He was ordered back down the slope. Later, Barton would receive the Military Medal for bravery in the field, the first Canadian to be decorated in Korea.

After they had been in action for some days, the PPCLI took a day off to relax, play sports, and catch up on the mail from home. The date was March 17, the birthday of Princess Patricia, after whom the Patricias were named. By this time the Chinese had started pulling back along much of the front and the Pats were moved into reserve near Chipyong-Ni.

For the most part the birthday was a lively occasion. There was a beer ration, a banquet, a pipe-band concert, and a singsong around a huge bonfire. In the official history of the Regiment, the day was a happy one, "the bleak landscape glowed and everyone went to bed well content."

"When I woke the next morning I was immediately informed

that there had been a great tragedy," recalls Colonel Stone. "There were four men dead, two blind, and several others having their stomachs pumped out. They got into the canned heat [methanol] and had been mixing it with fruit juice and drinking the stuff after the party was over. There was really no one person to blame. The whole thing was stupid and tragic. A few of the misfits we hadn't weeded out led the others perhaps. Today there are probably two blind men somewhere in Canada who can trace their blindness back to that night."

The tragedy had its effect. Colonel Stone ordered the bodies of the dead soldiers lined up and paraded his troops in front of the corpses. In the words of a private who was there that day: "He formed us up and addressed us and made us parade past so we could see the results of absolute stupidity. It was one hell of an effective lesson."

"We were really horrified then at what Colonel Stone did," another man recalls, "but nobody was going to argue with him. Now that I look back on what happened, I think he was right."

The way this incident was handled by the Canadians was noticed elsewhere, as alcohol was naturally a problem for the troops of all nations. René Cutforth of the BBC talked of it and Phillip Knightley in his book *The First Casualty* mentions the matter, although his description is somewhat inaccurate. He mentions that Cutforth believed Canadians were the only ones who managed to succeed in preventing their soldiers from drinking illegal booze because "they adopted the dramatic expedient of tying to a post the body of a soldier who had died from it and parading the Canadian troops in front of the unfortunate man."

When the Patricias returned to the line, they were without doubt a chastened group of soldiers. The time in reserve had been welcome but the tragedy helped to mould them into an even more cohesive unit. It was this unit that continued to be part of the U.N. sweep northward, a sweep through some of Korea's most rugged countryside, and ultimately to the 38th parallel and beyond. But on the way the Patricias would reach a town called Kapyong, where they would fight what would later be known as their greatest battle of the Korean War.

7

KAPYONG

At the same time as the United Nations troops were advancing toward the 38th parallel, intelligence reports were coming in describing a formidable buildup by the Chinese and North Korean armies. By the middle of April 1951, over 700,000 Communist soldiers were in Korea, facing a total U.N. contingent of some 418,000 men. Of these, roughly 245,000 were Americans, 152,000 were South Koreans, 11,500 were from Commonwealth nations, and 10,000 came from other U.N. countries.

The numbers of Chinese troops were, as always, approximate. From time to time deserters from the north blundered into the U.N. lines, and from these men, as well as from prisoners and through other channels, the U.N. high command was able to piece together a rough idea of enemy strength and intentions. But no matter how much they minimized the Communist capability, or depended on their own fire-power, the U.N. armies were outnumbered as much as two to one in most areas. In the case of the Princess Patricias at Kapyong, the odds were closer to eight or nine to one.

Kapyong is a quiet, sprawling country town in central Korea, now a two-hour drive northeast from Seoul. Some three miles farther on, where the Kapyong River meanders into a winding S curve, lies a series of brush-covered, eroded, interconnecting ridges, dominated by the feature known to the Princess Patricia's Canadian Light Infantry as Hill 677.

Today there is a PPCLI memorial there, in memory of the epic battle fought on the site between April 23 and April 25, 1951.

When I visited the battlefield during my research for this book, two old men who had lived in the vicinity all their lives told me, through an interpreter, that the area I was seeing was essentially unchanged since the Korean War. The winding river and the weathered hills were the same, of course, but the rice paddies at the foot of 677 and the dusty road along the river were also both there thirty years ago. And to make the location even more evocative in its historical significance, a long column of camouflaged ROK army trucks lumbered past, north up the Kapyong Valley, heading in the same direction as did Canadians years ago. In April 1951, however, ROK troops were streaming southward, fleeing before thousands of Chinese who had attacked some twenty miles to the north.

The massive Chinese advance began shortly before midnight on Sunday, April 22. Two regiments of the 6th ROK Division were hurled back, and when they realized the immensity of the army coming towards them, they simply turned on their heels and fled. All during the day on Monday, streams of Korean soldiers tramped southward along the river road towards Kapyong. As the Koreans fled, the Patricias were moving up, digging trenches, and positioning themselves on Hill 677 and on the mile-long ridge that was connected to it.

"I guess it was the morning of April 23 that somebody came shouting around for everyone to get the hell up," recalls one soldier. "We looked out and all we could see were South Korean troops flying past us along with all these monstrous American vehicles they were supplied with. We didn't know what the hell had happened."

Another soldier remembers going up to the lines: "The first part of the journey was by truck. I was sitting right in the back. There was just a stream of Koreans heading south and we were heading north. I began to think to myself, 'Lord Jesus, I am over here supposed to be helping to defend these people and they're running one way while I am going the other.' These guys were coming out as if they were piling out of a bank building. It was just like the staff going home at night. I've never seen fear and disorganization like those guys going down the road. It was on for hours and it wasn't all that encouraging."

Hill 677 and its interconnecting ridges are located on the west side of the Kapyong River. Hill 504 is across the river on the east side. When their defence collapsed in the north, the ROK troops moved between the two hills, down the mile-wide river valley. During the battle of Kapyong, while the PPCLI were occupying their position on 677, the 3rd Royal Australian Regiment was dug in on Hill 504. Behind and to the south of the Patricias was the British 1st Middlesex Regiment.

When it became obvious that unless they chose their defensive positions with care, his men would be driven back, Colonel Stone drove up the valley in order to get a look at 677 from the north side. "I took a large reconnaissance party with me," says Stone today. "We were able to look at the feature from the enemy side, which gave us a good idea of probable attack approaches. I kept thinking that if I was the one trying to take the hill, I would move in such and such direction, and so on. As I was working out a battle plan in my mind, we went up the hill, looked the area over, and I designated company positions. That night we started to move in."

"When we went in that night," says a soldier, "one of our half-tracks broke down. We were stuck halfway up the goddamned hill, waiting for somebody to get a new starter motor up to us. Every ten minutes Stone would say, 'If it doesn't get here in five minutes, I'm going to push this thing off the road.' But he didn't."

"It was getting late by the time we got into the positions we were going to occupy," recalls another Canadian. "I was with a fellow by the name of Ray Orford from Westville, N.S. I remember not digging our trench too deep that night. We went down maybe two feet, just enough to get underground.

"We spent the night in our shallow trench, sort of sitting down with our head and shoulders above ground. Early next morning, before daylight, a lot of firing broke out ahead of us. We heard that the Australian battalion had made contact with the Chinese and was being hit hard from a couple of different sides.

"I remember that from my position I could see a lot of tracers flying back and forth. At that point I decided that we'd better dig that trench a little deeper."

"I don't think you can ever dig a hole deep enough," says Gary Gurney. "I don't care if the damned thing is two feet deep or twenty; it's never big enough."

All during the day, Monday, April 23, the ROK troops surged to the south. Then, shortly after 10 p.m., the battle of Kapyong began. The Chinese, who had been right on the heels of the fleeing Koreans, first attacked the Australians on Hill 504. From their vantage point across the valley, on the higher 677, the Patricias watched the war, and waited.

Wave after wave of Chinese stormed the hill, were tossed back, and surged forward again. "The attack was so intense," recalls Jim Stone, "that I decided to change my deployment and ordered 'B' Company, commanded by Major Vince Lilley, to move from their position, which was partly dug in, and dig several hundred yards to the right, where they could overlook the valley of the Kapyong. As it turned out, the move was a fortunate one, because it helped bridge the gap when the Australians had to withdraw.

"I was listening over the Brigade radio and I heard the Australian commanding officer shouting that his command post was under fire and that he was going to have to pull back. This was after several hours of intense contact. The Chinese were all around him. His headquarters was gone and he had a lot of casualties."

The Australians had stood their ground all night and well into the following day. U.S. tanks who were supporting them had fired almost point-blank into the mass of attacking Chinese but were unable to stop them. Finally, at 5:30 in the afternoon on Tuesday, April 24, as the smoke of battle drifted across the shallow Kapyong River, the Australians were forced to retreat.

The Patricias now stood alone.

According to the official history of the war, the Canadians had by now deployed "to cover the north face of hill 677, with 'A' Company on the right, 'C' Company in the centre, and 'D' Company on the left. 'B' Company occupied a salient in front of 'D' Company."

Then, in the way that men who fought in Korea all remember, the Chinese signalled their first attack on the Canadians. "They started blowing bugles and whistles," recalls one man. "Then there was screaming, shouting, and they were coming through the brush towards us."

From then on, the next few terrible hours were a complete blur. Men who were at Kapyong recall some parts of the night, but have completely forgotten others. "I remember the attacks. I remember being surrounded. And I remember being more terrified than I ever was before or since," says Gary Gurney. "But it wasn't until I was in Winnipeg in 1976 at the twenty-fifth reunion of the battle that I really knew about the whole thing. I learned more in Winnipeg than I ever knew or learned at Kapyong.

"I think every man who was at Kapyong was a better man for it," he adds. "But I sure wouldn't want to go through it again. It was three days and nights of absolute hell."

The Chinese moved forward in waves. Some would fall but there were always others who came on. They slipped through the darkness with the ease of a panther through trees. Softly, stealthily, deadly. One minute a Canadian would be firing at shadows in the brush in front of him. The next moment he would have to fend off a bayonet attack from the rear. Over all, the sound of curses, screams, Bren gun chatter, half-sobbed prayers, acrid smoke, flashes of flame, bursts of fire, shouted warnings . . .

Bruce MacDonald of Peterborough, Ontario, and another Patricia manned a Vickers machine-gun that night. They positioned themselves so that their range of fire covered one of the easiest approaches to the hills. The Chinese realized this and scores of them moved up the draw towards the two defenders. Once, twice, three times they were driven back. Then, in a final, suicidal assault the enemy overran the Vickers gun and slaughtered the Canadians who used it. Two Korean houseboys who were there sobbed in the gloom when they realized their soldier friends were dead. No one remembers what happened to the youngsters when the position was overrun.

At one point during the battle, a moving platoon from "B" Company stumbled into a series of grenades placed on trip-wires around the Tactical Headquarters position. One man was killed on the spot and a second wounded when one grenade went off. A second flipped loose from its trip and rolled, smoking, along the ground into the middle of the platoon. For what seemed an eternity but in reality was only a second or two, everyone froze, and stared at the device, paralysed in mid-step. Then a young corporal yelled at his men to hit the dirt, grabbed the grenade, and started to heave it out of the way. There was a blinding flash and the explosive went off, blowing the corporal's hand away but saving the lives of the others. Later on, Corporal S. Douglas was awarded the Military Medal for what he had done.

The horror went on.

"Wayne Mitchell was number one on the Bren," said another soldier. "I was his number two. When we were overrun he was hit by shrapnel but he never gave up his gun for the rest of the night. We sat there and held them off as long as we could. I don't know how long we were there before we got the order to move out. I had three shells left, so I dropped back and fired them off. Just as I jumped up I fell over a Chinaman who was running up the side of the hill. He got me in the neck and then ran into the end of my bayonet.

"I was swung completely around. When I got my bearings I started back. I went as far as I could, then got weak and lay down. I tried to get up but I couldn't, so I crawled back. I was afraid they would shoot me, so I kept hollering. Mitchell recognized my voice and came out. Soon as I saw him I never talked for three weeks. Later I met him in hospital. He knew my rifle because I had a couple of notches carved in it. He told me, 'You got him. The rifle was still in him.'"

Mitchell himself was lucky to survive the night. His first wound had been in the chest, but as soon as he had it dressed he went back to the fight. Even after he was wounded a second time and losing blood, he stayed at his post. Finally, after it was safe to do so, an American helicopter flew him out. Later on, in a ceremony witnessed by many of the men whose lives he saved, Private Wayne Mitchell had the Distinguished Conduct Medal pinned on his shirt by Brigadier John Rockingham.

There were other brave men fighting that night.

The Commander of "D" Company was J. G. W. (Wally) Mills. His position was somewhat north and west of the others — and was perhaps the most exposed on the hill. During the evening and on into the night, hundreds of Chinese moved up, completely surrounded Captain Mills and his men, and then, in savage and desperate hand-to-hand fighting, moved over the entire area the Canadians were defending. To Mills and those around him, there seemed no hope.

"Wally Mills called me and said the Chinese had infiltrated and overrun his position," recalls Colonel Stone. "He wanted to pull out. I told him to stay there, that nobody could pull out. 'If we ever lose this hill,' I said, 'we lose it all.' 'Will you fire artillery right on top of my position?' Mills asked me. 'Are you dug in?' I asked. When he said he was, I told him to keep his head down and get ready. I got in touch with the artillery and our own mortars and we fired right where he was in this wooded area. He didn't have a single man wounded but it certainly got rid of the Chinese around him."

Captain Wally Mills was awarded the Military Cross for his actions that night.

Twenty-two-year-old Ken Barwise, a six-foot-four-inch PPCLI private, won the Military Medal. Just before the Chinese attacked his position there was a loud bugle call, then the sound of sticks being beaten together, and, as the first enemy soldier materialized out of the murk, the piercing sounds of shrill whistles. Within seconds the Chinese were less than fifty feet from Barwise, Sergeant Vern Holligan, Jim Waniandy, Private Peter Boldt, and others.

"We opened up with our Brens," said Waniandy to Bill Boss of Canadian Press. "We saw them [the Chinese] falling all over."

"They kept coming all night in waves," Barwise is quoted in a story in the *Vancouver Sun* on May 12, 1951. "They must have been crazy, or glory happy."

During the course of the night, Ken Barwise slaughtered six men in vicious close-quarter fighting: two with grenades, two others with their own guns, one with a machine-gun he retrieved from the Chinese, and a sixth with his own rifle. The former sawmill boom man had succeeded as a soldier. He never looked upon himself as a hero.

As the grim night wore on, fears that the Patricias would be annihilated gradually subsided. They held on until morning, and although they were heavily shelled during the following day, they were never attacked as they had been only hours before. With dawn, however, another problem arose. They were completely surrounded.

"Our supply route had been cut," says Jim Stone, "and I had no way of knowing how long we might have to hold our position or how aggressive the enemy might become. We were pretty well out of food, water, and ammunition. Around 4 a.m. I called for an air drop from Japan. We ordered what we wanted and sure enough, six hours later four C119s dropped, by parachute, everything we requested, including mortar ammunition."

To the men on the ground, the air drop was unforgettable.

"It was the most beautiful sight I can ever remember seeing," says one man. "I was so hungry my stomach was in knots. Then all of a sudden down came these big flying boxcars. They made a pass and then came back and made the drop. It was tremendous."

"We had Corporal Bishop in my platoon," recalls another man. "He had a metabolism like you wouldn't believe. We were issued two rations, two C rations per man. Bishop sat down on the edge of his trench and ate two C rations. There were three meals in each one. Then he went around seeing if anyone had any ham or lima beans they didn't need."

The battle was over. The supply route was opened and the gallant officers and men of the Princess Patricia's Canadian Light Infantry moved back into reserve. They had fought well at Kapyong, so well in fact that their gallantry was later recognized by the American government, who awarded them, as well as the Australians and a U.S. tank battalion, the Presidential Citation for "outstanding heroism and exceptionally meritorious conduct in the performance of outstanding services". This was the first and only time Canadians have won this award.

While no one may ever know the long-range plans of the Chinese in the actions of April 1951, it may well be true that, had it not been for the gallant stand by the Canadians at Kapyong, the U.N. lines might have been breached and Seoul might have subsequently fallen. "Kapyong was not a great battle," says Jim Stone. "But it was well planned and well fought. We were surrounded by the enemy. We could have run, panicked in some way, or surrendered. We stayed, fought, and withdrew in a soldierly fashion. In the circumstances, the Presidential Citation was earned."

The Pats lost only ten men at Kapyong, with twenty-three wounded, but the Chinese were not so fortunate. When the guns at last stopped firing, over fifty shredded corpses littered *one section* of Hill 677. Many others were removed later. No one knows how many were wounded.

8

MACARTHUR:
A CAESAR'S FALL

Even before the Princess Patricia's Canadian Light Infantry made their heroic stand at Kapyong, momentous developments had been taking place elsewhere. The capital city of Seoul, that sprawling, sacked, half-empty metropolis that had already changed hands three times, was liberated on March 5, by troops of the South Korean 1st Division. On the surface, the city was no prize. It had been burned, looted, ravaged, and shelled. Most of its citizens had fled, and those who were left huddled in pitiable hovels, scrounged scraps of garbage, and drank whatever filthy water they could find to slake their thirst. They were half-naked, cold, diseased, and without hope.

"Seoul was just a shattered, shattered city," recalls Pierre Berton. "People were all hungry; they were selling silver and brocade just to buy food. I drove all over the place but it was virtually empty. A few small armed bands of Chinese were here and there, carrying grenades. You could hear them firing at night.

"Some of the things that were happening were absolutely weird. For one thing, there was a policeman on every corner directing traffic. But there was no traffic, just my jeep. Once I saw a woman with a moth-eaten, bedraggled-looking ostrich and an American with a gun on his hip going after the bird. There were a few correspondents there, but everyone else was banned."

As he wrote in a story published in *Maclean's* shortly after he returned from Korea:

The silence of the grave hung over Seoul. When I entered the city ten days after the fourth liberation, its population, which once stood at a million and a half, had dwindled to fewer than 200,000. It had been looted of every grain of rice, every stick of fuel, every item of value. Its power plants had been wrecked so effectively that engineers despaired of getting electricity into the city in less than three months. Its water plants were ninety

79

per cent ruins. . . . Its citizens had been beaten, hunted, burned out, kidnapped, jailed, starved and shot by the tens of thousands.

Seoul had become a city of beggars and barterers, foragers and pimps. Children of nine plucked at my sleeve and promised to bring "sexy No. 1" in return for money or chocolate or rice. Women with smaller children strapped to their backs scrabbled in the ruins gleaning charcoal for fuel. Old tired men sat in the market place trying to sell silver cups . . . which they had hidden from Communist looters or looted themselves from the homes of the rich. There were few young men or women in Seoul. Those who had not fled south . . . had been herded north by the Communists into armies and work camps.

Berton wrote of another sight that was as unforgettable as the city itself:

I walked alone through President Syngman Rhee's fantastically lavish home, untouched by bombs or shelling, but looted of carpets, curtains and tapestries by the Chinese. Something of Seoul's lost splendour was mirrored here; in the inlaid floors which once shone like glass, now scratched raw by Chinese boots; in the faded flowers still in their vases; in the marble staircase thick with dust and the panelling and mosaics of walls and ceilings; and in the rare blue tiles of the roof — each reputedly worth ten thousand *won* in the days when this was a month's pay for a laborer.

In wrecked Seoul, which grew in its five and a half centuries to become the New York of Korea; a strange and sometimes beautiful jumble of Korean, Japanese, and Western architecture; a religious mixture of Christianity, Buddhism, Shintoism, Taoism and Confucianism; a city of proud, impassive people. I saw the familiar fatalism of the Oriental towards disaster. I listened while women told me how their fathers had been kidnapped and children told me how they were starving for want of rice as calmly and impersonally as if they were reporting the tribulations of a total stranger.

The stoicism described by Berton has never left the Koreans. In the summer of 1982, I also met men and women who told me of loved ones who disappeared forever during the war. Some who talked with me mentioned that they had tried to search for the missing, but that the search was totally futile. "The Communists came in here and if they did not kill people outright, they forced them to go to North Korea," one man said. Others told of missing fathers, brothers, uncles, and friends.

"My father was a lawyer here in Seoul," said Mrs. Kim Su Doc, the wife of the Director General of the Korean Overseas Information Service. "When the war broke out, he happened to be in North Korea on business. Since that day, I have not heard even one word from him. I have no way of knowing whether he is alive or dead. We cannot phone, as you can in Canada, or write — so I have no idea what happened to him."

This beautiful woman's story was the same story I heard over and over again.

"We are half a country," another person said. "Many of us have relatives in the north, but the war divided us for good. Some day we hope to be united, but I do not know when that will be."

Even though Seoul seemed little more than a city of despair at the end of March 1951, it was still the capital, the mecca of every Korean, the wonder-town of the land. For those reasons, south of the 38th parallel at least, he who controlled Seoul controlled the country. This was why, no matter how much of the great city had been destroyed, recapturing it was, to the Korean 1st Division who took it, the biggest prize of all.

But the news that the capital had been retaken was not the only news that involved Korea that spring.

Back in Canada, the Minister of National Defence announced on February 21 that the rest of the 25th Brigade would go to Korea after all, and join the 2nd PPCLI, who had been there for some time. Initially the conflict looked as if it would be over before these remaining Canadians had to go to the Far East. However, with the Chinese now in Korea, the war had taken on a new and more sombre cast entirely. The troops who had been training so long and hard at Fort Lewis were happy to be going — even though they all knew some would never return.

"In a war, you just assume that it will be the other guy who gets wounded or killed," says Doug Carley of Trenton, Ontario. Carley, who would later win the Military Medal for bravery in fighting against the Chinese, adds, "If you knew you would be killed, you'd never go in the first place."

"I can't think of anyone who was not eager to get going," says another Canadian. "We had been training, and all the while kept hearing that the war was going to be over soon. A lot of us were afraid it would be over before we got there. That seems silly now that I look back on it, but that's the way it was."

While the Brigade was completing training, Brigadier Rockingham, its forty-year-old leader, made a flying visit to the Far East.

"I flew from Vancouver to Tokyo," explains Rockingham today. "I wanted to see MacArthur as well as General Robertson, Commander-in-Chief Commonwealth, both of whom were in Japan. I also wanted to visit the PPCLI at the front and meet with General Ridgway, who was in Korea. Our Canadian Liaison Officer in Japan, Brigadier Frank Fleury, arranged my visits to both MacArthur and Robertson.

"At the Dai Ichi building, where I saw MacArthur, an aide who was a full colonel received me first and seated me in his own office, just outside that of his boss. At the precise second of my appointment, the aide led me into General MacArthur's presence."

Rockingham and MacArthur talked about the war effort in general, and about the heroic stand of the Patricias at Kapyong in particular. "The General was full of praise for the PPCLI," recalls Rockingham. "They had done a great job in that fight, and I was glad to hear MacArthur say so.

"Then he got around to talking about Korean strategy. He tried to justify the fact that he was under tension from President Truman and he said he [MacArthur] was very much in favour of bombing the Chinese over the Yalu River and not letting them into Korea at all. Then, in a most impressive voice he added: 'Never has a soldier been so interfered with by politicians. The Chinese and the North Koreans skulk behind their sanctuary north of the Yalu River and I am not permitted to attack them by air bombing. But some day when the dust has cleared — only it is not dust, it is blood — the politicians will have some explaining to do.' This sort of statement to a fighting soldier of my rank did not seem fitting to me.

"Next I visited General Robertson, an Australian, who told me he hoped the Canadian troops in Korea would be on Australian rations, as this would be to Australia's financial advantage. I explained that my cooks had been trained to cook American rations and my soldiers had become used to them and liked them very much. Their rations were excellent.

"It soon became clear that General Robertson and I did not see eye to eye and that he and his staff were about to give me a hard time. I explained, in an attempt to create a more harmonious atmosphere, that I was born in Australia and therefore should be able to get along with his staff. He replied, 'That is no qualification for getting along with Australian staff.' So the difference remained. Brigadier Fleury had made very good friends with General Robertson and his staff, and I seemed to be ruining the relations. However, it did not make much difference to me, as it subsequently turned out that all our operations were carried out under the direction of the Eighth U.S. Army or the Commonwealth Division. The Commonwealth Supreme Commander had some influence only over our administrative arrangements."

Rockingham then went on to Korea, and visited the PPCLI, although he did not see Colonel Stone on this trip. A few days before, Stone had returned to Canada on short notice because his eighteen-month-old daughter Moira had developed cancer in her eyes. As it turned out, one of the child's eyes had to be removed entirely. She later became totally blind at age four and died when she was only six. At the time of her death, she was living at a school for the blind in Brantford, Ontario.

Stone remained in Canada for six weeks, after which he flew back to Korea.

Following his visit to the Patricias, Brigadier Rockingham went to see General Matthew Ridgway, whose headquarters at the time were at Taegu.

"I flew from 27 Brigade's airstrip in a light airplane to the strip at Taegu. After landing and identifying myself to a young officer standing there, I asked the whereabouts of Eighth Army Head-quarters. On learning that I was to see General Ridgway, he said he was one of the General's aides and that the General was expected momentarily. In a few seconds the General arrived; but before the aircraft had stopped, the General was bursting out of the door. The Aide standing beside me dashed forward, took his map case and various bits of equipment and clothing which were being discarded as he ran along the strip. The airfield was surrounded by the usual debris of war, including a crashed aircraft. My thoughts were that perhaps a friend of the General's had recently crashed in the wreckage I could see and towards which he seemed to be running. Anxious to make a good impression and not allow anyone to think that Canada's Senior Officer in the Far East was not anxious to help, I fell into running file in third place. The General continued to dis-card bits of clothing and equipment, finally discarding his web equip-ment which had a field dressing on one of the front shoulder straps and a grenade on the other. Just as the situation had reached a great state of tension and as I was beginning to gain, General Ridgway rushed into a latrine at the side of the strip. I had heard that everyone in Korea got diarrhea sooner or later. In this experience I learned that the affliction was no respecter of rank."

Rockingham and Ridgway got along well with each other, and in Rockingham's words today, "I thought a great deal of him. I was always a bit amused by the fact that he wore the shell dressing, though. This seemed a bit melodramatic to me — particularly for a man of that rank. You never saw anyone else wearing that kind of thing. I guess he thought it made him look like a combat soldier to his troops.

"I remember one press conference," added Rockingham, "and a correspondent for one of the Canadian papers who was sitting next to me asked, 'What is he wearing the grenade for?' A chap on the other side answered, 'That's in case of enemy attacks.' 'What's the shell dressing for?' the first guy continued. 'That's in case the grenade goes off.' I always felt that Canadians weren't all that awed by the man."

There were also other stories related by Rockingham.

"One day," he recalls, "I was up at the front, looking out over no-man's-land through a pair of binoculars. As I did so, I noticed what appeared to be dark objects moving towards our lines. There was an artillery observation plane in the area at the time, so I asked a fellow on the radio to call the plane and have the observer check out what I had seen. To me the objects looked like tanks.

"It was a bright sunny day and the plane was flying at about 1,500 feet. But when he got over the enemy positions they really opened up on him with a hail of fire. The plane immediately swung back to our side and started climbing. He kept climbing and climbing, and all the while, I could still see the dark objects. When I looked up, the little spotter plane was so high it was just a dot in the sky. However, it was back over enemy lines.

"We radioed the plane and asked why he was so high. His answer came back, loud and clear. 'Because I can't get any higher!' I guess he had no intention of being hit."

Another time Brigadier Rockingham received a call from the commanding officer of 2nd Royal 22nd Regiment. "He said he knew where an enemy ammunition dump was located, and he asked permission to shell it," recalls Rockingham. "I asked him how he knew, since the intelligence reports had not mentioned it. The C.O. explained that one of his soldiers in a forward outpost had lived next to a Chinese laundry in Quebec City, and that the man had learned to speak Chinese. In the forward outpost, he had heard a Chinese transmission that happened to mention the location of the ammo dump. I could not really believe such a farfetched story, but because the C.O. insisted, I decided to order a shoot anyway. The artillery were told the location of the target and they fired a few rounds. There was a most wonderful display of fireworks and we knew they had destroyed the dump. The guy in the forward outpost had been right after all. I was amazed."

Rockingham remembers another incident: "Early one morning, before dawn, one of the battalions started calling for fairly large concentrations of artillery fire on what they described as an enemy patrol of bigger than platoon size. The firing was done, but the "patrol" turned out to be one of the big red Korean boars which, caught in the wire, had made a terrible racket. Naturally, the pig was pretty shot up, but I suggested that we could butcher it. The troops were not too keen on the idea, however, because the night before they had seen the boar chewing on the arm of an enemy corpse."

John Rockingham returned from Korea on April 3. On the fourteenth, Canada's Governor General, Field Marshal Viscount Alexander, along with the Minister of National Defence, Brooke Claxton, visited Fort Lewis, inspected the Brigade, and attended a mess dinner. The final inspection and the dinner went off without a hitch.

"We seemed to stand around that damned parade ground for hours," recalls one soldier. "But the whole thing came together at the end. I had never seen a governor general before, and this guy seemed to know what he was doing. It was Rocky who impressed me the most, though. My God, that man was a great soldier. Most of us would have gone anywhere for him."

While his men were trying to please their Commanding Officer, he was feeling justly proud of the men who marched before him. But he was inwardly worried about his duties as host to the Governor General.

"In an attempt to find out the preferred food and drink for our distinguished guest, I had wired Ottawa," recalls Rockingham. "Among the answers I received was the comment that he liked Irish whiskey rather than any other drink. None was available in Seattle or Tacoma, so I asked my friend the Canadian Wing Commander at McChord [air force base] if he could help me. I think a North Star roared up to Vancouver and returned with some Irish whiskey, which arrived in my mess of couple of seconds after His Excellency. Much to my dismay he said he would have bourbon — influenced I think by the fact that he was talking to an American general at the time. My very expensive (by this time) Irish whiskey was not drunk by His Excellency, so we took it to Korea with us."

During the period when the Canadian Brigade was winding up its training at Fort Lewis, events elsewhere were not at a standstill. This was particularly true in Washington, where President Truman clashed with his Commander in the Far East, General Douglas MacArthur. This clash, although it perhaps mattered little to the Canadians who were learning to be soldiers in Washington State, did none the less mean that the military leadership in existence in Korea would be changed before they got there.

In the early stages of the war, General MacArthur assured anyone who cared to listen that he did not expect the Chinese to enter the conflict. Once they did, however, MacArthur seemed to forget all his earlier assurances and instead asked for more and more troops so that he could "win the war".

By the end of March 1951, the Chinese winter offensive had

been stopped and U.N. troops were pushing into North Korea. For the second time in the war, the question of how far north the U.N. armies should advance was debated, not only at the Dai Ichi in Tokyo, but in Washington, at the U.N., and in capital cities around the world. At the U.N., attempts had been made to negotiate with the Chinese Communist government for the peaceful withdrawal of its forces from Korea. Canada supported the policy, but initially the resolution got nowhere. The United States wanted China named an aggressor and achieved their aim in a U.N. resolution passed on February 1, 1951. Peking countered with the view that the United States was the country guilty of aggression.

Into this debate was inserted the question of just how far north the U.N. armies should march. MacArthur wanted to push on into North Korea, and at the same time bomb military and other installations in Manchuria. This viewpoint was rejected by Washington, and, indeed, by other nations who supported the U.N. involvement in Korea. On the twentieth of March MacArthur received a message from Washington to the effect that Truman "was about to announce his willingness to discuss with the Chinese terms under which the fighting could be brought to an end."

Rather than supporting this decision, MacArthur called upon the Chinese to surrender unconditionally. It was this overture, in the view of Robert Smith in his book *MacArthur in Korea*, that earned MacArthur his dismissal: "Crudely, deliberately, with complete understanding of what would ensue, MacArthur undertook to sabotage Truman's effort . . . to open peace negotiations with the Chinese."

The message MacArthur sent the Chinese was, in effect, a taunt, a goading designed to cause them to increase their war efforts, to do almost anything but surrender unconditionally. MacArthur knew this. He "hadn't merely asked for an armistice in place; he had demanded that the enemy commanders admit that they had been beaten." In President Truman's view, "General MacArthur had openly defied the policy of his Commander in Chief, the President of the United States."

While his "surrender message" was only one of the areas where MacArthur and Truman disagreed, it was, publicly at least, the most well known. There were several others of lesser import, but whether any one of them might have been serious enough to topple MacArthur is debatable. Recently, however, a far more sinister aspect of the whole controversy has been unearthed by historian Joseph C. Goulden.

In his book *Korea: The Untold Story of the War*, Goulden mentions the fact that the fledgling National Security Agency (NSA) in the

United States, formed in 1947, was by 1951, and presumably earlier, intercepting messages of all kinds sent by foreign governments. Not all such intercepts involved powers judged to be hostile to the United States. In 1951 a monitoring station at the Atsugi Air Force Base in Japan collected all the information it could on the Chinese. As well, however, it also monitored diplomatic communications between embassies in Japan and other governments. Portugal and Spain were two of these, and both were, in Goulden's words, "countries run by right-wing dictators and countries for which Douglas MacArthur long had an affinity". Goulden continues:

> In mid-March 1951 President Truman was handed a sheaf of intercepted messages from Spanish and Portuguese diplomats in Tokyo in which they told superiors of conversations with General MacArthur. The gist of the talks was that the general was confident that he could transform the Korean War into a major conflict in which he could dispose of the "Chinese Communist question" once and for all. MacArthur did not want Portugal or Spain to be alarmed if this happened. The Soviet Union would either keep out of the war or face destruction itself.

Because the existence of NSA was rarely acknowledged in the early 1950s, and more specifically because its "mail-reading" activities were never mentioned at the time, Truman could not use MacArthur's conversations with the diplomats in a public forum in order to chastise him. The President's patience in the matter paid off, however, because MacArthur's public pronouncements, and in particular his "peace overture", were enough to bring about his downfall.

President Truman fired MacArthur on April 11, 1951.

This decision was undoubtedly one of the most controversial Truman ever made. Letters, telegrams, and phone calls poured into the White House, by far the greatest percentage of them reflecting anger, shock, and vehement opposition to the firing. The President was vilified across the country, denounced in newspaper editorials, burned in effigy, and opposed 69–28 in a Gallup poll which supported MacArthur. Prominent politicians, labour leaders, military officers, and business tycoons called for everything from Truman's impeachment to General MacArthur's reinstatement.

"A strong pillar in our Asian defense has been removed," was the way ex-President Herbert Hoover reacted to the firing. "It's a tragic thing to have happen at a time like this to one of the greatest soldier-statesmen America has ever had," said the famed flyer Captain Eddie Rickenbacker. Governor Thomas E. Dewey felt that the "dismissal by the President is the culmination of disastrous . . . leadership in Washington"; while Richard M. Nixon, then a senator from California, called for MacArthur's immediate reinstatement.

Other prominent people in the United States backed their president. "When you put on a uniform, there are certain inhibitions which you accept," was the way General Dwight Eisenhower responded when asked about the firing. Senator Hubert Humphrey felt that "it was MacArthur's obligation to stay within policy or resign his commission," while the former First Lady of the United States, Eleanor Roosevelt, stated flatly: "I do not think a general should make politics."

Elsewhere, reactions to the firing were also mixed, though probably more supportive of Truman than of MacArthur. Members of the House of Commons in London cheered when they heard the news. In Italy, France, and Holland, the firing was debated in the streets, but Truman's decision was felt to be the right one. The Vatican newspaper, *Osservatore Romano*, called the dismissal "a decisive act, proclaiming a desire for peace. . . . The President of the United States refused a policy that presented such a risk for the United States and the world." As expected, Communist countries were glad to see MacArthur gone.

In Canada, "the general feeling in Parliament," wrote Lester Pearson, "was one of relief." Our External Affairs Minister had been worried about MacArthur, and in particular was concerned about some of the warlike statements attributed to the General. As well, Pearson had spoken publicly about Canada's fears with regard to U.S. foreign policy. "The days of relatively easy and automatic political relations with our neighbour are, I think, over. . . . Our preoccupation is no longer *whether* the United States will discharge her international responsibilities, but how she will do it and whether the rest of us will be involved." This statement was part of a Toronto speech made only hours before MacArthur was let go. Across the country, Canadians who admired MacArthur's fighting qualities nevertheless feared what he might do next. No one wanted war with China, and, unless checked, MacArthur was moving closer and closer to that eventuality.

In the preparation of this book, I asked almost everyone I interviewed whether Truman was justified in firing MacArthur. "Absolutely. He probably should have done it months earlier," was the answer I got from George Ignatieff, now Chancellor of the University of Toronto and for years one of this country's most respected diplomats. "I think he had to fire him," said Pierre Berton. "I would have fired him long before. I never had much use for MacArthur; I think he made a goddam mess of things. In many

Wasp flame-thrower used
by Princess Pats, June 1951.

14

15

Following a night patrol:
men of "B" Company,
1st Battalion, RCR, who
survived a Chinese attack
on Little Gibraltar Hill,
October 1952.

16

The harsh Korean winter came as a bitter surprise to Canadian recruits expecting a tropical climate. Two privates of the 2nd Battalion, Princess Pats, Bren-gun crew, March 1951.

American Brigadier General Haydon L. Boatner, in charge of the North Korean prisoner compound at Koje, was ably assisted by troops of "B" Company, 1st Battalion, RCR.

Ken McOrmond with skull of Chinese soldier.

Combat Kelly comics, written for the U.S. market, were also popular with the Canadian troops.

22

A welcome taste of home: happily, Canadian soldiers did not have to number beer among their privations in Korea.

A familiar symbol from the television series M*A*S*H, similar signposts were also erected by Canadian troops in Korea. This shot was taken at Brigade Headquarters, 25th Canadian Infantry Brigade, January 1952.

23

Many of Canada's top entertainers performed for the ''boys over there''. Comedians Wayne and Shuster on a visit to the Maple Leaf Club in Tokyo, April 1952.

Soldiers wounded at the front in Korea stood a good chance of survival, chiefly owing to the use of helicopters that evacuated the seriously injured to mobile army surgical hospitals in a matter of minutes.

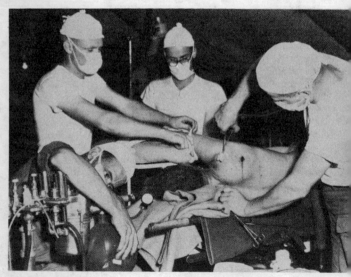

26

Hockey championship match between teams of 1st Battalion, Princess Pats, and 2nd Battalion, Vandoos.

27

Staff of Radio Maple Leaf, which kept the troops in touch with news from home.

Quebec Premier René Lévesque was a correspondent in Korea for CBC Radio. He is seen here interviewing a Canadian soldier in Communist territory near the Imjin River, August 1951.

ways he was a good general, but in so many ways he wasn't. He was always out for himself."

"I believe MacArthur was right," explains General Jacques Dextraze, "but in a democracy, the military must be subordinate to the civilian in authority. It must be that way. While I had the greatest admiration for MacArthur, he lost a lot of my respect because he was insubordinate."

Other Canadian soldiers said much the same thing, but the view held by Dextraze is far from universal. Several men who were in uniform in 1951 told me that they were shocked when the firing took place, but looking back at the world since April 11, 1951, are of the opinion that Truman was right. American soldiers didn't seem to understand what the controversy was all about.

"I was in Pusan the day MacArthur was fired," Pierre Berton recalls. "A lot of the GIs were wandering around the streets, looking bewildered. 'Why did he fire MacArthur?' a lot of them asked. Yet I don't think they were all that crazy about the General. I didn't sense any great upset or horror at the firing; just a sense of bewilderment."

But whatever the reaction, Douglas MacArthur's military career was over. He returned to the United States, amid emotional outpourings that were so effusive that even he must have been surprised. On April 19 the General addressed a joint session of the U.S. Congress, where, according to the Toronto *Telegram* banner headline that evening, he urged the United States to "ATTACK RED CHINA". MacArthur had other proposals in mind, but he was already whistling in the wind. As we look back on his speech that day, perhaps the most memorable part of it was its conclusion:

> When I joined the army, even before the turn of the century, it was the fulfillment of my boyish hopes and dreams. . . . The hopes and dreams have long since vanished, but I still remember the refrain of one of the most popular barrack ballads of that day which proclaimed most proudly that "Old soldiers never die. They just fade away."
>
> And like the old soldier of the ballad, I now close my military career and just fade away, an old soldier who tried to do his duty as God gave him the light to see that duty. Goodbye.

Within a short time, shorter than even he could have predicted, MacArthur faded into obscurity. He did, none the less, leave a legacy that some remembered, if for the wrong reasons. To columnist Jack Anderson in Washington, the entire upheaval in the Far East was something that could be described with the utmost simplicity — a simplicity that irrevocably included MacArthur. In Anderson's view, "the Korean crisis reduced itself to two components: a charismatic, always decisive general boldly in pursuit of the wrong policy, and a pedestrian, sometimes indecisive President who haltingly supported the right one."

But the last word in the Truman-MacArthur controversy comes from the man who fired the flamboyant general who wanted to widen the most unpopular war the U.S. had ever entered. In 1961, writer Merle Miller interviewed Harry Truman at his home in Independence, Missouri. Miller asked the ex-President why he fired Douglas MacArthur. The peppery 77-year-old Truman answered: "I fired him because he wouldn't respect the authority of the President. . . . I didn't fire him because he was a dumb son of a bitch, although he was, but that's not against the law for generals."

With MacArthur gone, Matt Ridgway moved into the Supreme Commander's office in Tokyo. As the U.N. senior officer in the Far East, he did what he was told.

9

NORTH FROM PUSAN

A few days before the three troop-ships carrying the 25th Brigade arrived in Korea, six other vessels with stores, equipment, and vehicles for the Canadians tied up at the docks at Pusan. Twenty-one officers and 171 other ranks of the Advance Water Party (a unit that had come earlier by sea, rather than by air) began to unload them. The task was a laborious one — hot, dusty, seemingly never-ending, and complicated by several irritants, most of which were unavoidable.

For one thing, the compound where the Canadian equipment would be stored was almost nine miles from Pusan, in an abandoned prisoner-of-war camp. Although some stores were housed in a prefabricated warehouse a little closer to the sea, most of the supplies and all of the 1,500 vehicles that had to be landed had to be moved to the fenced enclosure out of which the Canadians would operate — and they had to be moved quickly.

Because of the upheaval in the country brought on by the war, thousands of homeless, transient, starving refugees had flocked to Pusan, crammed every available living space, and begged, bought, or stolen whatever food they could find in order to remain alive. They also stole anything that could be exchanged for food, or the means to buy food. This included goods belonging to Canadians.

"We had to guard everything, day and night," recalls one man who was there, "and even then we lost a hell of a lot of stuff. I never thought something could be stolen as you watched it. You'd blink your eye and a box you had just set down would be gone. It was unbelievable."

"On one occasion a tandem of five vehicles was being towed from the dock to the compound," recalls John Rockingham. "On arrival, the last vehicle was found to be missing. It was the Brigade Provost Marshal's jeep complete with red lights, sirens, and so on. There was no sign of it until later when the siren was found on the black market. Jeep-stealing was quite common. The vehicle was quickly stripped into small components, carried on Korean backs into the mountains, then sold on the black market."

Pusan was a filthy place in 1951. "Tiled roofs, corrugated iron, adhesive dust . . . not especially squalid or awful . . . no age, no beauty, no attractive vice, only lean-tos and laundries and signs: 'Well come Unitted Nations!' 'Hurra Demo Cracy!' " The bulging of the narrow, dusty streets with refugees, the stench which hung over the town, and the apparent casual disregard for human life bothered the Canadians.

"I remember coming into harbour on the *General Edwin P. Patrick*," says Doug Carley. "We were on deck waiting to disembark and we could see American MPs literally beating kids with 45s and rifle butts. We were booing them and we thought that this was so terrible. They told us to mind our own business because sooner or later we would be doing the same thing ourselves. I never saw a Canadian hit a child, but you did become very callous with the kids because they were always under your feet, stealing your stuff or urinating in your drinking water. Sometimes we found them carrying grenades under their clothes."

"It seemed to me," writes James Cameron, "to be a war of unprecedented dirtiness. One disliked seeing helpless old refugees put down with a bullet in the skull, but equally one disliked seeing nice old men reaching into their bundles for a couple of grenades. . . . It was ludicrous to suppose there were any conventions left. . . ."

"One day in Pusan I noticed a truck driven by an ROK soldier run over and kill a Korean child of about seven," says John Rockingham. "The driver got out of his cab and dragged the child by its foot to the side of the road and then headed back to his truck. The ROK truck was being followed by several Canadians who would not let the Korean just drive away. I intervened in the incident and made a report to the Korean army. They didn't actually say 'so what' but managed to convey that impression."

The movement of Canadian equipment from the docks to the fenced compound was a big job, and it went on for several days. The task was made even more onerous because many of the vehicles which had just arrived had been sealed for the long sea voyage. Their batteries had been taken out, a sticky substance had been placed on all electrical wiring, and even the windshields had been taped so that it was impossible to see through them. As a result, most of the vehicles that were soon lined up on the Pusan pier were not in running order. They had to be moved as quickly as possible, though, so every available soldier became a truck driver. At this time, the troop-ships had still not arrived.

"Because I had arrived before the main body of the Brigade," recalls Brigadier Rockingham, "I and some of my staff were accommodated in the U.S. Officers' club in Pusan. But with the rush to get the vehicles off the dock, I decided I should try to help. I drove a 2½-ton truck for two days, towing four or five of the non-running vehicles on each trip. The men who were working with me did a good job, and I really don't think they minded having me as one of the drivers. We worked long hours, but I was used to that, so it didn't bother me. At the same time, the few engineers who were around were busy fencing the compound to keep the looters out."

As soon as the Brigade arrived in Pusan, the troops were taken to the newly fenced enclosure. Once inside, they were amazed at the curiosity of the Koreans. "We were interested in them, and in all that we were seeing," says Ken McOrmond, "because everything was so new to us. But the Koreans would come up to the fence and watch us for the longest time. It wasn't until we were there a while that somebody discovered that half the people who were peering at us were spies. They were taking an account of our people, looking at the weapons, looking at the type, counting us, and reporting all this to the enemy.

"Later we found that the prostitutes, and there were lots of them, were probably the worst spies of all. We then put a twenty-four-hour guard around the place and warned outsiders to stay away from the fence. It didn't take the hookers long to get around this restriction, however. They suddenly became wash-women who came in to do the laundry.

"One day I was on guard duty and a young guy was actually halfway up the outer fence when I saw him. I yelled at him to halt but he took off. I ran after him, but when I was just about to lose him, I raised my rifle and cracked the bolt as hard as I could. The guy stopped and I grabbed him. I then took him to security and I imagine they found out what he was doing. They had their methods. . . ."

At least one other person remembers the fence at Pusan. Saskatchewan-born Dr. Earl Russell recalls that the first case of syphilis he ever treated in Korea was contracted by a soldier who "managed to acquire the disease through the wire at Pusan. This was obviously a highly skilled feat and said something for the abilities of the Canadians who went to the Far East. He was also the only person in my entire career in medicine whom I treated later in the same year for a fresh case of the same disease."

While his men were getting used to Pusan and working themselves into shape after their long sea voyage, Brigadier Rockingham received an invitation to lunch from Korean President Syngman Rhee. "I had heard that he was unusual, but I was not really prepared for my experiences that day," says Rockingham.

"Rhee was as western as it is possible to imagine, but our lunch was served and eaten Oriental style. I am fairly tall and my legs are rather long. The first problem I had to cope with was how to cross and fold my legs under a table about eighteen inches high. I finally told the President that I was simply unable to get my legs under the table. I had to stick them out at the side.

"Korean meals are something else. I remember in particular trying to eat the national dish, which is called Kimch'i. This is a peppery food made of hot, white pickled radishes, cabbage, red peppers, garlic, and God knows what else. It has to be the hottest thing on earth. The concoction is buried underground in an earthenware crock for quite some time until it's ready for consumption. After that meal, my mouth burned for years afterward. We washed the lunch down with tiny glasses of sake, but even that didn't help. I was very uncomfortable but I think Mr. Rhee was highly amused.

"At the end of our meal, the President told me that he thought the Canadians might as well go home, as we were no longer going to be needed because the war was almost over. I told him I had just arrived and couldn't very well go home so soon. As it turned out, it wasn't long until we were needed."

Less than two weeks after they landed in Pusan, the first of the Canadians were in action. The 2nd Regiment of the Royal Canadian Horse Artillery (RCHA) joined the 28th Commonwealth Brigade and fired their first shots on May 17. This action was north of the Han River.

By May 20, the 25th Canadian Brigade had travelled northward by tracked vehicle, truck, and train. To most of the new arrivals, this was their first real look at Korea, in this case Korea in the spring. While many of the impressions are long forgotten, others are as vivid as yesterday.

"I was most impressed by the Korean people," says Ed Haslip, stretcher-bearer with "C" Company, 2nd RCR. "They gave me a greater respect for humanity. After all, the fact that a little nation such as Korea could go through as much over the years, and still refuse to be beaten down and give up, taught me a lot. We learned patience, honesty, and respect from the Koreans. They had nothing but they made do with what they had. Their villages were burnt around them, but still they hung on and never gave up. I loved the Korean kids."

"We moved up from Pusan," recalls Ken McOrmond, also with "C" Company, 2nd RCR. "Our first contact with the enemy came as a bit of a shock. We got into war sooner than we really expected. We were marching along and turned a corner and there was an anti-tank gun wrecked beside the road. There were several dead Koreans lying around it. These were the first dead we had seen and they were not very pretty. We didn't care to look too closely.

"We marched another couple of miles and came to a stream. Our section commander told us to sit down for a breather and to soak our feet. After a couple of minutes of doing so, the Lieutenant came running back, told us to get our shoes on fast. The Communists were on a hill right above us. Then we were ordered to take the hill.

"As soon as we started to go up, you could see arms in the air and grenades coming down. We climbed higher and higher and the fire became heavier. It was coming out of these little caves on the hillside. Finally we got to what we thought was the top — except that there was another higher hill in front of us. We then started up that one, and as we did we passed dead and wounded Communists. We just left them there because they were already out of action. Some of our guys were also hit.

"Finally we moved back and the tanks started shelling the hill and aircraft came over and strafed the top. While they were shelling the hill, we took cover beside the tanks. The whole thing was very impressive. The smoke rolled back and up the hill, then the jets came screaming over us, blasted the slope, and roared away.

"Then there was a sound like raindrops, except that the noise came from shell casings from the aircraft, dropping on top of us like hail. These were 50-calibre casings and a direct hit at that speed from any one could kill you. That was one of the scariest things. Going up the hill was bad, but the idea that we could be killed by our own planes when they weren't even shooting at us . . ."

Private Don Muir went up through central Korea as one of several PPCLI reinforcements. "I remember the dust," he says, "and the mosquitoes, and the look of the first man I saw killed. I suppose I was a bit scared, but I got used to it. I'll never forget the hills, though. One after the other and they seemed to go on forever. The poverty bothered me, especially when we saw hungry kids. We often shared our rations with kids on the road or gave cigarettes to the older people. The country was so poor. I couldn't believe the change I saw when I went back a couple of years ago. Korea is so modern now."

Capitaine J. P. Savary, now with the Corps Canadien des Commissionnaires in Quebec City, went to Korea with the Royal 22nd Regiment and recalls being afraid as he went into battle for the first time. "We were shelled many times," he recalls, "and we had close calls many times. When you can't hear a shell, it's dangerous. When you hear it, there's no problem because it's going over you. After a while you start to get used to what's happening. Then you can identify shells by their sound; you know the calibre by the sound. I remember one day a shell I didn't hear landed right beside me. It didn't explode, though, so now I can tell you about it."

When Dr. John Beswick arrived at the Pusan compound, a friend of his who had been there with the advance party gave the doctor a bottle of Japanese beer. "It was the most beautiful bottle of beer I ever drank," he says. "It had been on ice, and was really cold. As I drank it, I remember talking about the war, about the trip over, about Pusan and so forth. But then when we started to move farther north, half the time we didn't know what the hell was going on or where we were. Guns and airplanes and trucks and guys running and cursing. It reminded me of being in Sicily in the last war and a guy saying, 'I'd give fifty dollars for an *Evening Telegram* [a Toronto newspaper] to find out what's going on.' The ordinary soldier just went from place to place, took that hill or crossed that stream. He didn't know where he was most of the time."

As I researched this book, Dr. Beswick's words came back to me time and time again. Most Canadians who went to Korea knew approximately when they went there. Some, however, who were wounded and went to Japan to recuperate, often confused their time of return. Several talked of crossing one river or holding a particular hill when both the river and the hill were somewhere else — occasionally miles from where the front might have been at the particular time. Often names, ranks, and incidents were long forgotten in the passing of years.

Jim Brown of Egmondville, Ontario, was with the advance party in Korea prior to the arrival of the Brigade. "I was with the 191 workshop originally, but when the Royal 22nd wanted a workshop set up, I went with them. I was at Pusan when Old Rocky started driving trucks. That was great. Later on I became a dispatch rider at headquarters and got to know the man well. He was a beautiful man, every inch a soldier. He also loved his booze, but that never stopped him.

"On the way north, part of my job was to keep the trucks running. If they broke down we had to get them mobile as soon as possible. That went for all the vehicles. Often we had to cabbage parts from vehicles that our guys had died in. I never really liked that but it was necessary."

Jim Brown recalls that as his unit approached the front, they witnessed an incident he will never forget.

"One nice, clear, sunny day we were moving toward this little village in the middle of nowhere — I've forgotten the name now. Anyhow, the people had been ordered out because the word was around that the Communists were close. The railroad ran through the place and the people were massing on the tracks. I was going along a road that ran right beside the railway and I noticed the people up on the tracks. Why they were there I don't know, the roads or the fields would have been much safer. The next thing I knew, the train was coming and then it was on top of the people. I figured they'd get off the tracks but they never did. The damned engine ploughed right through the crowd. Ten people were smashed to bits. One young girl must have been thrown twenty-five feet but she lived. Others were strewn all along the right of way. The whistle never blew and the train never stopped."

Another Canadian witnessed a similar type of accident. Don Randall, a private in the Royal Canadian Electrical and Mechanical Engineers (RCEME) was one of a group of twenty-eight soldiers on board a train that pulled into Seoul en route to the 191 Infantry workshop at Uijongbu. "Just as the train was slowing to a stop at the station, it hit an old lady who was standing beside the track," says Randall. "One of her legs was cut off, and as we left our coach, a bunch of Koreans were standing around looking at her. Nobody did anything, because I guess nobody knew what to do. They just kept staring at her. One of our men placed a blanket over her, but we didn't have time for first aid or anything, we were being put on trucks and taken out of there. I noticed one Korean chap who went down the track and brought the woman's leg up and laid it beside her, as though that would do some good. I was shocked by the casualness of the whole event. The woman just lay there, fully conscious, with her eyes wide open. I never knew if she lived or died, or bled to death, or what."

As the Canadians moved up through the central part of Korea, they were often impressed by the people on whose land they fought. The man who would later become Chief of the Defence Staff, General J. A. Dextraze, during the Korean War Lieutenant-Colonel of the Royal 22nd Regiment, recalls his feelings about Korean family life: "The Korean people were a happy people, or at least they were until we got there. If you stood up on a hill and took your binoculars and looked into the compound of a family inside a fence, of a family dwelling, you could see the grandmother and the grandfather and their son, daughter, or daughter-in-law, and their little children — being a happy bunch of people. Lots of laughing and behind-slapping, of little kids receiving tender loving care from their grandparents and parents, and you could see they were a happy people. If they saw you, they immediately became very passive, very bland, and you couldn't detect any feelings at all.

"At other times you could see how the children were being educated. You could see great respect for one's elders. You could see the grandfather — the grandmother would stay in the house if she was very old — everybody would go to the rice fields and the grand-father would gather all the children of his family and would go along to the rice paddy and sit under a tree, and I don't know what he was telling the little ones, but they were all listening. There would be little children of eight or nine, with other tiny ones, and they were getting their education in this way.

"To me, it was a bit romantic and was very peaceful. I am an emotional man, although my men rarely saw that. They just saw me as a soldier. Anyway, as the father of three children myself at the time, I could see and appreciate the happy life of the Koreans before we got there. They are also a very frugal people. I was always sad-dened when I saw what our modern weaponry did to those people, to that country."

General Dextraze remembers certain incidents that illustrated for him the real brutality of the war.

"We would attack a village, level the place, and then go on to the next one, the next, and the next. One day we were approaching this place and I called for an air strike. A few hours after, I moved into the village with my scout car. The whole place was a burning, shattered, smoking ruin. Almost everything was destroyed. As we went along, we were passing buildings that were almost all gone and I could hear somebody crying. I told my driver to shut off the motor and we listened, and then we walked toward the sound. In what had been a house was a grandmother, a grandfather, and a mother lying dead with a little baby trying to feed at the mother's breast. I went inside to take the baby in my arms. As I did so, a bigger brother, of about six or seven, who had been hiding in a corner, came and started beating on me. While I held the baby, one of my signallers took the little boy. We brought both of them back with us.

"I gave the baby to my medical officer and the padre and they placed him in an orphanage. The little boy stayed with me for months. We took some of my shirts and pants and cut them down so he could wear them. I grew very attached to the little fellow, and he would sit and wait for me, morning and night, and bring me tea and so on. I missed him when we had to say goodbye.

"The boy was eventually placed in an orphanage and he was educated. I paid for his education, but lots of our soldiers did the same thing. Most of us sent money for these kids. It was always sad for me to see this type of thing, to see a cripple without a crutch, and so on. Such things bothered all of us. Canadians soldiers are tough, but we are not tough inside. Whether we're French or English, we are all basically very sensitive. Canadian soldiers are really all a bunch of emotional bums.

"I remember another day when we were in North Korea and lots of refugees were coming down. I had been in the rear for something or other, and as I was moving back up towards my battalion, I came to a crossing in the trail. There was one woman there, all alone, sitting on the ground with a little boy and girl of four or five, I suppose, with her. She had a baby in her arms. The two little ones were sitting.

"There was a bag of rice that she had been carrying on her head but the bag had fallen and the rice was all spilled in the dust. I stopped and had my interpreter ask her what she was doing there. She told us she had given up, that she didn't want to go on any more; she didn't want to live any more. She said she had nothing but her rice, and now it was gone, and she wasn't able to feed her children any more, to keep them alive.

"That bothered me a lot because the woman was so terribly pathetic, so totally discouraged. I knew we had tons of rice and here was this poor creature, ready to die because she had none.

"We brought her back to my headquarters, fed her, and gave her the things she wanted. She stayed with us for three months."

Others also remember their journey up through Korea to the front.

"I was on a train going north when snipers started to shoot at us," says Don Eager. "We all hit the deck and crawled under the wooden seats. Because the terrain was so mountainous, the engineer would go like hell between tunnels. By the time we got to the end of the line, the old engine looked like a sieve.

"As we went along, we saw hundreds of refugees moving south. They were starving. It broke my heart once when we had stopped to eat, out of range of the snipers. We were eating out of tins, and the poor people were grabbing the empty lids and licking them off. That bothered me. It really bothered me."

The war was cruel in other ways.

Captain H. C. (Bud) Taylor remembers being at Uijongbu when he observed what he later referred to as "one of the most poignant incidents I've ever seen". Taylor, who in 1981 retired from the Canadian Forces as a full colonel, was standing outside a Canadian medical facility one morning when he saw a tiny moving figure some distance away.

"It was a beautiful Korean morning," he recalls. "Away off in the distance I could see somebody trudging along a dusty path towards me. As the figure came closer, I realized it was a little Korean boy, in short pants and without shoes. He couldn't have been more than six or seven. His head was down, and as he plodded along I noticed that he seemed to be carrying something. When he finally got to where I was, I realized that there was a tiny guy of perhaps three on the older one's back, his arms locked around the older fellow's neck.

"The poor little guy was not crying. He had been riding on his brother's back for God knows how long. They were actually beside me when I realized the little one's right foot was gone. It had been blown off by a Chinese mine. The older one had tried to bandage the shattered stump, but the pathetic-looking little bandage was trailing down. The medics took over then and I almost cried. It was times like that when you wanted to curse the very idea of war."

By late May 1951 the Canadian Brigade had moved northeastward over the high ground to a position immediately south of the 38th parallel. Some four miles farther on, past the junction of the Yongpyong and Pochon rivers, was a small North Korean village known as Chail-li. To the 2nd RCRs, Chail-li and a nearby hill, variously called 467 or Kakhul-Bong or Old Smokey, were names they would not easily forget. Because this area was a main supply gateway for war materials shipped down from Manchuria, and was also an important Communist communications centre, it was vigorously defended by a highly trained and well-equipped Chinese army.

At six o'clock in the morning on Wednesday, May 30, it fell to the Canadians to attempt an advance on Chail-li, on Kakhul-Bong, and on two smaller hills on either side of the village objective. Under battalion commander Lieutenant-Colonel R. A. Keane, four companies of RCRs moved out, buffeted all the while by a wild wind- and rain-storm that not only obscured the intended objectives, but denied the force any air support. The advance, however, did have a measure of success.

The two small hills and Chail-li itself were taken with relative ease. But on the rugged, misty, wind-swept slopes of Kakhul-Bong the attack foundered. The RCRs, who had slogged through mud and filth at the base of the hill, now clambered around rocky outcrops, exposed knolls, and through stunted, blasted underbrush as they started up 467 itself. High above on the ridge, where sheets of rain and mist hid them from view, Chinese marksmen dug in and waited with a patience that was as confident as it was deadly.

The Canadians never reached the top.

Out of camouflaged bunkers and slit trenches that criss-crossed the higher elevations of the hill, a withering barrage of machine-gun and mortar fire poured down on the hapless RCRs. Men who had joined the army on a whim in Halifax or Hamilton bled and some died on that forsaken slope, before the order came for them to pull back.

While the blistering fire fight was in progress on Old Smokey,

Ken McOrmond and others with him on the lower Hill 269 felt somehow removed from the action. "We could hear the firing on Old Smokey," says McOrmond, "and we knew the guys were in one hell of a fight. The only thing about it, though, was that we couldn't see anything in the fog and rain. Later, a friend of mine, Vern Roy from Sudbury, told me how terrible the fight had been. It wasn't long before we had our own problems, though.

"As we looked down the slope in front of us, we could see a platoon of soldiers moving toward us along a pathway, and then in single file over a rice-paddy dike. As we watched, two of them, both wearing ponchos, came closer and closer. Every few seconds the mist would get so that we couldn't see them, but we didn't dare shoot in case it was our guys. Then suddenly a gust of wind blew one fellow's poncho back and we could see puttees on his feet.

"'They're Chinese,' somebody said, 'they're wearing puttees!' None of us wore puttees, and that was the only way you could tell. One of our fellows said we should fire, but when he stood up to see where the two were, they ducked down on the other side of the dike a few feet in front of us.

"So here we are. We have two people pinned down but we don't know for sure who they are. They're not firing and we're not firing and our officer [Major J. F. Peterson] hasn't seen them. He's got the glasses and he wants to see who they are. So we started to watch where they came from. Sure enough, another group are coming the same way. They also have ponchos. Then the wind came up again and we saw the puttees.

"'They're Chinese!' Peterson hollered. 'Fire!'

"As soon as he yelled, everyone heard him, Chinese as well. We swept the hill and never hit a one. They all flopped down in five hundred years of human waste in the rice paddy. Now it was a stalemate. We couldn't move and they couldn't either. We didn't have any great desire to try to grab prisoners because we knew what they were lying in. But then they started to throw mortars at us and we backed off."

Meanwhile, the Canadians who had taken Chail-li also had to relinquish their prize. By late morning, more and more Chinese were seen approaching the village and the RCRs who were there moved back as they came under increasingly accurate fire from small arms, artillery, and mortars. The pull-back continued in all areas until by nightfall the day's gains were gone. So were the lives of six Canadians who had moved reluctantly forward in the mists of morning. Twenty-three men and two officers were wounded, but two Military Medals were won.

10

THE GREAT IMPOSTOR

While Ottawa was trying to decide whether Canadian ground troops would be sent to fight in Korea, the Royal Canadian Navy had not been idle. The three destroyers assigned to the U.N. Forces in July 1950 had carried out patrol and escort duties through much of the first phase of the war. On July 4 a blockade of the entire coast of Korea was ordered by President Truman, and after the blockade was in force the small "gunboat navy" of North Korea was soon rendered ineffective. There was some danger from enemy planes, but no Canadian ship was ever attacked from the air. The biggest danger in the early stages of the conflict was from mines, and later, particularly after the Chinese entered the war, from shore batteries.

As has been mentioned earlier, the three Canadian destroyers originally sent to the Far East were the *Cayuga*, the *Athabaskan*, and the *Sioux*. Captain Jeffry Brock, the 37-year-old Vancouver-born captain of the *Cayuga*, was also Commander, Canadian Destroyers Pacific. In actual fact, however, all three ships rarely worked as a unit in Korea. It was felt that, because only the three were involved, they could better serve the U.N. operation if they operated individually. And because they were involved primarily on escort and patrol duties, they had a relatively quiet time during the first days in Korean waters. However, shortly after 6 p.m. on Tuesday, August 15, the *Cayuga* became the first Canadian ship to fire a shot in anger.

Fighting at the time was concentrated in the Pusan Perimeter, and enemy troops had captured the port of Yosu on the south coast of Korea. In order to ensure that the Communists would be unable to make use of certain waterfront warehouses bordering the harbour, the *Cayuga*, along with a British vessel, the *Mounts Bay*, was ordered to destroy them. The port bombardment went on for two hours and the operation was successful. Later on, the brass shell-casing from the first Canadian round fired was moulded into an ashtray and presented to Prime Minister Louis St. Laurent.

Patrols continued for some time, up to and long after the Inchon landings on September 15. The Canadian destroyers did operate together at Inchon, but in somewhat of a peripheral role — providing escort services, enforcing the coastal blockade, and guarding against possible interference from enemy submarines. (None appeared.) In the first volume of his memoirs, Captain Brock comments on the Inchon landings, and talks of the orders he was given as a commander of a task group for the operation. "A few days before the event," he writes, "I was presented with two enormous volumes of top-secret operational orders." Calling the orders an "extraordinary example of American staff work gone mad", Brock discovered they even specified "the exact number of typewriters, boxes of paper clips, and other stationery supplies, that somebody had reckoned to be necessary for the conduct of operations after . . . landing."

Even though such support materials were probably important, Brock was unable to find "any reference to the possible nature of enemy resistance, fog or other forms of adverse weather conditions, the action to be taken in the event of heavy mine laying . . . nor other considerations of basic interest to an operational commander." The Captain then adds, presumably tongue-in-cheek: "It was comforting to know that the logistics planners had done their work so thoroughly that there would be no shortage of good food, clean water, chocolate bars, and Coca-Cola machines."

No wonder the landings were a success.

Late in September, when mines in the coastal waters of the Yellow Sea became too much of a menace to the safe operation of the U.N. ships, men from the *Athabaskan* resolved to eliminate the danger. But because the inshore waters were often too shallow to allow their ship to get close enough to destroy the mines with 40 mm fire, a handful of personnel from the *Athabaskan* took a motor cutter from the ship in to the explosive. They towed a small row-boat behind the cutter and then paddled the row-boat up beside the mine itself. The cutter moved back while David Hurl, a demolitions expert in the small boat, gingerly fastened an explosive charge on the bobbing bomb. The task was extremely dangerous, because even the smallest jarring against the mine could set it off. Had that happened, Hurl and those with him would have been blown to bits.

While the demolitions team worked, men in the cutter, and others using high-powered binoculars on the *Athabaskan*, watched the operation and prayed to God the row-boat would stay still, the sea would stop heaving, and the dead bomb would remain dormant for *just a few more seconds*. Finally, as soon as the charge was securely fastened to the mine and the fuse lit, those in the little boat dipped their oars and shot away. When the blast came, the shattered silence gave way to cheering, laughter, and boisterous back-slapping on the

Athabaskan, in the cutter, and, most of all, in the tiny row-boat, where the nonchalant Mr. Hurl sat with an ear-to-ear grin across his face. Some time later, after he and his helpers had demolished several deadly North Korean mines, Hurl received a Mention in Dispatches for his courageous endeavours.

At the end of the third week of November 1950, the Canadian ships were busy patrolling the west coast of Korea, particularly the area from Inchon north to the mouth of the Yalu River, the border between North Korea and China. It was at this time that the North Koreans, reinforced by the thousands of Chinese that Douglas MacArthur said would never enter the war, pushed southward to launch their great winter offensive.

U.N. troops pulled back and back until it looked as if Chinnampo, the port for Pyongyang, the capital of North Korea, would have to be evacuated. Because two of the Canadian ships, *Cayuga* and *Athabaskan*, as well as other vessels under his command, were in that area of the Yellow Sea at the time, Captain Brock was notified on the morning of December 4 to be ready to render whatever assistance the retreating troops might require. Other messages followed, each one more alarming than the one before it. At the same time, other ships under Brock's command converged on the scene. By nightfall these included vessels from Korea, the United States, Australia, and Britain. The *Sioux* had also arrived.

The port of Chinnampo is situated near the mouth of the Tae Dong River but some twenty-three miles inside a treacherous, shallow, winding estuary. The estuary had also been mined, although both Korean and American minesweepers had cleared a path through the mines and indeed had been able to erect unlit marker buoys on either side of the navigable channel. However, no one could guarantee that the mine-clearing had been totally effective. But whatever its efficacy, anyone taking a destroyer, or even a smaller vessel, up the estuary would need nerves of steel. Nevertheless, under the expert seamanship of Captain Jeffry Brock, six destroyers set out for Chinnampo at 10:30 p.m. in a snowstorm on the night of December 4.

Brock had originally intended to wait until the following morning, but after he received an emergency call from an American escort vessel in Chinnampo harbour itself, he decided he should attempt to reach the apparently beleaguered city as soon as possible. He did not look forward to the journey. "The night was as black as the inside of a cow," he wrote later, "and the snow of a little earlier had turned into a blinding blizzard. Never before had I experienced such fear. . . ." He also wondered to himself if he was "justified in taking such hazardous action, involving not only the total Canadian contribution to the war effort but also the ships of four other countries."

The journey took four hours. To the chagrin of Captain Brock and those with him, Chinnampo was found to be "a blaze of lights and all peaceful and serene". This impression was somewhat illusory, however, as the Chinese were known to be coming ever closer to the city and its evacuation became necessary.

All during the daylight hours of December 5, U.N. troops fleeing the Communist advance, along with thousands of Korean civilians, poured onto the Chinnampo waterfront. The soldiers and as many civilians as possible were loaded onto evacuation vessels, while hundreds of packed Korean junks set sail down the channel to the sea. At 5:35, the systematic destruction of all military and strategic installations in the city began. *Cayuga* participated in the bombardment, although both *Athabaskan* and *Sioux* did not. The former had been sent downstream earlier to locate a safe anchorage for ships after the shelling, while the latter had run aground on the estuary bottom the previous night. At 6:45 p.m. the bombardment was over and the port for Pyongyang was a city in ashes. The entire "Chinnampo Affair", as it came to be called, "was without a doubt the most important mission performed by the Canadian Destroyer Division . . . during the entire Korean conflict."

Less than a month after the fall of Chinnampo, Inchon was also taken by the advancing enemy. During the Christmas season, hundreds of civilians fled this port of Seoul, and while the Canadian ships *Athabaskan* and *Cayuga* did not play the dominant role here, they were none the less involved in assisting the fleeing civilians in every way possible. Inchon fell to the Communists on January 5.

Later on in the same month, the Tokyo High Command ordered several ships to stage a bombardment of Inchon in the hope that "this might mislead the Reds into thinking that another amphibious assault was planned and cause them to divert troops there." The shelling may or may not have had the desired effect, but it certainly damaged the town. Lorne Barton was there on the *Nootka*, the first destroyer from the Canadian east coast to reach Korea. "After the shelling, there wasn't much left of Inchon," he says. "The place was really flattened."

It was at Inchon that Canadian ships were fired on for the first time in the Korean War. "We were there, and so was the *Cayuga*," recalls Barton. "Then, just as we were leaving the place, somebody started shooting at us. The Old Man ordered us to swing around and we moved in closer and opened up on them." Within minutes a shore battery on Wolmi Island fell silent. A couple of days later the *Cayuga* was back at Inchon as part of a second bombardment intended to soften up resistance for U.N. troops farther inland. This time the Canadian destroyer was again under fire from the heights above the town, where the park and the statue of General MacArthur are today. The shelling from the shore was again ineffectual; however, splashes were seen less than the length of two football fields from the ship.

As time went on, Royal Canadian Navy vessels continued their role as support for commando operations behind the enemy lines. These operations went on for varying periods and at one time or other were carried out by every ship we sent to the Far East. Because one commando raid was much like another, men who participated are often hard pressed to remember when a particular landing took place, where the action was, and what results, if any, derived from it. For the most part, the "mother ship", whether the *Athabaskan*, the *Huron*, or any of the other six Tribal Class Canadian destroyers that saw action in Korean waters, would sail in reasonably close to enemy-occupied territory and then ships' personnel would use motor-boats to go in to the shore. From time to time they encountered resistance, but often the area would be quiet. If one is to take an over-all view of the war, these raids were perhaps most beneficial for their nuisance value.

"I went in a couple of times when we were blowing up bridges," recalls Lorne Barton. "We always had a couple of ROK guides who told us where to go. Then there would be three or four ROK commandos and about the same number of us. The demolition guys would set the charges and then everyone would run like hell. My job was to operate the motor cutter.

"The guys going in just took the explosives and their own weapons. They didn't take much equipment. I just carried a 38-calibre revolver. The others had sub-machine-guns. From time to time we would hear some firing but we never stayed around too long. We took turns going in. I always thought the whole thing was fun. . . ."

"I don't think there was ever any raid that could be called 'typical'," says Commodore James Plomer today. The former captain of the *Cayuga* during her second tour in Korea is of the opinion that the raiding was worth while. "It was also rather exciting," he adds. "We worked with a number of guerrilla officers in several raids above the 38th parallel. One of my officers, Don Saxon, did a lot of work with the U.S. Marines in connection with the raids. He did a great job and later won the DSC for his efforts.

"I was always impressed with the Korean guerrillas. My God, they were tough. Tough, and when they had to be, brutal as well. And they were very, very courageous. I suppose when you have been treated as a dominated nation for so long, you tend to react in kind. But I admire the Koreans. They kept their language and culture under the most difficult circumstances, and for so many years.

"I never thought the British were too enthusiastic about the war, and I know one senior British officer, whom I was never impressed with anyway, who sure didn't think much of our raids. He told us to stop fighting our own private wars. When our own Admiral W. D. Creery came out to see us, he spoke to this British chap. There was no problem after that."

Bob Johnson was a leading seaman on the *Crusader*. His chief memory of landing in Korea was not the danger or the excitement but the poverty of the people he saw. "I saw one family who were actually living in this tiny chicken-coop," he says. "They had nothing, and as a result their only recourse was to move into that little coop. They may have ended up with a bit of shelter, but they were left with the lice and whatever diseases the chickens might have had. One poor chap was so lousy his head was bleeding."

Denton Wessels was on the *Iroquois*. "I was only an eighteen-year-old kid when I was in Korea," he recalls, "but I still remember the poverty. We went on shore someplace and I remember helping to evacuate some people. I had never seen poverty until I saw Korea. On the other hand, if that kind of a war ever broke out again, and I was younger, I'd be the first to go. I learned a lot from it. I learned how good we have things in this country." Jim Chapman of the *Iroquois* echoes the same sentiment.

Along with the commando patrols involving several of the Canadian destroyers in Korea, another popular form of harassment used against the Communists was "train busting", or the shelling by the navy of trains along the northeastern coastal railways of the country. A "Trainbusters Club" was formed which was made up of any ship that destroyed a train through bombardment. After an American destroyer wrecked two trains in one day in July 1952, the Canadians, who were not to be outdone, "entered into the spirit of this game with the greatest enthusiasm, and before the end of hostilities had destroyed proportionately far and away more trains than had ships of any other nation." In all, twenty-eight trains were destroyed after the club was formed. Canadian ships wrecked eight of these, and the destroyer *Crusader* four of the eight. Two other Canadian ships, *Haida* and *Athabaskan*, each scored twice.

By the end of the war the Royal Canadian Navy had sent 3,500 men to Korea; three men were killed in action, and several wounded. The eight Canadian destroyers had steamed some 725,000 miles and fired over 130,000 shells in the cause of peace. The record was a proud one.

Perhaps the most bizarre story of all involving the Canadian navy in Korea concerned a rotund, jovial, masquerading misfit named Ferdinand Waldo Demara. Demara, the son of a French-Canadian father and an Irish-American mother, was born into relative affluence in Lawrence, Massachusetts, in 1921. By 1929, the father, who had owned a string of movie theatres, fell on bad times and was forced to dispose of most of his holdings. The loss of status apparently bothered young "Fred", as he was called, and he became silent, sullen, and stubborn. At the age of sixteen he ran away from home and entered a Cistercian monastery in Rhode Island.

Fred Demara was a failed monk, but he did not give up easily. He tried at least two other religious orders but dropped out of both. According to the Associated Press account of his life published in the Toronto *Globe and Mail* on June 9, 1982, the man was at various times "a doctor of psychology, dean of the school of philosophy at a small college in Pennsylvania, a law student, a zoology graduate, a career researcher, a teacher at a junior college in Maine, an assistant warden at a Texas prison and a teacher in a Maine village." He was qualified for none of these. Without a doubt, Fred Demara's greatest career "role" was that of Surgeon-Lieutenant J. C. Cyr, medical officer on the *Cayuga* during the ship's second tour in Korea.

Shortly after he entered Canada as a tourist at St. Stephen, New Brunswick, Demara, or "The Great Impostor" as he would later be called, entered the novitiate at the Brotherhood of Christian Instruction at Grand Falls, New Brunswick. Not long afterwards he met and cultivated the friendship of Joseph Cyr, a pleasant, unassuming local medical doctor. The friendship grew, until one day Demara disappeared. So did Dr. Cyr's medical certificates.

On Tuesday morning, March 13, 1951, he offered his services as a doctor to the Royal Canadian Navy at Saint John, New Brunswick. He told the recruiters there that he was Dr. Joseph Cyr, and he produced the real Dr. Cyr's medical credentials as proof.

"I told them that if they didn't take me in a hurry I'd join the Canadian army," he related later. "Within two hours they had me on a train to Ottawa and I was commissioned there the next day. I passed the physical exam without taking off my clothes and they never even bothered to take my fingerprints. One of the admirals on the selection board told me the processing that I went through in a day usually takes ten weeks."

Demara then worked in naval hospitals in Nova Scotia for three months. He also read every medical journal he found. Robert Crichton, author of *The Great Impostor*, wrote: "Whenever he saw a sore throat, heard a serious-sounding cough, or saw someone who looked very bad, he rammed them full of penicillin and, after that, with whatever miracle drugs happened to be current and choice. If a patient persisted in being sick, Fred would manage to maneuver him to any one of six or seven other doctors, using each one as sparingly as possible."

Finally, after a short period of duty on the aircraft carrier *Magnificent*, then tied up at Halifax, Fred Demara received orders to report to Esquimalt, British Columbia, for assignment to Korea. At Esquimalt he joined the *Cayuga*.

"I was the Captain on her second tour to the Far East," recalls Commodore Plomer today. "We left the west coast on June 19, 1951, so we were at sea for quite some time on the way to Korea. Shortly before I took command, I had been on a course in northern England and while I was there I had some problem with a tooth. However, because I was too busy at the time I let it go. That was a mistake. We were halfway to Korea when the damned thing started to hurt. That was when I sent for the doctor and told him to pull the tooth for me."

The man calling himself Surgeon-Lieutenant Cyr arrived at Plomer's cabin, took one look at the Captain's mouth, and went to get equipment to extract the tooth. This time there were no doctors to consult, no wonder drugs that would suddenly stop the tooth from aching or pop it out on its own. Demara was all alone and he was scared. Looking after a sailor with a cut on his head was one thing; playing dentist for the Captain was another.

Alone in his cabin, Demara found himself actually shaking with fear. Though he had worked for a time as a hospital orderly, he had never pulled a tooth, had never given anyone an injection anywhere near the mouth; though he had pretended to know what he was doing when he looked at the Captain's teeth, he had no idea which one was aching. Finally, realizing this might be the greatest performance of his career, he picked up what dental equipment was at hand, walked resolutely to Captain Plomer's cabin, and tapped on the door. The Skipper yelled at Demara to come in.

"He really did an excellent job," said Plomer recently. "I had to show him the bad tooth, but I really never thought anything of it at the time. He filled my jaw pretty full of freezing, I believe, but the tooth came out easily and in all the years since then, I've had no complications whatsoever. I seem to recall hearing that he looked up the instructions for pulling teeth in a medical book he had on board."

Demara felt better after his first real test of skill. With the Captain on his side, the future looked bright. And indeed it was — for a time.

The *Cayuga* steamed steadily westward, crossed the International Date Line, and one month after departing Esquimalt arrived off the Korean coast. For several days the ship was on carrier screen for the

British aircraft carrier *Glory* and the American vessel *Sicily*. The screening duty was rather monotonous and for the most part was disliked by the Canadians. The job involved protecting the huge ships from attack from either the air or the sea. "We used to call it the Dick Tracy run," recalls Bob Johnson. "Just like the detective in the old comic strip; we found the bodies." The bodies were flyers who ditched in the sea during carrier-based missions.

As time went on, Fred Demara established himself as a bona fide doctor as far as the ship's company was concerned. He looked after routine illnesses on board, occasional accidents, and at times even bothersome cases of sunburn. Finally, however, he was given an opportunity to really practise his illegitimate calling. In early September the *Cayuga* had supported a guerrilla raid on the Korean west coast near Chodo. The operation had been a success and a reported 150 enemy defenders had been killed. No guerrillas lost their lives and indeed only three had been seriously wounded. According to the Royal Canadian Navy's official history, "The three seriously wounded, one of them with a rifle bullet through his lung, were treated by Surgeon-Lieutenant J. C. Cyr, *Cayuga's* Medical Officer. . . ."

The three men survived and Demara later bragged about the removal of the bullet.

"Maybe it was true, but I am not sure," says Commodore Plomer today. "Dr. Cyr, we called him, didn't mind exaggerating a bit. But the bullet was never found. Everyone liked Cyr, and in my opinion he did his job well. I used to see him a lot because on a warship the doctor must report to the captain every day on morale and things like that. He was an intelligent chap. He would come in and chat. I liked him very much and I never, ever, suspected he wasn't the man he claimed to be. In my opinion he was a hell of a lot better doctor than a few real ones I've encountered. In another case he amputated a man's leg. That did happen. As far as I know, there were no complications later either. Dr. Cyr was a brilliant man."

Unfortunately for Fred Demara, his glory days in the medical profession came to an abrupt end.

Halfway around the world, the real Dr. Joe Cyr was reading a newspaper one afternoon in Grand Falls, New Brunswick, when he happened to see a story about himself — or at least about a doctor who had the same name. "I had lost all track of Demara, or Brother John as I knew him," recalls Cyr today. "Just before I met him I had moved down from Quebec, and because of the move, a lot of my stuff had been in a state of flux. But then when I couldn't locate my own credentials, I had a pretty good idea where they had gone. Both my certificates and Brother John went missing at the same time. In a way, though, I thought he just might be in the state of Maine. But then when I read this story about a doctor on a Canadian ship in Korea, I began to get suspicious. That's when I went to the RCMP and asked them if they could find out what was going on."

The newspaper account that Cyr read came about because a navy public relations man heard about Demara's skills on the *Cayuga* and felt they should be publicized. At first the impostor was a bit leery about allowing the story to be published, but he finally relented, and thus brought about his own unmasking.

The message reached the *Cayuga* on the morning of October 24, 1951 — Korean time. It stated simply that the man who claimed he was the medical officer was an impostor. The reaction, according to the official history of our navy in Korea, was as follows: "Everyone . . . who had anything to do with 'Cyr' found this information hard to credit, but further investigation proved that it was completely accurate."

"I couldn't believe what I read in that message," recalls Captain Plomer. "I knew and liked Cyr, or whoever he was, and I needed him. I decided that I would call him in, and if he denied it, I would take his word. He was doing a good job.

"He came to my cabin. I said, 'Good morning, Doctor. I have some bad news for you.' Then I read the message. He looked a bit staggered and said, 'I should never have joined the navy. I knew I shouldn't have.'

"'Are you Dr. Cyr?' I asked him. He told me he was. I then told him we would be supporting another shore raid that night and I wanted him to be ready, that there likely would be guerrilla casualties. 'Very good, sir,' was all he said and away he went.

"That night we were busy, but the next day I got another message about our doctor. By this time they knew he was a fake and I was ordered to put him on board another ship, the *Ceylon*, and send him back. I regretfully told the man the bad news.

"The *Ceylon* came alongside and I was up on the bridge. Then I remember looking aft, and noticed two of my people carrying 'Dr. Cyr', getting him ready for the transfer to the other ship. He was out cold. We later found that a lot of drugs were missing and I know he tried to do himself in. His records and some letters were all scattered around his cabin. I felt sorry for him but there was nothing I could do. He was never belligerent with me. When I gave him the second message he looked shocked and terribly, terribly sad."

The unconscious Demara was placed on board the *Ceylon*, and the *Cayuga* was without a doctor. The flat, brief, rather cold wording in the ship's log notes the passage: "1400 Surgeon Lieut. J. C. Cyr left ship to join *Ceylon*." Demara was taken to Japan and then back to Esquimalt, where a navy hearing into his activities was held. At the end of the hearing, he was given $1,000 in back pay, drummed out of the navy, and deported from Canada.

"I was asked if I wanted to press charges," recalls Dr. Cyr, "but I said no, leave him alone. He has done a good job and helped people and that's all that is important."

Twenty-seven years after Fred Demara's infamous naval career ended, Dr. Cyr moved to the United States and opened a medical practice in Anaheim, California. Shortly after his arrival, he was accorded hospital privileges in nearby Good Samaritan Hospital.

"At noon on my second day at the hospital, I was having lunch in the cafeteria," says Cyr. "There were several people in the room at the time and I was talking to another doctor. I'm not sure what we were talking about now, but I will never forget what happened next.

"A door opened from an adjoining corridor, and the man I'd known as Brother John, Fred Demara, walked in and sat down. I could hardly believe my eyes. At first I thought, 'My God, he's still posing as a doctor,' but the man I was with told me Demara was the hospital chaplain.

"I went over and started a conversation with him but he pretended he didn't know me. Nevertheless, I knew he knew. At no time did his past, or his use of my papers, ever come up, and I got to know him well, and saw and talked to him almost every day over the next couple of years.

"The only time *anything* was ever said was in the same cafeteria several weeks later. I was having a cup of coffee with Fred and right out of the blue he said, 'Do you know where I was last weekend?' I told him I didn't know and he went on, 'I was at a Canadian Navy reunion in British Columbia.' With that, he changed the subject and went on talking about something else. Nothing else was *ever* said — by either of us.

"While I am not sure I would have called him my friend, he did give me a lot of publicity over the years. When the book *The Great Impostor* came out, and then the movie about the whole thing with Tony Curtis, a lot of people heard of me. The publicity brought me a million dollars' worth of work."

During my research for this book, I interviewed Fred Demara, via telephone, at his office at Good Samaritan Hospital in Anaheim. He told me he had been an ordained Baptist minister and had been at the hospital for the previous eight years. He no longer pretended to be someone he was not, he told me, and he was now known by his proper name. He had good things to say about Canada, the Canadian navy, and the officers and men he knew on the *Cayuga*. He thanked me for my call and ended the conversation with the words "God bless you." On June 7, 1982, at age sixty, he died of a heart attack.

11

NORTH STARS
VS. MIGS

On July 25, 1950, as the body of Mackenzie King lay in state in the rotunda of the Peace Tower in Ottawa, six Royal Canadian Air Force transport planes passed in formation overhead. The six North Stars dipped their wings in a final salute to the late Prime Minister, then broke formation and set course for the Pacific Coast. Their destination was McChord Air Force Base in the state of Washington, where they would become the first Canadian aircraft to see service as part of the United Nations effort in the Korean War.

The decision to offer the first of twelve aircraft to the U.N. had been announced by the government only four days earlier, but for some time rumours had abounded in Ottawa that there would be some RCAF involvement in Korea. As it turned out, 426 Transport Squadron, the unit chosen, would not fly to Korea itself, but would, in the course of 599 round-trip flights, carry thousands of tons of supplies, equipment, and mail between McChord and Tokyo, Japan. In addition, over the lifetime of the trans-Pacific shuttle, 13,000 people would use the service. In all, the operation involved 34,000 flying hours, but not a single life was lost — nor was any cargo destroyed. This achievement has never been properly applauded.

The first commanding officer of "Operation Hawk", as the airlift came to be called, was Wing Commander C. H. Mussels, a decorated, no-nonsense professional pilot whose spirit and drive were ideal for such an endeavour. Even after the command passed to successive C.O.s, the example shown by the first commanding officer continued. The performance, morale, and dedication of the officers and men in the various sections of the operation were always apparent.

During the summer of 1950 in particular there was such an immediate need for supplies for the Korean campaign that the original six planes and their twelve crews were flying much more than had

113

been expected when the move to McChord was made. Many of the
air crew were logging over 150 hours per month, and each plane
was in the air for as much as 300 hours in a similar period. With so
much air time involved, crew rest and machine maintenance became
critical.

During the summer, the northern or Great Circle route was the
one generally used: McChord to Elmendorf, Alaska, to Shemya on
the remote tip of one of the Aleutian Islands, to Haneda Air Force
Base, just outside of Tokyo. During the winter, the planes flew
farther to the south: from Tokyo to Wake Island, to Honolulu, to Travis
Air Force Base in California, and then back to McChord. Servicing-
units of fifteen to twenty men were located at each stop, as was a
fresh air crew. The incoming air crew turned over their ship to the
rested crew, then got some sleep and relaxation so that they would
be prepared to fly the next plane out. The system worked well, and
each stopover point on the route acquired its own folklore, much of
which was invented by the first group of men who got there and
was passed successively to each greenhorn who came through.

For most of the men who were there, "Shemya meant days of
boredom alleviated by continuous card games. There was also
opportunity of swimming in the Bering Sea and the North Pacific,
but this pastime never became too popular." The remote island
always seemed to be blanketed in a bone-chilling, sweeping fog that
drifted for days over the barren landscape. Because of the fog,
landings were often made on the island that, had it not been for the
pressure of time, would never have been attempted. Even on days
when there was no fog, biting, shrieking winds swept across the
bleak terrain and played havoc with landings, where shifting cross-
winds were so common they became the norm.

By contrast, however, Wake Island — "seven miles of coral and
snow white sand" — was equally remote, but far more popular. Here
the crews sunned, swam, ate tropical fruit, and in the words of a
man who was there, "worked like hell and loved every minute of
it." The men stationed there also took a perverse delight in seeing
visiting crews and even the occasional dignitary sunburned within
minutes under the searing tropical sun.

The favourite posting, of course, was Japan. Then, as now, the
food, shopping, bargaining, and sightseeing were unparalleled anywhere. From the time the noisy North Stars entered Tokyo air space,
glided down past the beautiful Mount Fujiyama, and pulled up at
the ramp at Haneda, until they were airborne and headed for Wake,
the Japanese stopover was more than just special; it was unforgettable. Perhaps this is why men who were stationed in Japan during
the Korean War, those who were on leave there, or those who were

simply passing through, look back on their time in that country with a kind of misty, fond recollection they will never lose.

Other memories of the airlift are not so pleasant.

"My wife and I, with our small son Rob, were only two of many who had to pack up everything and truck across Canada to Tacoma, Washington," recalls George Kightley, who was a squadron leader flying North Stars out of McChord. "The journey to the coast was rushed, as so many service moves sometimes are. We got the word that we were going and they wanted us there yesterday. There were so many last-minute details, so many arrangements, and so many snap decisions that had to be made that I sometimes wonder how we got everything done."

Kightley's cultured, soft-spoken wife Evelyn also remembers the turmoil of the move: "It seemed that everything was in a state of upset for days. Our son was quite little and his needs had to be looked after, of course. But there were a lot of other families who had more children and far more dislocation than we had. We all packed up and shoved off, like lemmings I suppose."

Mrs. Kightley laughs today when she thinks of the time. "It was like that old movie *Follow the Boys*. We followed them, all right, and then they just flew away. When Korea was finally over, we followed them somewhere else, and somewhere else. I know most service wives will tell you the same thing. A lot of us followed the boys for a lot of years."

During the Korean airlift, the flying was sometimes unpleasant, often boring, and on some sections of the journey both taxing and dangerous. Shemya was bad, and so was the last leg west, between the tiny Aleutian Island and Japan. The journey was over water, often under cloud so thick that that astronavigation was impossible, and far beyond the range of any navigational aids then in existence.

There was another kind of flying done by Canadians during the Korean War. No sooner had hostilities erupted in Korea than fighter pilots in the RCAF began hoping one of their squadrons would be dispatched to the war zone. As it turned out, no fighter squadron was ever sent from Canada, but "between November 1950 and July 1953, 22 RCAF pilots were attached to the United States Fifth Air Force and flew with Sabre-equipped fighter-interceptor squadrons."

The day war broke out along the 38th parallel, the North Korean Air Force had a total of 132 combat aircraft. The men who flew these machines were Russian-trained and for the most part were enthusiastic about their jobs. In some respects their enthusiasm must have been greater than their skills, however; by the end of August 1950, 114 of these planes had been destroyed. Even when the Chinese entered the war, the U.N. air supremacy was never seriously threatened. The Russian-built MiG-15 aircraft which the Chinese used were not equipped for long-range sorties, and because the airfields of North Korea were persistently wrecked by U.N. bombing, the Chinese were forced to fly from bases in Manchuria. Because of this state of affairs, United Nations ground operations were never unduly hampered by enemy air attack.

It was always frustrating for U.N. pilots operating along the south bank of the Yalu, the border river between North Korea and Manchuria, to see opposing MiGs take off, attack, and, as soon as they were threatened, turn tail and scoot back into Chinese air space where they knew the U.N. pilots had been ordered not to follow. During the first autumn of the war when the Chinese ground forces were pouring into North Korea, U.N. fliers were sent to bomb several of the Yalu bridges, but were forbidden to enter China as they did so. Nevertheless, retired U.S. Air Force Brigadier General Noel Parrish would later admit that he "ordered his pilots to fly due-north courses, release their bombs as they reached the limit of North Korean territory, and then cut sharply back to the south.

"The pattern necessitated the B-29s flying over Chinese territory to a depth of several miles. So, too, did fighter escorts. . . ."

The first Canadian fighter pilot in Korea was Flight Lieutenant J. A. O. Lévesque of Montreal. In the fall of 1950 Omer Lévesque was on exchange duty in the United States. When his unit, the 334th Fighter Interceptor Squadron, was sent to the Far East in November of that year, Lévesque received authorization from the Canadian government to go along.

Because Defence Department officials believed that RCAF fighter pilots would gain valuable combat experience through spending time in the Korean war theatre, an agreement was worked out with the United States whereby qualified Canadian flyers would go to Korea on a rotation basis. It was subsequently decided that any pilot wishing to apply for combat duty would have to have flown jets for a minimum of fifty hours. Once accepted for exchange, the pilot would fly fifty combat missions, or remain in Korea for a period of six months. As it turned out, several pilots flew fifty missions and three flew several more. One officer, Bruce Fleming of Montreal, actually completed eighty-two sorties.

The most effective Canadian flyer in Korea, on the basis of combat kills, was a shy, handsome, slim, 29-year-old Flight Lieutenant named Ernie Glover. Born in Niagara Falls, Glover had resided in several Canadian cities, but when the Korean War started, he gave Leaside, a Toronto suburb, as his home. During the Second World War Glover had flown Hurricane fighter planes for the Royal Air Force on raids over occupied France. One night as he was about to strafe a freight train, an enemy ack-ack crew opened up on him. "It was about four in the morning and I was rather surprised that they were awake," Glover says today. "I was only about fifty feet in the air when they got me. I pulled up as much as I could, but then when I knew the ship was going to go in, I blew the canopy and got the hell out of there. Fortunately, the chute opened, but I was almost down to the treetops when it did.

"A French family found me behind their barn. They gave me a hat and trench coat but said they couldn't hide me as they were being watched. A bit later another Frenchman found me and turned me in for something like 3,500 francs. I was in a German prisoner-of-war camp for the rest of the war until we were liberated by the Russians. In all, I had been away from home for just under four years."

When he learned that Canadian fighter pilots were going to get a chance to fight in Korea, Glover applied for the job, but neglected to let his wife know what he had done. She learned of the application from another service wife. "She sure wasn't pleased," says Ernie Glover today, "but she finally accepted the whole thing. Now that I look back on it, she had plenty of reason to be upset. I did intend to tell her, of course, but I'd let the thing slide."

Before he left for the Far East, Glover was given a final briefing at St. Hubert at Montreal and from there flew to Chicago on what was then Trans-Canada Air Lines. Because he had five hours to kill before a subsequent flight to California, he found himself wandering rather aimlessly around O'Hare airport.

"As I was eating in a restaurant there," he says, "an American chap and his wife noticed me. I could see them looking at the uniform and the insignia and finally they came over and asked me who I was and what I was doing there. When I told them, they seemed surprised because they thought only Americans were fighting in Korea. The couple then took me sightseeing in their city and later wrote to me while I was in the Far East."

Glover went on to Travis Air Force Base in California, to Hawaii, Wake Island, and Tokyo, and finally to Seoul, where he joined the 4th Fighter Interceptor Wing operating out of Kimpo airport. This was in June 1952.

"The ground forces were at a standstill around that time, just above and below the parallel. There wasn't much activity in the air either, so about the end of August I was getting bored doing reconnaissance sweeps so I asked for a five-day R and R [rest and recreation] in Tokyo. I no sooner got there when I found out that the Wing was knocking down MiGs right and left. I grabbed the next flight out and got back to Kimpo on August 29. The next day on my first mission back

I got two damaged. For the next while we saw MiGs every day."

During his time in Korea, Glover shot down three enemy fighter planes and damaged three others, with two of the three kills coming on successive days. What was it like to shoot down another plane, to possibly kill another man?

"You are very excited. The adrenalin flows very quickly and you know your heart is pumping a mile a minute. Your head is on a swivel and you are trying to keep track of your own guys, as well as trying to watch the plane you're after — or you are trying to get the hell out of the way if somebody is shooting at you. If you do get a strike, you feel like walking on water. You get back and want to talk, talk, talk. You are laughing, joking, really high. It takes some time to unwind.

"When you are shooting at another plane, you never think of the human being inside it. You are after another machine. It's an airplane against an airplane. I can never remember any feeling of pity or sadness or even fear. You are just too happy. Of course, if the guy you have just hit bails out, you see the parachute and then you remember that there was a man in that plane. I can't even recall any remorse when one of the aircraft I destroyed hit a granite cloud [a mountain side] and blew up. You are just too busy to have too many second thoughts."

Glover and the other Canadians who flew jets in Korea went on sorties that usually lasted about an hour and a half. They rarely flew on overcast days because when there was a lot of cloud, the MiGs rarely left their Manchurian air bases. Occasionally as flights patrolled the area immediately south of the Yalu River in an area of north-western Korea dubbed "MiG Alley", the weather closed in. When this happened, the U.N. pilots simply returned to base.

One afternoon, as Glover was doing a reconnaissance run along the Yalu River, he almost didn't make it back. "I stayed along the river too long," he says today, "and I almost ran out of fuel. I headed for Kimpo, along the coast. I'd go so far, then shut the motor off and glide. Then I'd relight it, climb a bit, and glide some more. My plane was an F-86 and its gliding ration was good. Finally, though, when I flamed out for the last time, I didn't have time to go around. I had to come straight in. There was a problem ahead of me, though. Another plane had crash-landed on the runway. So here I was. Out of gas and nowhere to go but down, except that there was no place to land. Then the tower told me to hold on. Somebody roared out to the strip with a bulldozer and scraped the crash out of the way. I came in a couple of seconds after. I later was roasted because I had returned without sufficient fuel."

Not everyone was as lucky. "When I was at Kimpo," recalls Glover, "there were some forty-six houses of ill repute lining the airport. One day twenty-four aircraft were flying in formation, doing a low pass over the field, when one guy's plane flamed out at about six hundred feet. He tried to relight it, failed, and came down into a row of whore-houses. Nobody was hurt at all, but suddenly there were fifteen or twenty guys in various states of undress bailing out of these houses and running like the devil. The whole thing was hilarious, particularly because every one of those places was strictly off limits.''

Some time later, after his return to Canada, Flight Lieutenant E. A. Glover was awarded two Distinguished Flying Crosses, one Canadian and one American. The Canadian medal was the first DFC ever awarded in peace-time. (The "police action" in Korea was never technically called a war.)

The air war over Korea brought with it a number of other "firsts". The first-ever jet air battle took place in Korean skies on November 7, 1950. The first-ever jet ace (a pilot with five or more kills) won the title in Korea. He was an American named James Jabara and his fifth strike came on May 20, 1951. The first rescue by a helicopter of a downed pilot from behind enemy lines happened in Korea on the morning of September 4, 1950. Here again the principals involved were Americans.

But while the fortunes of two courageous Canadians involved in the Korean air war may not have made any of the record books, the stories of an air force squadron leader from Montreal and an army captain from Ottawa were certainly out of the ordinary.

The squadron leader's name was Andy MacKenzie. When the Korean War broke out, MacKenzie was busy forming 441 Sabre Squadron at St. Hubert, Quebec. The thirty-year-old father of four had been in the service for ten years at the time, and fully expected to make the air force his career. He had been a successful Spitfire pilot in the Second World War, with 8½ kills, and a DFC behind his name. When he learned that some Canadian fighter pilots would be sent to Korea, he jumped at the chance to go.

"There should have been an entire Canadian squadron in Korea," he says today. "The Americans had asked this country to supply one, but the decision was made to place the defence of Europe first, so the aircraft were sent there. Unfortunately, while a lot of us had World War II experience, none of us had operational experience flying jets in a war. The whole approach to air combat is different with jets, and even though a pilot might have some luck in a Spit, there was no guarantee he would be so great in a Sabre."

The fact that MacKenzie would want to increase his skill came as no surprise to those who knew him. Years before, he and the legendary Canadian fighter ace Buzz Beurling had been close friends. "We were on the same squadron and he taught me how to shoot," explains MacKenzie. "Once I understood what to do, the rest came easy."

"In just three weeks I had three . . . [aircraft] burning in twenty seconds," MacKenzie told author Brian Nolan. "Christ, I couldn't believe it. It was like shooting ducks. It was so easy."

Beurling, who shot down twenty-seven aircraft in fourteen days during the Second World War, was a good teacher. His technique involved the use of a little model plane and a good knowledge of angles of deflection and aircraft speed. "Once I got the hang of it, I did okay," recalls MacKenzie, "but if it had not been for Beurling, I might never have hit a thing. But I wanted to see what I could do in a jet.

"When I got to Korea, I was based at Suwon with the American 51st Fighter Interceptor Wing. I arrived there about the middle of November 1952. For the first two weeks they checked me out, took me up over the parallel, showed me where the enemy were, and so on. My first four sorties were uneventful. Then, on December 5, I left on my fifth."

It would be his last.

"They gave me what I later realized was a tremendously bad briefing. I was told that if anything were to go wrong, they didn't know what would happen to me because nobody had ever come back to tell them. They didn't tell me there were any prison camps in North Korea. I believed all of our fliers who were shot down were dead. The Americans knew there were seven prison camps along the Yalu River but they didn't tell me. They said they didn't know.

"I still admire the Americans, but they lied to me."

At noon on December 5, sixteen Sabres, four flights of four planes each, roared down the runway at Suwon. Flying in the number 2 position was MacKenzie as Cobra 2. Even the code name seemed to be a premonition of trouble. "I hated snakes then and I still do," he says today. "Perhaps I should have expected problems.

"After we gained altitude, we headed straight for the Yalu. That day we stayed about five miles south of the river, although a lot of guys had flown over it on other occasions, although they generally stayed rather quiet about where they had been. We weren't supposed to fly into China but a lot of chaps did. A lot of them shot down MiGs in China but they were later deliberately vague about the exact location.

"The radio transmission discipline in Korea was terrible. In World War II we didn't say anything unless we had to, but in Korea everyone was on the air at once, babbling away, telling jokes and so on. I remember one fellow who got lost over China. He panicked, I guess, and he started crying on the radio — asking his mother to help him, all kinds of baby stuff. A British exchange pilot heard a lot of this and finally had enough. 'Oh, for Christ's sake,' the Brit yelled on the radio, 'shut up and die like a man.' The fellow who was in China shut up but I don't know whether he died or not."

As MacKenzie's flight headed east, some few miles south of the Yalu, several of the pilots noticed jet contrails. This was the sign they had been hoping to see. Obviously Chinese jets were in the vicinity.

"Suddenly I saw two MiGs shoot under me," recalls Andy MacKenzie today. "They were going into North Korea, so I knew they'd have to turn and come back. I decided to follow."

MacKenzie transmitted his decision to his flight leader, but because of radio interference only part of the message was heard. The next thing he knew, the flight leader was asking for cover as *he* went after a group of MiGs up north near the Yalu. MacKenzie turned to follow.

"Because I was so far behind," he says, "I had to try to catch up. The only way to increase my speed was to dive down and then zoom up. Because the leader was climbing and I was diving, I figured I could increase my speed enough to catch him. I would be going seven hundred miles per hour or so and I figured I could zoom up to where the leader was. As I did this I dropped down through the other three flights of our own airplanes. Just as I went to pull up, there were tracer bullets coming at me. Then all hell broke loose."

One of the tracers blasted the canopy away over MacKenzie's head. When this happened, the explosive decompression tore his instrument panel to shreds, causing the pieces to fly out of the cockpit. A second bullet sheared off part of the right wing, while a third thudded into the fuselage, wrecking the hydraulic control system. The plane shuddered and went into a wild screaming, spinning dive. MacKenzie slammed the control column to the left in a vain attempt to stop the spin. Then he pulled the ejection handles and blasted himself out into space.

A split second before he did so, he saw the American who shot him down.

As soon as MacKenzie was free of his plane, the terrible slipstream tore at his body. Because he was falling at seven hundred miles per hour, his face was horribly contorted, his helmet and goggles disappeared, his arms and legs flailed wildly. The watch on his wrist was ripped off and he went careening, out of control and unconscious, towards the rocky hills of North Korea, forty thousand feet below.

"When I came around, I was still a long way up but I was dropping like hell, so fast I couldn't control my hands. When I was at last able to do so, I got the seat away. It wasn't automatic in those days. Then I finally got the chute out above me. That was a beautiful feeling. In all my years of flying, I'd never bailed out, but when I had to, the damned thing at least worked. But then it was cold, so terribly cold, but at least I was alive, scared as hell, half frozen, still excited from all I'd just come through, but alive, alive. I started looking around to see where in hell I was."

Another man whose experience over Korea was not exactly routine was Joe Liston.

Captain Liston had arrived in Korea towards the end of July 1952. Two weeks later he was a prisoner of the Chinese.

"My battle career in Korea was rather brief," laughs Joe Liston today. "I had hardly arrived there when it was all over for me. I was an artillery observer and I was flying a little aircraft called an Auster VI. My job was to fly up over the lines, select targets for our own artillery, and then radio back. The artillery would open up and from the plane you could see whether they hit anything or not. It was all quite simple. That same summer an Australian guy who was in the same type of plane as I was had been killed because when he was hit by anti-aircraft fire he was without a chute, so he couldn't bail out. After that, I took a parachute.

"Anyway, at noon this day, my thirteenth day in Korea, I took off on my thirteenth mission. I sent back a couple of specific targets and our artillery started firing. Then I got a radio warning that there would be jets in my area, one of our own air strikes. As soon as they came in, they started to draw a reasonable amount of anti-aircraft fire, so I started to get out of the way. They were never going to see my little plane and I didn't want them to hit me.

"As I went along, I was paying attention to the jets and watching their targets so when I was debriefed I would know if the jets had hit anything. Unfortunately, as I watched the strikes, I apparently wandered too far over the enemy lines. Suddenly I started to notice some bigger than usual shells exploding all around me and I knew I was the target. I immediately headed for home and went into a steep dive down to about five thousand. Just when I thought I was safe, I heard a crash.

"It was a direct hit and apparently I was knocked out for a minute or so. When I came around, the aircraft was in a spin and I didn't have any controls. I later found out I didn't have any tail either. The back end had been shot off and was dangling from the rudder controls. I tried the radio and it was dead, but at least there was no fire. The plane was still spinning wildly and I realized that if I didn't get out of there soon, I was going to go down with half an airplane.

"The next thing I knew, I was dangling from the parachute and coming closer and closer to the ground. I knew I was behind enemy lines and I could see Communist soldiers standing around and waiting for me. Then I became a prisoner of war."

12

"MISSING — PRESUMED DEAD"

The parachute carrying Joe Liston into captivity glided smoothly out of the cloudless Korean sky. The descent was swift, and the Canadian army captain had no opportunity to hide. The same Chinese who had seen him bail out now stood transfixed as they watched him fall. Occasionally he could see them place their hands in front of their eyes, like a baseball outfielder who had lost a fly ball in the sun.

At first there didn't seem to be many of them, but the closer he got, the more he saw. First one or two near a clump of trees, then double that; then a lot more. Scores of light-brown uniforms swarming out of nowhere; out of caves, or trenches, or bunkers so well hidden they were almost invisible. By the time he was bracing himself to land, he saw that soldiers seemed to carpet the ground *wherever* he might go. He knew he had little hope of escape. A kilometre away, the little wrecked Auster aircraft ploughed into a barren hillside.

"When I saw how many troops were waiting for me," recalls Liston, "I was certain I would be captured, so I tried to figure out where I was. There were really few landmarks, or at least none I could really see, but I think I came down a bit less than a mile behind the Chinese lines.

"Even with the reception committee waiting for me, I tried to hide the chute because I was in shock, I suppose. But this just made them mad, so I guess it wasn't such a smart thing to do. This was something of a reflex, though, as they told us in training to get the chute down fast so it is hidden. In my case it didn't help. The chute was caught up in some shrubs and the Chinese started shooting at it. I must have been in shock, because the next thing I knew, I was frantically trying to dig a hole with my fingertips in order to hide."

As Liston was attempting to conceal himself from the encircling

123

Chinese, Canadians a mile or so to the south realized that the little Auster had been hit but were relieved when they saw the parachute balloon below it. Within hours, this somewhat bittersweet news reached Helene Liston at her home at 105 Carleton Avenue in Ottawa. The telegram told her that her husband was missing in action but "was observed to bail out when plane was shot down."

"I recall vividly that when the boy brought the telegram to the door he asked for me — but then he asked if there was anyone with me," says Helene Liston today. "I asked him why he wanted to know if I was alone. I could see that he was embarrassed. It never entered my head that there would be anything the matter with Joe. But then I insisted that the boy give me the telegram. He did so, and he left. When I saw the message, my hands started to shake; I felt cold, and suddenly very, very tired.

"I had worked in External Affairs before I was married and I knew Lester Pearson well. He made a lot of inquiries for me, trying to find out what happened to Joe. Unfortunately, there was no more news. I was pregnant at the time and had two other children, the oldest only three, so I had to go on from day to day. Because the parachute had been seen, the men in the army were hopeful. That was the one thing that gave me hope as well. I never lost that. It wasn't easy, though. Like any wife or mother in that type of situation, there were days when I was pretty low."

Seconds after he touched down, Joe Liston was surrounded by the Chinese and captured.

"One or two were making rather violent moves towards me with their rifles," he recalls. "But others were controlling them. Then they marched me off the hill and motioned for me to sit down. One chap handed me two cigarettes and I smoked them, one right after the other. It was after I finished the second that I *knew* I was in shock: I was a non-smoker.

"I was then marched for what seemed like miles. Their slit trenches went on forever, on the flat and up and down hills. As I went along I kept wondering how I was going to handle interrogation. I'd been given basically no briefing in case of capture, other than the name, rank, and serial number stuff, of course, all of which was completely impractical there.

"They seemed to be looking for someone who spoke English who could question me, so they marched me from bunker to bunker. In one, I recall that the whole back of a hill was dug out, but they had tunnels through the hill and they were firing out the front. While I was there, our own shells were coming over. The Chinese just ignored this shooting but it scared the hell out of me.

"Finally they found a young NCO who spoke halting English.

He had a little mimeograph book and asked me to pick out my unit. This was the best break I had because I had a chance to go through the book and see what they knew about our positions. This guy wasn't a regular interrogator, because if he had been, he would never have let me see the book. Anyway, I was actually surprised and shocked to know how much they knew about us. They had the names of all our commanders, and even though the information wasn't up to date, they sure had lots to hang us with. I did my best to memorize as many of the names as I could, so that if they really went after me, I could tell them stuff they already knew.

"They had also located my plane, which I guess didn't burn because they produced my Very pistol. The guy thought the pistol was for signalling our gunners and I wouldn't tell him differently so he threatened me with it. When I saw that he was trying to push a shell in through the muzzle, I wasn't too worried. He made no other threats."

Liston was then placed on a truck and taken seven or eight miles back from the front and lodged under guard in a Korean house. He was kept there for over a month and given nothing but rice to eat. The rice was washed down with hot water.

"This seemed to be an interim interrogation camp," he continues, "but the best interrogation I received was there. The guy who questioned me sure knew what he was doing. At first I told him I was French and couldn't speak English. But then he switched to flawless French, so that line of approach got me nowhere. At first he didn't even talk about anything having to do with military matters; it was all Canadian politics — and he *knew* them.

"I guess he was trying to put me at ease because he knew I didn't want to talk. He would ask questions that had nothing whatsoever to do with the war. I tried to keep stalling him as long as I could so I could decide carefully what I was going to say. I kept thinking that it was the time element that was important — but I knew in the end they would have ways of making me talk. . . .

"One day in particular they brought me into this little shack where they did the questioning, sat me at this table between two guards, and asked me to tell them about the Canadian line positions. When I told them I couldn't read their map, they handed me my own map out of my plane. When I kept stalling, they reminded me that no one back home knew if I was alive or dead, and that they had made a decision about what to do with me. They would put me on public trial.

"By this time I was terrified. I had heard stories of their trials, although in my case the threat of a trial was only a bluff. I didn't know that then, though."

At night Liston was left on his own — with the hundreds of large rats that overran the camp. During the day the rats didn't bother him, but at night, as he slept on the mud floor of his hut, they ran across his legs, over his body, and from time to time even against his face. He would wake up, brush them away, and fall back to sleep. He was never bitten.

From time to time he noticed other prisoners but for the most part was unable to communicate. "I once was able to steal a couple of words with an American and, a bit later, with three Australian guys. They had all been captured together. Most of the time I was alone. There was no recreation, and the sleeping hut was so small I had to lie corner to corner to stretch out.

"I remember lying there for hours and hours, worrying about Helene and the kids, wondering what I had done to them. I also knew that with her pregnancy and all, the time would be tough for her. Throughout my whole imprisonment the worst part of the mental torture for me were the times the Chinese would remind me that they alone knew I was alive, that no one at home knew. That bothered me a lot."

One morning the Chinese came in and told Liston and others that they would be moving to another camp. On the way, he met a man he will never forget.

"Along the way, at one of the stops, we picked up some more prisoners. One of them wore a Canadian army shirt. He was paralysed completely on one side and I offered to help him because I wanted to talk to him. But because the poor chap was in such bad shape we never did communicate much, and at the time I didn't know his name. I told him mine but I wasn't sure if he understood. We were in the back of a truck together at one time and he would look at me quite intently. I remember that he seemed fascinated by the fact that I was wearing a pair of cowboy boots. Later on we were separated and I never saw him again."

The new camp to which Liston was taken, and the one in which he would spend the remainder of the war, was located in a small valley, isolated from the outside world by a ring of hills. Thirty-five Americans were there, and a day or so after Joe Liston's arrival, one Australian and one South African were brought in. Not only was Liston the only Canadian, he was the senior officer as well.

"A day or so after I got there, the Chinese came to me and told me they wanted us to build a fence around the compound. I told them we would never build it. Why should we fence ourselves in? Then they put the fence up themselves — in one night! We could have done so but it would have taken us three weeks.

"Every so often somebody got the bright idea that he should try to escape. Several of us would review the escape plans and if they looked at all plausible, went along with them. As far as I know, however, no one ever made it back to our lines. There were just too many things against it. For one thing, we didn't know where we were. We couldn't speak the language. We couldn't go unless the grain was ready to eat. We had to have food. On top of all that, our beards grew quickly enough so that within a day or so at most, we stuck out from everyone else. One fellow did get away and almost made it to the sea before he was caught. Another hit a guard on the head and took off. He was caught soon afterward though, and shot. That discouraged a lot of breakouts."

Each day the prisoners were fed, counted, and ordered to clean their quarters and then sweep the compound. They were idle much of the time, but occasionally were marched to a local schoolyard and allowed to play softball. After some weeks of captivity, the Chinese produced playing cards and allowed a few books into the camp. Most of the reading material was propagandistic. "They would only let us read a chapter at a time," recalls Liston today, "and then we had to give the book to someone else. It was one hell of a way to read a book."

From time to time, selected prisoners were interrogated, and on two occasions Liston was asked to make a tape recording. "They told me they would send the tape to Canada so that my wife would know I was alive and well cared for. This was propaganda of course, so I refused. I told them I wanted her to think I was dead so she could remarry and forget me. When they heard this, they told me I was a bad man. After that, they forgot about the recording.

"Sometimes they got angry when their questioning wasn't producing any results. I recall one day a colonel interrogating me started to lose his cool. His face got red and he started yelling. At that point I began taunting him. Finally he jumped up from behind the table where he sat, grabbed an ashtray, and flung it at me. I saw it coming and refused to duck. It just grazed my face, so the guy stormed out. I'd made my point.

"On another day, though," says Liston, "they got to me. They were demanding that I admit something or other and I refused. When one guy started into a screaming fit of abuse, I started to get up, but a guard slammed me in the back with a rifle butt. That day he made his point. For the most part, though, they left me alone and time dragged."

Liston was not the only Canadian who found that time dragged in prison. Moments after his F-86 Sabre was wrecked in the skies over North Korea, Andy MacKenzie was floating down towards a brush-covered mountain side. "I could see the Yalu River off to my right, and the sun shining on the mountains all around me," he recalls. "And it was so *quiet*. One minute there was all the roaring and excitement of battle; the next I was hanging under the parachute and there wasn't a plane in the sky. I thought I was completely alone. Then I happened to look down, and a few feet from where I was going to land, I could see an old Korean woman picking up sticks. She glanced up at me with a rather blank expression on her face but then turned and went on about her business. I didn't believe anybody could be so stoic. She hardly even *paused* in her work.

"I saw a couple of trucks in the distance and realized they were coming towards me. By the time I was out of my parachute harness, they were pretty close, and I could see soldiers in the trucks. I tried to get out of there but they took a couple of shots over my head so I stopped running."

The soldiers surrounded MacKenzie and one of them motioned for him to put his hands in the air. They then ordered him down the mountain side to one of the trucks.

For the Canadian squadron leader, the days and weeks that followed are now a hazy, jumbled memory, like a half-forgotten horror movie. He was moved from place to place, from camp to camp, until he finally found himself taken into Manchuria, where he would spend many long, terrible months in Chinese prisons, accused of being a spy. During much of this time he was interrogated, threatened, half starved, and left in solitary confinement for weeks on end.

Often the solitary cell was cold, so cold he couldn't even sleep. "All I had was my light flying pants, flying boots, socks, light sweater, shirt, and nylon flying jacket," he told a reporter later. "This may sound like a lot of clothing, but the room was not heated and the only protection against the zero weather outside was the four mud walls. In one was a latticed door covered with thin paper. I huddled Indian squat-style wrapped in my single blanket, shivering continuously. Between the cold and the mental strain of not knowing what was going to happen to me, muscular spasms developed in my back, causing severe pains. . . ."

During another period, MacKenzie was placed in a tiny solitary cell and ordered to sit on the edge of his bed. He had to place his hands on his knees and stare at a bare wall six feet in front of him. He was not allowed to lie down, stand, or even fall asleep. This form of persecution went on from dawn until dusk, and lasted ninety-three days. Each time he attempted to get up, a guard screamed at him to sit down.

"It is difficult to describe the mental torture that went on during this period," he would say later. "My main occupation was to reminisce about the things I had done as a boy and in my later life. Some distasteful incidents out of my past would arise. I would re- proach myself and sometimes break into tears. I was always thinking of my wife and children, and I would recall how, during the last war, I had written my mother and dad only once every month or so, and I mentally vowed that I would make up for the anguish I had caused them."

Unfortunately, he would never see his mother again. She died while he was in prison.

"Being locked up sure made me appreciate life in a free world," continues MacKenzie today. "When they put me in solitary, I really never expected to leave that cell alive. I reminisced about almost every day of my life — and for the first time really came to understand what a good life I had had. My dreams of being at home became so vivid. I would be there with my wife, playing with my kids, going sailing with them, enjoying our family life. This dream came almost every night. But then I would awaken in the morning and I would be so shocked. I was still there in that same hell-hole."

As time went on, MacKenzie became more and more convinced that if he didn't at least pretend to go along with whatever his jailers wanted, he would rot in his cell. "I called the guard and told him that I was ready to be questioned."

At first nothing happened.

Then, about two weeks after he made his request, he was led from his cell into an interrogation room. There were eight Chinese officers already there, seated in a semicircle. MacKenzie was ordered to sit in a wooden chair in the middle of the room. The man he believes was the senior officer opened the session by asking about the big American bombers then in use in Korea. MacKenzie told his inquisitors that, as a Canadian and a fighter pilot, he was unfamiliar with the B-29 and B-50 bombers.

The Chinese didn't accept the explanation and had their prisoner returned to his cell.

The solitary continued for several more days. Then, with no prior announcement, MacKenzie was moved to another cell, this time a larger one. He believes this was around the beginning of April 1953. "I had no way of knowing for sure," he explains, "but I had been scratching a mark in the paint on my bed, under the mattress, so I think the date was reasonably accurate. Anyway, things started to improve around that time. Whether it was because the war was winding down or not, I don't know. I was given warm water, tobacco, and several magazines. Then one day three prisoners were moved into the cells to the left of me."

As soon as he felt it was safe to do so, MacKenzie started to tap the left wall of his cell. The tap was answered, and at first nothing else happened. But because he was now allowed to move around his room, he often stayed near the tiny slot in the front of his cell to see if he could learn who his neighbour was. A few more days went by. Then one morning he had his ear against the door slot and found that not only could he hear the man next door talking, he recognized the voice!

"It was an American named Harold Fischer," says MacKenzie. "Fischer was a captain then and had been in my squadron. He is now retired as a colonel. In Korea he was my closest friend. You can imagine the joy of that reunion. We found a friendly guard and started passing notes back and forth because they wouldn't let us talk. Fischer told me that no one had seen me bail out and that they had assumed I had been killed. All my belongings had been sent home.

"He also knew the secret I kept for thirty years. He knew the name of the American pilot who shot me down. The day I was hit I had dived down to attack a pair of MiGs. When I got separated from the flight leader, I was trying to catch up. One of our own guys saw me off by myself and mistook me for an enemy plane. Then he shot me down. After I was released from prison I learned that the guy returned from that mission and went right in and told our commander what had happened. The pilot was a religious person and apparently he felt terrible. He asked to be taken off operations.

"They put him ferrying planes from Korea to Japan. This was a routine procedure when major overhauls were needed. It just wasn't feasible to do the work in Korea. Anyway, seven days after he had shot me down, he died when he crashed his plane into a mountain in Japan. Apparently he was preoccupied.

"After I finally got home, I was called in by some of our brass and told to keep quiet. 'We're friends with the Americans, and talking about this will only make them look sillier than they are. Why don't you forget the whole thing?' I agreed to do so because I am not a bitter man. I'm not bitter because they told me to shut up, and I'm not bitter towards the poor chap who shot me down. He made an honest mistake.

"There were quite a few stories written about me years ago, after I finally got back to Canada. In all of them, I simply said I had been shot down. Anyone who wrote about me just assumed the shooting was done by the enemy. A couple of years ago I told John Picton of the *Toronto Star* what really happened. The *Star* was the first paper to carry the story and I guess this will be the first book. I have no qualms about telling you now because the war has been over for a long time — so what the hell — we all made mistakes."

In his story about MacKenzie, published by the *Sunday Star* on

December 21, 1980, John Picton states that the pilot refused to tell his captors "the circumstances of how he bcame a prisoner because the propaganda would have been invaluable." In all probability that would have been true, because, as it was, the Chinese were putting MacKenzie through hell to get at information that was of far less value to them. It is highly unlikely that they even suspected how he met his fate. They were interested in what they called the "truth".

"They wanted me to admit that I had been in Chinese air space when I was shot down," explains MacKenzie. "They wanted me to tell them I had been ordered to fly over China, that I had been captured in China. This was what they called 'the truth'. Finally, they wore me down to the point that I gave them what they wanted. I just couldn't take any more. A number of us were ultimately forced to do the same thing.

"I had been taken into China illegally, but that aspect of 'the truth' never seemed to be important to them. The prison where I was, at Mukden, was the place where they took people who didn't interrogate properly. I also tried to get away a couple of times and that didn't help either. The first time I was running out in the night, screaming because of what I was going through. I ran into a guard. He took me back to the cell and in the next while they told me I had done something very bad, that I should not have tried to run. So then I was sure I was going to be killed. They kept hinting this but they never actually came out and said it. After another period in solitary, I started screaming again, and when the guard unlocked the door, I ran again. I was covered in body lice, great big half-inch body lice. A million of them on my body, and I was going crazy. I just couldn't take it any more.

"I realized later, of course, that if I had given them what they wanted, the propaganda stuff they wanted, I could have been out of there a lot earlier. But I kept thinking of what was going to happen when I got home. What would happen if I gave them a so-called confession? Would I be court-martialled? and so on. Their truth was what they wanted to hear. Finally, when I gave them what they wanted, things started getting better."

But Andy MacKenzie's troubles were far from over. He saw others released from prison long before him, and he never knew why. One or two of the men that were let go informed Mrs. MacKenzie that her husband was still alive. This was the first hint she had of what had happened to him, and the best news she ever received.

"The Chinese never actually laid a hand on me," says Andy MacKenzie today. "It's what they hint they're going to do. That's what drives you crazy. The torture was all mental. Being alone for days on end. I heard sounds that were not there. The loneliness was terrible. My body ached but my mind kept on working, wondering what was coming next, what they would do with my body after it was all over, that sort of thing. Then I went on long, protracted crying jags. I cried for days and couldn't stop.

"Much later, when I was able to receive a bit of mail, my father's first letter told me of the death of my mother. That almost killed me. I would never see my dear mother again. She had gone to her grave believing I had been killed. I really felt sorry for myself. But one day I had a letter from a chap who had also been imprisoned. He had broken his leg bailing out, and he knew how hard I was taking my mother's death. He simply told me I was being selfish. He said I should revere her memory instead of crying about my loss. He told me I should feel fortunate because I had had such a good mother. This approach helped me a lot and I felt better after that."

During the last eight months of his stay in prison, MacKenzie's situation improved a great deal. He and the three Americans in the cell block with him were given the use of the entire wing of the building they inhabited. They were able to talk, visit each other, read, and play cards. But just being able to talk was the greatest relaxation of all.

"We talked for hours and hours," laughs MacKenzie, "and we became quite close friends. The day, right out of the blue, when they said I was going home was a happy day for me, of course, but saying goodbye to the others was hard.

"They put me on a train, under guard, and we travelled for four days through China, to Canton. Then they marched me across the border into Hong Kong and I was free. The date was December 5, 1954 — exactly two years to the day after I was shot down — and long after the Korean War ended."

Andy MacKenzie and Joe Liston became POWs when they parachuted into enemy territory. Other Canadians were captured on the battlefield. One of them was George Griffiths, a blond, 22-year-old, clean-cut kid from Brighton, Ontario. On the night of October 23, 1952, Griffiths was with "B" Company, 1st RCR, when their position on Hill 355 (or Little Gibraltar as it was called by the Americans) was overrun by attacking Chinese. The capture took place after approximately thirty Canadians were cut off from company headquarters following an intensive bombardment by enemy artillery.

During the fierce shelling, Griffiths received a minor wound in the foot, not serious enough to prevent him from walking, but bothersome to the point that he was unable to keep up with other soldiers as they moved forward in a trench. As he lagged farther and farther behind, he realized the Chinese were right above him.

"Just as I came around a corner in the trench, a Chinese soldier jumped down from the parapet and stood in front of me, his rifle pointed towards me,'' recalls Griffiths. ''I ducked back to the corner, trying to figure out what to do next. The whole thing happened so quickly, and of course it was dark and it was hard to see. Then the next thing I knew, the guy threw a grenade and it blew up and hit me in the face and chest. The wounds were rather superficial but I realized right away that my face was bleeding and I was getting mad. I rammed back around the corner and blasted the guy from about four feet. I imagine he died, because I shot him in the gut. He just fell over. He had to die. He made no sound.

''I was trying to figure out how I was going to get myself up the trench. I knew the Chinese were just above me, so I threw a couple of grenades and stumbled along until I came to a dead end, a bunker with a blanket across. As I half turned to try to escape, another grenade came over the top and hit me in the left knee and left shoulder. By this time I hurt like hell, I'm trapped, and I figure it's all over. There's all this flashing, explosions, just like lightning, and I'm scared — no, terrified.''

Griffiths then pulled the blanket aside and climbed down into the bunker — with four dead men. ''I don't know who they were,'' he says, ''and at first I didn't realize they were dead. But then the blanket was pulled back and two Chinese soldiers filled the doorway. One was carrying a flashlight and the other a burp gun. I was back to one side and I didn't even breathe. I was hoping they would see the dead and perhaps not see me — and for a minute I thought I was okay. The guy with the gun went to each body and pushed his bayonet through the corpse. But when they came to me I turned and they realized I was alive, although I was smashed up and covered with blood by that time. They motioned for me to drop my rifle, get my hands up, and get out of the bunker.''

The climb up and out was steep, and the entrance-way was awash in blood as Griffiths stumbled into the night air. As he did so, he held his right arm above his head; his left was immobilized by the shoulder wound. ''I may have just slipped or I may have started to pass out,'' recalls Griffiths today, ''but I instinctively slid back and my good hand grabbed the guy's bayonet. I even remember that it was triangular, with three sharp edges. He pulled it back, but didn't shoot.''

As Griffiths was being pushed and prodded down the trench, he came upon other Canadians who had also been captured. Ahead of them were several corpses, lying every which way, and a number of wounded, many of them Chinese with legs, arms, or hands missing. The sickly-sweet stench of warm blood, dust, and cordite mingled with the cries of the wounded and dying, the gasping for breath, the thud of mortars, and the staccato bursts of machine-guns. At one point in the slow procession down the hill into no-man's-land and finally into Chinese-held territory, the trench became narrow, too narrow for Griffiths. In his wounded state he stepped on the stomach of a corpse, and the swoosh of air from its gut chilled him to the bone. "That sound will stay with me to my dying day," he says with a shudder of aversion, "and I never, ever, want to hear it again."

The underground trench and tunnel system being used by the Chinese ran for miles, and was as much of a revelation to the Canadians captured on 355 as it had been to Joe Liston and to many other U.N. soldiers taken elsewhere in Korea. In places the tunnel had been bombed, but apart from minor damage it remained virtually undisturbed. For the most part the ceilings were a little over six feet high, the walls three or more feet apart. Every so often a larger excavation of perhaps eight feet across provided sleeping space for troops. The tunnel itself connected to a room, roughly ten feet square, into which George Griffiths was led. The room, like the tunnel, was entirely below the surface of the ground.

"There was a table there, some chairs, and six Chinese soldiers," explains Griffiths. "One guy gave me a cigarette and I took it and smoked it even though I don't smoke. At that point they apparently did not know whether I was Canadian or American, so they drew pictures of the Canadian and American flags on the table. They motioned to me to point to which one was mine. When I indicated the Canadian, all six Chinese pulled out their bayonets and stabbed the Stars and Stripes. I sure picked the right flag! That incident told me what they thought of Americans."

While George Griffiths was enduring his hell on earth during the Chinese attack on 355, and his subsequent capture, he might as well have ceased to exist as far as the rest of the world was concerned. As it was, he was half dead with battle wounds and loss of blood. His "dog tags" (military identification tags) had been lost, possibly when the first grenade had exploded in the air in front of him; the stone in a ring he was wearing had been blown out; and he was dragging one leg behind him. The next day his wife would receive a telegram informing her that he was missing in action. And, as if she might hold in her heart a flicker of hope, dashed that with two more words, "presumed dead". Ten long months would pass before she would be told that he was not dead but was a prisoner of the Chinese.

"But I was not the only one who had a bad time that night," Griffiths says, deliberately down-playing what he experienced. "A lot of our guys were just as bad off as I was. The Chinese gathered twelve or thirteen of us together, and we sure looked like a beaten army. One chap was wounded in both wrists, for God sakes. How in hell would a guy get wounded in both wrists? I saw another fellow who was far too young to be there. He'd lied to get in, so he ended up with wounds, disabilities, and a pension, all before he was eighteen. He was just a child. Another guy had been wearing his tin helmet during the attack. A bullet had taken the helmet off, but the whole front of his head had gone with it. He was a pathetic sight, but he was alive."

From the time they were wounded and captured until they were pushed, driven, and dragged the mile or so into Chinese territory to the prisoner collection point, most of the young Canadians had been in shock. As a result, they had not experienced the full pain of their wounds. Now searing, burning, numbing pain assaulted them. Pain that coursed through their bodies in blinding spasms. Pain that was worse than anything they'd ever known. Pain that was always there. Pain that made death seem almost welcome. Pain that would drive them to try anything for relief — even if what they tried would likely get them shot.

"We were in pretty bad shape, but we still thought we should do *something*," says Griffiths. "So the next day, even though none of us were given medical help, they decided to march us farther up into North Korea. Here we are, stumbling along in single file, being taken farther and farther back from the line. At a rest break, I suggested to Don Orson, a friend of mine who was helping me, that after the break I could lag behind and he could help me. Then we might be able to kill the two guards near us and get away. We talked about the idea a bit and then decided that just past a clump of trees ahead of us we would see if our little plan worked.

"I started to fall farther and farther back, and Don pretended to help more than necessary. Then, right out of the blue, this goddamned American jet who obviously has taken us for the enemy roars overhead and starts shooting at us. This is broad daylight, so when the shooting starts, we all had to go for cover. Nobody was hit and the guy up above buzzed off for coffee down at Seoul. The guards then tightened the line up and we couldn't get away after that.

Griffiths and the other prisoners, many of whom were Canadians, were marched farther and farther north. As they went, the bedraggled group were fed cabbage and potatoes and lodged in abandoned houses, a coal mine, and during a later night, a hillside cave. That night, from another cave far above them, they heard someone singing "The Blue Canadian Rockies", but they never learned who it was. The sound was reassuring because, in its mournful simplicity, it told each Canadian who heard it that he was not completely alone, that a countryman who understood was there in that foreboding place.

"That was where they put three of us in a dark hole," recalls

George Griffiths with a shudder, "and we had to crouch down along one wall. None of us wore shirts. Then they had some kind of a tap above us that allowed drops of water to fall on our backs, slowly, for hours. The water was ice cold, and gradually it became extremely painful. I am certain that if they had continued it long enough, we would have gone insane. We couldn't move, even to stretch. A soldier with a burp gun sat in front of us and screamed if we moved. The torture was effective, and it left no marks. As this went on, they kept telling us that if we did not co-operate, if we did not tell them whatever it was they wanted, they couldn't guarantee our safety. The mental torture, the unknown, was worst of all."

Some hours after they were driven into the black hole, Griffiths and his companions were allowed out, and the march northward continued. Finally, some ten or twelve days after their capture, they arrived in a prisoner-of-war camp, a village somewhere in north-western Korea, "reasonably close to the sea," Griffiths believes, "because occasionally we could hear naval guns, and they have a different sound.

"This was where the real questioning went on. They asked me over and over and over again why I came to Korea. 'To stop Communism' was my answer, or 'to kill Chinese'. When they asked me what a Communist was, I told them I didn't know. 'You are here as cannon fodder for the Americans,' they told me. 'You don't even know why you are fighting.' This type of thing led to requests that I go back home and tell the Canadian government that the war was unjust. I told them to forget that idea; that I didn't want to listen to that kind of horseshit. You know, I don't think they liked that."

Griffiths lived in this camp for ten months.

"There were a lot of characters there, and we tried to be as supportive as we could to one another. A few guys became a bit strange, though," says Griffiths. "There was a British chap who thought he had a motorcycle and a dog. He did have a stick about two inches thick and two feet long. He called this the motorcycle. He would hold it in front of him and tell you he was driving this big bike. Then he would make noises like a motorcycle, pretend to steer the thing, and then he'd race around the camp. The dog he thought he had did not exist at all, but he would call it, pet it, feed it, and so on. Every night he would roar up to our hut, park his stick, open the door for the dog, and then both would come inside. When he left, he would tell the dog to come on, and the two would leave. The bike would start and they would roar away. Poor guy."

As time went on, Griffiths' wounds healed, although he still carried shrapnel in his foot. Each day he walked as much as possible around the camp, because he had joined the escape committee and had no intention of being left behind if they decided to take off. As he walked, he grew more and more accustomed to this prison without bars, this home for "180 misfits who wouldn't believe in communism". He saw Greeks, Americans, Puerto Ricans, Turks, and a dozen or more Canadians.

"The Puerto Ricans were in on an escape attempt that involved eight of us. The night we tried to get away, the Puerto Ricans kept singing songs at the tops of their voices in one part of the camp while we crawled through the guard line, then along behind some houses to the outskirts of the camp. There was no perimeter fence, but there was a deep trench that we had to get through. As we went down into it, we were almost beside a guard. Suddenly he rattled his gun and saw somebody. I really think they knew we were coming and they caught a couple of Americans. The rest of us sneaked back in before we were caught.

"Then all hell broke loose. Guards came running from somewhere, and they formed us up for a count. Fortunately, they started counting at the front row. Here I am, at the back — loaded with food for our escape. Luckily, by the time they got back to me with the count, we had passed the food out and eaten it. Don't forget, this is all in darkness. At the end of the count, everyone was present. They knew there were Canadians involved in the attempted breakout, but they didn't know who."

Towards the end of the war, a number of sick and wounded prisoners on both sides were exchanged in what has been called Operation "Little Switch". Two Canadians were released at this time, and in all probability Griffiths might well have been the third. However, in the first seven months of his captivity he had never received any medical treatment whatsoever for his injuries. The Chinese knew this, of course, but they had no intention of letting the news reach the outside world.

"They called me in right after 'Little Switch'," he recalls, "and told me they had decided to attend to my wounds. I figured 'better late than never' so away we went. They froze my foot, gave me a few opium seeds to chew, and put a pillow-case over my head so I couldn't see. I nearly smothered under the pillow-case, so I took it off and watched them digging away at me. They took six hunks of steel out — but I wouldn't want to have them do a heart operation. My foot still gives me a lot of trouble.

"As I was recuperating, they kept supplying me with opium seeds and half the time I was higher than a kite. I would walk along a pathway and a little stone would look like a boulder and I would take a huge step over it. At other times when I was high I felt so carefree I'd get up in the middle of the night and go out and throw stones at the guards. They didn't bother me, because we were just looked upon as cannon fodder. They hated Americans, though, and some of them were punished for less.

"Because I was wearing glasses when I was in prison, they decided to give me an eye test. One day this guy showed up, and all he had was a little case in his hip pocket. He had no other instruments. He sat me down, looked at my eyes, and said I didn't need to wear glasses unless I wanted to do so. I didn't know whether to believe him or not. Later on, after I got out, they examined my eyes in a million-dollar building in Kure, Japan. They told me the same thing but it took twice as long and was a hell of a lot more expensive. It was too bad the dental guy in the compound was not as good as the eye doctor. While I was in prison, all my teeth rotted out. They ached and ached. After a while the ache stopped."

When the end of the war finally came, Joe Liston, George Griffiths, and all the other U.N. prisoners who were released with them, were shuffled around from camp to camp until one day they were taken to what became known as Freedom Village at Panmunjom, Korea. There they crossed a bridge, the Bridge of No Return, separating the two Koreas. Then these men, who had endured such appalling conditions for so long, were cleaned up, examined by doctors, fed, and given new clothes and new boots. While each man who returned to freedom had his own thoughts, hopes, and dreams for the future, George Griffiths was particularly happy about the new boots. "I sat there and looked and looked at them," he recalls. "I was so proud of my new boots."

Then he climbed on a truck and began the journey home.

13

"BLOOD ON
THE HILLS"

From the summer of 1951 until the end of the war, almost all of the fighting done by Canadians in Korea was centred in a small area north of Seoul, between the 38th parallel on the south and the town of Chorwon on the north, and from the Sami-Chon River east to Chail-li. At its widest, the area is perhaps thirty miles across, although the bulk of the Canadian action was within an even more limited section along the United Nations front. Many Canadians died here; many more were wounded; some were captured, but most were unharmed. A few were heroes.

Private Doug Carley was a signaller with "D" Company, 2nd RCR, who was involved in a fighting patrol near a hill called 166 on the night of December 13, 1951. The patrol's task was to move across a valley under cover of darkness, make contact with the enemy, and if possible bring back one or two Chinese prisoners. The job was unpleasant, unwelcome, and unsafe, but it was not unnecessary. There had been an increase in Chinese shelling along parts of the U.N. line, and it was felt that if a prisoner could be captured and questioned, his answers might assist the Commonwealth Command in determining what the enemy was planning.

"It was long after dark when we moved out," recalls Carley today. "There were twenty-five of us, and we all had our faces blackened and nobody was making a sound. Before we left, we had been briefed on where the minefields were, but even so, you had to be careful. My radio, which weighed about forty pounds, with an extra battery, was strapped on my back."

The patrol moved silently down into the valley that separated the lines, then proceeded in single file along the dikes between rice paddies. The column moved slowly as each soldier gingerly picked his way and watched for any movement, prayed, and hoped to hell he would come back alive. There was no moon, and, save for the

139

sawing of a mournful breeze through the stunted grasses, almost no sound. For a while the silence seemed unreal. But then it was shattered.

"We were no more than twenty yards from them when they opened up on us," Carley explains with a shiver that takes him back to that night. "I couldn't see the Chinese, but the flashes of the machine-guns were awfully close. My mouth was dry, as if I was chewing cotton. My hands were cold, clammy, and those bullets were all around us. All I could see was blue flame, feet up in the air, arms all over the place, just like rag dolls. We all hit the dirt, of course, and then the sergeant sent the get-away man, the last man in the patrol, for help. He was only a few yards away when he was hit. Bullets are crashing all over the place. My short radio antenna was shot off and so were the epaulets from my uniform. Then the sergeant ordered us to get the hell out of there."

The Canadians scrambled backwards, through the waist-deep filth of frigid rice paddies, to what they believed might be the relative safety of a river bank. During this mad retreat, Carley fell far behind, weighed down by his radio, utterly alone in front of the stuttering deadliness of the Chinese guns. He fell, heaved himself out of the putrid muck and water, and fell again.

"I kept saying to myself, 'Oh Christ, why me, why me, why me,'" recalls Carley today. "I'm not a religious person and I don't know whether you'd call that praying or not, but I was damned scared. I knew the other guys were getting farther and farther ahead of me, and I sure felt like getting rid of the radio. I could hardly move — it was so heavy, but somehow I caught up."

As soon as he found his companions, Carley calmly crouched down, dried out the handset on his radio, pushed up the longer ten-foot antenna which had not been damaged, and called for artillery support. While he was doing so, he was exposed to the steady and increasingly accurate fire of the enemy. For this selfless courage, Doug Carley won the Military Medal. In the words of his citation, his "coolness and efficiency under heavy fire was a very steadying example to the remainder of the patrol. . . . His conduct was an example to all signallers, in particular, and to the men in general." What the citation did not say was that D. W. Carley, MM, saved the lives of over twenty men. Years later, when I interviewed him for this book, he was most reluctant to talk about his own exploits at all, and only produced his citation after I pleaded with him to do so. He modestly claimed that so many others had performed far more deserving feats of courage that night.

As soon as the artillery barrage that Carley had called down was over, the patrol again surged forward, overran the Chinese position, and riddled its defenders. The Canadians also got their prisoner.

"We got lucky," says Carley. "The guy we grabbed had more holes in him than a tramp's shoes. He was a huge man, a Mongolian or something, because his head hung over one end of the stretcher and his feet over the other. We got him back, but how they kept him alive I'll never know. I guess the doctors pumped him full of blood so they could get the information they wanted. It must have worked, because we heard later that the guy was quite helpful."

On March 19, 1952, Corporal Ken McOrmond, RCR 2nd Battalion, "C" Company, along with a sergeant and eight men, was sent on a fighting patrol to destroy an enemy machine-gun post. As they attempted to cross a valley leading to the gun position they ran into a large number of Chinese. At one point McOrmond, who was in charge of number two group of the patrol, was lying face down in a rice-paddy sump making his reconnaissance for his position when he sensed a presence in the darkness to his left.

"I could tell that there was something out there," McOrmond recalls, "but I couldn't tell whether it was a man or an animal. The longer I waited, the more I wondered, but because of the darkness I couldn't see *anything* unless it was highlighted. Then the form came closer and I held my breath. I saw the outline of a man, but I didn't dare shoot in case it was one of our guys. I knew if I said anything, and the man was Chinese, he'd let me have it."

McOrmond had to actually creep forward to within five feet of the figure before he knew.

"I peered into the man's face," says McOrmond. "He was a squat, thick-set man in a bulky uniform, and he had a burp gun in his hand. As soon as I saw that, I started shooting. My only immediate thought was to hit the guy before he could pull the trigger. I know I killed him. But then several machine-guns started firing from our left."

The patrol sergeant was wounded by the barrage, and then McOrmond assumed command of the entire patrol. Although he now plays down his actions as not being particularly courageous, he was responsible for leading the unit back to safety. "Corporal McOrmond displayed exceptional ability to think fast and clearly during the heat of the battle," says the citation for the Military Medal he won that night. "He subjected himself continually to heavy enemy fire. . . . Due entirely to his efforts the patrol was able to fight its way clear of the numerically superior enemy, inflicting undetermined casualties while suffering none."

A few days later, a Canadian Broadcasting Corporation news report from Tokyo on April 22, 1952, stated: "If McOrmond were told he was a hero, he'd reply that he didn't know what you were talking about. And he'd mean it. The fact of the matter is that Ken McOrmond is . . . a hero, and not an accidental one." The men McOrmond led to safety would agree.

There were others whom both Carley and McOrmond and every Canadian in Korea knew who, though they never received medals, exhibited behaviour that was exceptionally meritorious. Many of them were too modest to mention what they had done. Others performed courageously but their deeds went unnoticed by those in command. Some brought a lifetime of pain from the battlefield, and have been in and out of hospitals ever since. Many others enlisted and never returned. Perhaps these are the real heroes — the men whose remains lie today in the peaceful plots of the United Nations Cemetery at Pusan. These are the young men whose reward for war was a grave.

Don Muir remembers Emerson Patterson (PPCLI) who died a few days before he was to come home. "We were in danger of being overrun," recalls Muir. "Emerson was beside me on a machine-gun when he realized three of our guys were out of ammo. He tapped me on the shoulder and said he'd be right back. He grabbed some ammunition and started to take it down front. He got halfway to the men when the Chinese opened up on him. He died trying to save his three friends. He was twenty-three at the time and I watched him die."

Keith Aiken lost three close friends in Korea. All were with him in the PPCLI and all three died on the same day — October 23, 1951. "This involved an attack on a hill," says Aiken. "The object was to take a prisoner. That was the last day on earth for my friends; Donnie [E. F.] Bradshaw, Bobby Arnott, and Sergeant [C. J.] Currie. Donnie was on a Bren gun when he was killed. He had emptied a clip at a machine-gun nest, and instead of getting a new position right away, decided to put in another magazine. As he did so they got him. Then Sergeant Currie stood up to wave some more men up the hill and he was gunned down. When things quietened down and the whole thing was over, Bobby Arnott was helping to carry a stretcher on the way out. On the way he stepped on a land mine. . . .

"Years later I thought I would go and visit Donnie Bradshaw's mother, just to tell her how I felt about him, and what a wonderful guy he was. I was living in the west and I hitchhiked from Calgary to Kirkland Lake, Ontario. I checked into a hotel in the evening and intended to go and meet her the next morning. You know, I was not able to do it. I left the next day and never saw her. I just couldn't go through with it."

Ed Haslip will never forget his friend Pat O'Connor, a 27-year-old stretcher-bearer with the RCR. On the second-last day of May 1951, O'Connor's company was overrun by enemy troops, and several men were hit. O'Connor moved through the dead and dying, giving them comfort, bandaging wounds, occasionally praying with them, all the while ignoring his own exposed position. In a couple of cases, dying men held his hand and whispered their final words in his ear. To others who were wounded he gave support, told them they would be okay, and occasionally dried the tears of pain and fear that he saw on so many of the young faces around him. Finally, when his medical supplies ran out, and the situation started to look more and more desperate, he told Haslip he would go and get help. "I watched him start to run back," says Ed Haslip bitterly, "but before he'd gone fifty yards a Chinese machine-gun cut him down. He died trying to save the lives of the men with him. In my opinion, he should have received the Victoria Cross. He was a completely selfless and dedicated soldier, as well as a wonderful human being."

A few hours later, when Private Howard Root was gathering up O'Connor's few personal belongings for shipment to his widow in Sarnia, Ontario, a sheaf of tattered paper fell to the mud floor of the bunker where the young Canadian had spent his last day on earth. On one of the pages was a poem, a poem Private O'Connor was seen writing the night before he was killed. The paper was passed around the bunker, and a clutch of misty-eyed young soldiers with trembling hands read the heart-wrenching words that might well be an epitaph not only for Pat O'Connor, but for all the brave young men who lost their lives in Korea, fighting Canada's forgotten war.

Korea

There is blood on the hills of Korea
Tis blood of the brave and the true
Where the 25th Brigade battled together
Under the banner of the Red White and Blue
As they marched over the fields of Korea
To the hills where the enemy lay
They remembered the Brigadier's order:
These hills must be taken today
Forward they marched into battle
With faces unsmiling and stern
They knew as they charged the hillside
There were some who would never return
Some thought of their wives and mothers
Some thought of their sweethearts so fair

And some as they plodded and stumbled
Were reverentially whispering a prayer
There is blood on the hills of Korea
It's the gift of the freedom they love
May their names live in glory forever
And their souls rest in Heaven above.

The experiences of men who were wounded in Korea were generally just as traumatic as the sufferings of the wounded in any other war. The major difference, however, was the use of the helicopter in the evacuation of severe cases. For the first time in history, dying men could be moved from the line of fire to the operating theatre, sometimes within a matter of minutes.

Art Johnson was wounded the day he was to go home. "I actually was told I would be leaving the day before," he says, "but they had some kind of a transportation foul-up and I was told to come back the next day. Anyway, we were on 355 and the Chinese had been shelling our positions all night. Colonel Peter Bingham, a hell of a great guy, was in charge. At about ten o'clock in the morning, mortars were coming in and one hit the roof of a bunker near me. Nothing much happened, other than a lot of dust came down, because we had the roof reinforced with steel bars.

"A few seconds after the hit, a chap by the name of Mason, who had been in the bunker, came running out, covered with dust from head to toe, and cursing so loudly you'd hear him in Seoul. He looked so funny that I had to just stand there and roar laughing at him. Then the next thing I knew, I'm lying on my back and one leg and one arm hurt. My arm was really whacked. It was all smashed up, and had somehow got draped backwards over my shoulder the way you might carry a coat.

"Then a guy from our medical corps by the name of Phillips, from Winnipeg, came running over, took one look at me, and I thought he'd throw up. I was contorted like a pretzel. He ran for his morphine and because he was so nervous, broke the first needle he tried to push into me. The second one went in okay and soon I was floating. Five or six guys put me on a stretcher and toted me down the hill. As they were putting me in the back of a jeep ambulance, I asked the corporal how my leg looked. All he told me was that it wasn't bleeding a lot. I could see by his face that all was not well.

"The jeep came to the casualty clearing station and they'd already ordered a chopper for me. At 8055 MASH as they were carrying me inside, I remember that it was starting to rain."

Johnson's arm was put together, but one leg had to be removed.
Tom McKay was not only Art Johnson's close friend, he was

wounded the same day and taken to the same MASH. His injuries were accidental, but they were equally severe. A young soldier who had just arrived in Korea was examining a loaded Bren gun in a bunker on 355. McKay, who had been in the war zone for some time and was already a battle-tested veteran, warned the new man to leave the gun unloaded unless he took it outside. Just as the kid started to unload the weapon, it went off, and shattered both the silence and McKay's right leg. "After that, I remembered very little of 355," he says now.

McKay, ordinarily a cheerful, happy guy, was semi-conscious when they pushed him into an ambulance for an eleven-hour, pain-wracked trek to the nearest MASH. The rain which was just starting as Johnson was brought in had grounded all helicopters when McKay's turn came.

The harried medical people at 8055 MASH put McKay's leg back together, but his troubles were far from over. A few days later, his big toe turned black and the right foot had to be removed. He was shipped to the south to a hospital at Taegu. Here even more of the leg was taken off, this time at an inch or so below the knee. Still later, as he lay in a ward in a Toronto military hospital, two doctors examined him, stepped a few paces away from his bed, and one said to the other, "What an abortion."

"I overheard the remark, even though I wasn't supposed to," says McKay. "Things seemed to be going okay, but that comment hurt me. I was really shattered."

Finally, many weeks after the initial injury, Tom McKay's right knee was also amputated. By that time, however, the boy who did the shooting in the bunker in Korea was beyond the realm of recrimination or pain. His body had long since been interred on a hillside near Pusan. He had been killed by the Chinese on 355.

Stu Meeks was on 355 during the fierce fighting of October 23, 1952. He had been in and out of the line earlier, including a seven-day stretch at a Norwegian MASH where he recovered from phosphorus burns to his arms and hands. "I was treated well," he recalls, "but I've still got scars on my wrists because of the phosphorus. Awful stuff. It burnt so severely I actually tried to cut it out with a knife.

"When we were attacked on 355," he continues, "I was still some distance back. But I was there for the counter-attack. They called for a barrage on the hill, and I'll never forget the noise. We started to move up in the darkness, with all this yelling and screaming and explosions and so forth. I figured I was going to die for sure and I started to forget my fear and began to act like a soldier. I kept thinking, 'I'm going to kill as many of those little bastards as I can before they kill me.' I had lost my fear and I had nothing else to lose.

Then I remember seeing one Chinese soldier, then another and another. I know one guy I hit just spun like a top and seemed to disappear. When you hit them like that with a Bren gun it picks them up and they flip over backwards. Finally, though, I ran out of ammunition and still they were coming on. Some of us started heaving rocks and even beer cans that were all over the hill.

"The next thing I knew, a squat little guy was standing in front of me with a burp gun. I could see the fire from the goddamned thing because he was only twenty-five feet from me, and I was wondering how he could miss me at that range. My nose was bleeding and my ears were bleeding from all the concussion and I just assumed I was going to die. I felt weak and tired, as if I was trying to run in a dream or in deep water and I couldn't get anywhere. Then I put my hands down and knew my intestines were falling out and my knees wouldn't hold me up.

"Everything became fuzzy and the next thing I knew it was morning and I was strapped under a helicopter and all I could see were clouds. I thought I was in heaven and I remember thinking, 'I can't be, soldiers don't go to heaven.'"

Today Stu Meeks is a veteran alderman in Belleville, Ontario, where he runs an ambulance business. During my interview with him, he showed me his battle scars, the "souvenirs from 355". His stomach looks like an old soccer ball that has been kicked and gouged in a thousand games.

"Yes, my stomach looks like hell," admitted Meeks, "but at least they patched me together. My first memories after I came around in the MASH concerned the pain caused by the dressing they had on me. Then a few days later I was so hungry but I could never seem to get enough to eat.

"The chopper took me to an American MASH, and when a lot of us were getting fairly healthy, some of the Yankee brass came around and gave us all Purple Hearts, the U.S. medal for guys who'd been wounded. The hell of it was, though, that half an hour later they came and took them all back when they found out we were Canadians. I tried to hide mine as a souvenir but they were too fast for me. Probably would be worth a couple of bucks too."

During the war, several Canadian doctors and nurses, as well as other medical personnel, spent time in Korea. Major Flora Brohman, now Mrs. Mike Dolan of Ottawa, worked at No. 25 Field Dressing Station; Betty Neil was a nursing sister, Jean Mickle a physiotherapist. John Beswick, E. K. Fitzgerald, and Earl Russell were doctors attached to Canadian units, and, in the case of Dr. Russell, later on to American medical care facilities as well.

"The Field Dressing Station was at Uijongbu," Jean Mickle explains today. "We lived in Nissen huts, four to a room, and we had a short walk to our work. We took turns on duty roster, and part of that involved getting up and starting the stove each morning. The huts were cold and water left in a basin in the room was always frozen solid in the morning. We slept on camp cots. The floors were wooden — but that place was cold! Dr. Larry Lawson, one of our surgeons, used to tell us to cheer up and forget the cold. He said we'd pay good money for the same thing in the Laurentians. I suppose he was right. In a way, it was a good place to be — particularly for a woman. There were a lot more men.

"We always had Korean women around who helped to look after the place and do the laundry and so on. We called them 'Mamma Sans'. They were nice people and we grew attached to many of them.

"During my time there, silk stockings were a bit of a luxury and they were popular on the black market down in Seoul. One night when the four of us in my hut were sound asleep, I wakened to find somebody going through my clothes beside my bed. I screamed and a little Korean boy of about twelve scampered out. The next morning I realized he had taken my underwear with him. The others with me still laugh about that."

Dr. Earl Russell worked at 8055 MASH for several months. There he saw young soldiers, fresh from the battlefield, who died on the operating tables. He also saw others who looked as though they were gone but who survived and went on to lead healthy lives. And he recalls a third group who were overjoyed because they had been wounded.

"This last category were sometimes annoyed when we patched them up and sent them back to their units," he recalls. "They looked upon a wound as a ticket to home. Their tour might not have been up for some time, so they felt the injury would allow them to leave Korea. I recall one young GI who came in with his helmet still on, a bullet hole in the back of it, and a lot of blood running down his neck. Initially it looked as if the helmet was holding him together. But when we got it off, there was really little injury. A bullet had gone through the helmet, cut a little crease in his scalp, and caused a lot of bleeding. We put the equivalent of a Band-Aid on the guy and sent him back to the front. Was he ever upset!

"For a time I worked in the Pre-Op and Receiving section of the MASH. Through there were accepted all of the patients who came in. I assisted in the resuscitation. At that time we had what we called six surgical trestles. As each man came in he was on a litter, and the litter was simply carried from one surgical station to the next. I got to know the surgeons pretty well and I knew their particular abilities and interests, so I was able to channel the patient appropriately. These doctors generally came out from time to time so that we could decide which cases had to be done with the most urgency.

"I was at the MASH during the wintertime and the weather was bitterly cold and raw, although we had little snow. We worked under conditions that were pretty primitive, though — and at the time I was there we were doing something over 1,700 operations a month."

In the years since the outbreak of the Korean War, others have talked of the cold of Korea. James Michener, in his novel *The Bridges at Toko-ri*, wrote: "From the vast empty plains of Siberia howling winds roared down to lash the mountains of Korea. . . . Then with furious intensity the Arctic wind swept out to sea, freezing even the salt spray that leaped into the air from crests of falling waves." BBC correspondent René Cutforth talked of the flats along the Han River at Seoul, exposed to "the sweep and triumph of the wind". And later, "It was so cold that it made you afraid." But it was W. L. White who described the cold as it affected the practice of medicine at the front. According to White, at least one MASH borrowed space heaters from the U.S. Air Force and used these to heat the operating tents. Unfortunately, these heaters were not designed for long-term use, and they often seized up when least expected.

The Diesel generators used for operating-room lighting sometimes clogged in the intense cold — particularly at temperatures of less than seventeen below zero Fahrenheit. When that happened, the lights would fade to the point that operations were sometimes finished "using three flashlights, focused by nurses on the open incision. You could see warm, moist air rising from the patient's belly and then, condensed by the tent's chill into steam, curling up through the flashlight's yellow beam."

Dr. Earl Russell recalls what it was like to go for a shower during the Korean winter. "We had a shower every day, but I know there were times when going to the shower, getting into it, and coming back were not exactly pleasant. You had to hustle through the winter to the shower tent, but the tent itself was not heated. All around the showers were ridges of ice, sometimes a foot high. You climbed over the ice and had your shower. The area around the drain was free of ice because of the warm water, but the sides built up higher and higher. Then you had to scramble back to a warm room."

Often ROK soldiers, Chinese prisoners, and Korean civilians were given treatment at United Nations medical facilities. Sometimes these patients wanted help; at other times it was forced upon them (particularly if they were prisoners the intelligence people wanted alive);

and at other times, the "help" was more than they ever expected.

An Associated Press story originating in Korea on August 21, 1952, told of the plight of an unfortunate Korean farmer. "Somewhere in Korea there is a farmer who will never forget this day. He was plowing a field when his ox stepped on a mine. The ox was blown to bits, the farmer scratched on the chest. Allied troops took him to a nearby hospital. A little iodine and some bandage patched him up nicely, and he offered to help around the hospital tent. He got sleepy, lay down on a stretcher and soon was fast asleep. A helicopter landed to pick up a wounded marine and fly him to a hospital ship at Inchon. Medics picked up the first stretcher and lashed it to the outside of the helicopter. The farmer awakened high in the air. His beloved earth lay far below him. Only a thin piece of canvas held him aloft. On the ground at Inchon, the farmer finally made his plight known. The pilot flew him back, this time inside the helicopter. The farmer trudged slowly back to his field, shaking his head."

One operating-room complication that at first startled U.N. doctors was accepted as commonplace as time went on. Because of the human manure used to fertilize Korean and Chinese fields, people of these countries pick up round-worm parasites which live in the intestines. For this reason, North Americans and other visitors from abroad are still warned about what they should or should not eat in the Far East. (During the Korean War, Canadian soldiers received similar warnings.) From time to time during the war, doctors doing stomach or other operations on Orientals often encountered these worms. When the intestines of the patient had been punctured, the worms were almost always present. They were anywhere from a few inches to a foot in length, and "would move slowly, rather like angle-worms in sidewalk puddles after a heavy rain." According to surgical nurse Captain Genevieve Connors of 8055 MASH, "within the first ten minutes of an operation, you would find seven or eight. . . . As they crawl out, all you do is pick them up, drop them in a pail, and go on."

Dr. John Beswick recalls going to a MASH for clinical meetings. "That was where I picked up most of my first knowledge of the worms," he says. "We were told that ninety to one hundred per cent of the population had worm infestation. Almost everybody. Yet they were good-looking people, strong, sturdy — but they had worms. I heard one case presented at the MASH where they operated on a chap for a bowel obstruction, a Korean civilian, and he was going to die. They opened him up to clear the obstruction and found a whole mess of worms. He could have lived with all of them but they had all moved to the one place. Then the poor chap was out of luck."

Conducting operations during the intense heat of the Korean

summer was also difficult at times. Operating facilities in the field were not air-conditioned. Some were lucky to have even a fan. Doctors worked for hours in sweltering heat, with few breaks, and often at the end of these ordeals lost the young men they tried so desperately to save. The strain, the tension, and the ever-pressing need for more time, much more time, was only aggravated by the stifling heat and oppressive humidity.

During the months of July and August, in particular, the heat was often so blistering that a surgeon's "sweat-soaked white gown might have to be changed three times during one operation. Sweat filled rubber gloves so quickly that . . . surgeons had to discipline themselves to keep their fingers, during an operation, always lower than the glove's mouth; otherwise half an ounce of sweat might pour into the patient's belly."

Because the reality was so stark, it is perhaps not at all surprising that the medical people I talked with who worked in Korea have had little affinity with either the movie or the long-running television series *M*A*S*H*. The television program ran a total of 251 episodes and along the way picked up fourteen Emmy Awards. It also played almost eleven years, but in all that time, and with all the adulation the program received, it failed to win wholehearted applause from those same men and women it attempted to depict.

John Beswick watched it occasionally. "I didn't mind it really — and some of it was clever. There was a lot of wisecracking, and I have seen some things that were quite comparable: relations with civilians, relations with other ranks, with fellow officers, and so on. Parts were too far-fetched, though.

"One day I had a call from a writer for the series in California. He wanted a few story ideas relative to what happened to Canadians who were in Korea. I took the time to write out a number of things and I sent them on to him. As far as I know, they never used them. However, I'm told that a year or so ago they ran a story about the quality of food. Apparently somebody stole a side of beef that had been reserved for a general. I'm also told that this general was a rotten guy. His name was Beswick. They didn't use my stuff, but as a booby prize or something they used my name. I guess that's what they thought of my ideas."

Dr. Earl Russell was even less enthusiastic about *M*A*S*H*. "I was never a fan of the series, and I have really seen very little of it. It is okay as entertainment, I suppose, but it certainly does not reflect the actual situation. They have eliminated the pain. There were also a lot of pretty tense times and on those days it was no fun being in a MASH. They have filtered out all the stress and strain and agony. If the series was accurate, or true to life, nobody would watch it. Years ago, the author of the book *M*A*S*H* told me that the end product on television was so far removed from what he had actually intended that he could hardly recognize it. There were jokes and wisecracking, of course, but I recall one officer who worked in a MASH who committed suicide because the strain was so great."

The First Secretary and Consul at the Embassy of Canada in Seoul is Eber Rice. I asked Dr. Rice if *M*A*S*H* was popular in Korea, where it is shown on the U.S. Armed Forces Korean Network. "It probably has its share of viewers among the English-speaking community here," he answered, "but I doubt if many Koreans watch it."

There were hundreds of Canadians who received medical attention in one form or another while they were in Korea. In many instances the visit to the doctor was not the result of shelling by the enemy. Colonel Peter Bingham, who quite deservedly has been called one of Canada's most respected soldiers, was injured shortly after he and his troops arrived in the war theatre.

"Peter Bingham was an impressive man," says Tom McKay. "He made you proud to be an RCR. He was the sort of guy who, on parade, or just before a patrol or something, would say, 'You're my tigers. This will be a piece of cake.' But in Korea he was one of our first casualties. He had just given us a big lecture and ended by saying: 'Now go up to the hills and dig in for the night, and watch for booby traps.' The next thing we knew, there was an explosion. Colonel Bingham himself had walked into a booby trap and he had to be away for some time. I imagine he was quite embarrassed about the whole thing."

"The Colonel was laid up for around ten days, I believe," recalls Bud Taylor. "It is probably fair to say that his injury caused him a good deal more anger and frustration than it did pain. It has been said that evacuating him to the hospital was probably the toughest problem that medics ever had."

The medics faced other difficult problems.

"There were so goddamned many rats everywhere that I used to think that all the rats in Asia came down to Korea because there was a war on," says one Canadian. "They were in our supplies, in our bunkers, in our beds, and in our dreams. But then you'd waken and the dream would be real. A half-dozen beady eyes would be staring at you."

"Sometimes we would waken and the whole place would be full of rats," recalls Frank Cassidy. "They were so big, it would make you think they were wearing combat boots. It was as if somebody was marching a platoon by your bed. I know some guys who were bitten by them. That was no joke."

"While I was in Korea I picked up a disease called Manchurian

Rat Fever," says Jim Brown. "A rat bit me on the arm and it became infected. I had had lots of other bites but this one was the bad one. I was in a field dressing station for a while, then a MASH, and finally a hospital down at Taegu. The doctors had quite a bit of trouble curing me. They shoved a lot of liquids in front of me and pumped me full of antibiotics, but time seemed to be the only cure. A lot of guys died from that fever, though. I know of half a dozen whom I saw in the hospital at Taegu. They all died. I was out of it for almost two months."

There were also medical advances made in Korea. This was particularly true for kidney-related diseases, battle fatigue, types of pneumonia, operative techniques, and diseases spread by lice, rodents, and insects. Battle fatigue was always hard to handle.

"It has been called shell-shock," says Dr. Beswick, "but that's a misnomer. I had a guy in Fort Lewis who went into acute battle fatigue on the rifle range. They brought him in to where I was and he just crawled under the table and screamed. No one had ever fired at him.

"People get squirrelly in a war. There is nothing the matter with a guy who draws ducks on the wall. However, when he starts to feed them, you have trouble."

As has been the case in all wars, venereal disease was always a problem. It was never eradicated, and presumably never will be, as long as there are wars and soldiers who go away to fight them. Nevertheless, the Canadian government of the day decided in its infinite wisdom to design a form which was supposed to be a small cog in the Canadian Army venereal-disease-eradication program. "They called the form National Health One," says John Beswick. "The form was a great long thing that had to be completed by the doctor following every case of venereal disease he treated. The form mentioned the type of disease, the contact person, the place of contact, date, follow-up information, and so on. Now, this might be okay with a stable population, but as far as being effective, or even applicable to an army on the move — that was another thing.

"A friend of mine, Dr. Andy Anderson, sent a bunch of these forms back to Ottawa and told them that under the circumstances it was impossible to fill them out in full. But some joker with nothing better to do was insistent and sent them all back to be properly completed.

"So Andy sat down and for a couple of hours one afternoon became quite creative. Under 'Contact Person' he wrote such names as 'Tokyo Rose', 'The Queen of England', 'Lady Godiva'. For 'Place of Contact', he scribbled 'In a ditch', 'On the other side of the ridge', 'Under a tank'. The dates ranged all the way from the year 1066 to 1492 to 1984. Under 'Hair Colour' he put things such as 'had none',

29

The Royal Canadian Navy sent 3,500 officers and men to Korea. The photo shows sailors preparing for minesweeping at Sonjin.

Ferdinand Demara, the Great Impostor, who posed as a doctor aboard the Canadian naval ship Cayuga.

30

One of the first flights of 426 Squadron, Royal
Canadian Air Force, on the Korean airlift,
July 1950.

Recipient of two Distinguished Flying Crosses,
Flight Lieutenant Ernie Glover shot down
three enemy fighter planes in Korea.

33

34

Propaganda signs mounted by the Chinese at night just in front of the U.N. lines.

Mr. Moneybags is in Florida this Christmas.

35

Chinese propaganda photo.

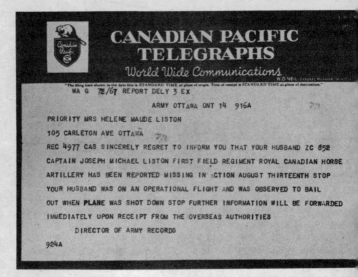

CANADIAN PACIFIC TELEGRAPHS
World Wide Communications

"The filing time shown in the date line is STANDARD TIME at place of origin. Time of receipt is STANDARD TIME at place of destination."
WA G 72/67 REPORT DELY 3 EX

ARMY OTTAWA ONT 14 916A

PRIORITY MRS HELENE MAUDE LISTON

105 CARLETON AVE OTTAWA

REC 4977 CAS SINCERELY REGRET TO INFORM YOU THAT YOUR HUSBAND ZC 852

CAPTAIN JOSEPH MICHAEL LISTON FIRST FIELD REGIMENT ROYAL CANADIAN HORSE

ARTILLERY HAS BEEN REPORTED MISSING IN ACTION AUGUST THIRTEENTH STOP

YOUR HUSBAND WAS ON AN OPERATIONAL FLIGHT AND WAS OBSERVED TO BAIL

OUT WHEN PLANE WAS SHOT DOWN STOP FURTHER INFORMATION WILL BE FORWARDED

IMMEDIATELY UPON RECEIPT FROM THE OVERSEAS AUTHORITIES

DIRECTOR OF ARMY RECORDS

924A

Telegram received by Joe Liston's wife Helene reporting her husband missing in action.

Private Pat O'Connor, whose poem (printed in Chapter 13), written the night before he died, is a moving testament to the men who sacrificed their lives in Korea.

38

...sed from a Chinese POW camp in April 1953, Lance-Corporal Paul Dugal brought happy news of ...Canadian captives, long believed dead.

Twenty-two-year-old George Griffiths was captured in October 1952 and spent several months in the primitive conditions of a Chinese POW camp.

Toronto Telegram *headline announcing end of Korean War, July 27, 1953.*

41

atriation of Canadian POWs, Panmunjom, August 1953.

Of the 25,000 Canadians who fought in Korea, 312 Canadians were killed in action. Many of these rest in the United Nations cemetery at Pusan.

'gun-metal grey' or 'sometimes'. Anyway, he sent all the forms back and he never heard another word about them. I don't know if anyone ever looked at them or not."

In general, the Canadians had a good record of looking after the medical needs of their soldiers. The record extended all the way from the preventive-medicine programs, to the efficiency of stretcher-bearers in the field, to the staffing of the treatment centres in Japan, to the veterans' hospitals in Canada. In many cases the doctors wanted to keep men who were injured for longer periods of time, but these soldiers insisted on returning to their units as soon as they could. In some instances, however, they returned too soon and have lived with the effects of battlefield injuries ever since.

"A good friend of mine was an orthopedic surgeon," explains Earl Russell. "One day the two of us were present when a chopper came in with a young fellow who had fractured his femur. By the time they got the soldier off the helicopter, he had died. As we looked at the soldier, the surgeon said to me, 'Well, he's not a Canadian. I haven't seen his tags, but if he was a Canadian, he would be alive. Canadians who come in here are properly splinted before they're sent.' I regarded this as a pleasant thing for an American doctor to say when I was at an American MASH."

While the wounds of war were being looked after in 8055 MASH and in the other medical facilities in Korea, in Japan, and in Canada, the war itself was still being fought along the Imjin River, up the Chorwon Valley, and on the tortured slopes of 355. The struggle seemed endless, at times needless, and yet went on from day to day, seemingly without respite. Then, one afternoon, men who thought they might live in a bunker forever were told they were moving out. No one told them where, or why — or even how. But they welcomed the change, so they gathered their gear, said hurried goodbyes, climbed on trucks, and left.

A few days later they found themselves in Pusan. Then they boarded ships and headed for a tiny speck of land off the Korean coast. There they saw another kind of war, a kind of war none of them knew. They saw a war behind barbed wire.

14

INSURRECTION AT KOJE

Thirty miles off the south coast of Korea lies an island called Koje. Though largely unknown today, this jumble of mountains and brush was once mentioned on the front pages of the world. In the spring of 1952, a series of unfortunate events here gave the 150-square-mile island as much fame and notoriety as it had ever known. The fame was fleeting, but the circumstances that spawned it were not taken lightly at the time. But with the 20–20 hindsight of history, we might say that the events were exaggerated out of all proportion when they happened.

In the first frantic weeks of war, North Korean prisoners were housed in compounds and jails in and around Pusan. As the front came inexorably closer to that city, both prisoners and civilian refugees were moved even farther south, to Koje, and, in the case of hundreds of fleeing civilians, to several of the other islands in the Korea Strait. Later on, following Inchon and the breakout from the Pusan Perimeter, more and more North Koreans fell into U.N. hands. Still later, with the Chinese entry in the war, prisoners from that nation were also taken. Finally, by March of 1952 there were over 150,000 Communist POWs on Koje alone.

On the island were seventeen prisoner enclosures, each designed to hold about one thousand men. Because these were soon terribly overcrowded, discontent and trouble became inevitable. On February 18, 1952, a battalion of U.S. troops entered Compound 62, where an insurrection had occurred. The trouble came about because the prisoners were being screened for possible patriation back to North Korea or China. Some POWs refused to return, and those who did want to return made life as difficult as possible for the first group. They also made the screening a nightmare for the guards.

Knife-wielding fanatics ran screaming at the U.S. troops; others threw rocks, hunks of wood, bottles, rock-filled tin cans, and spears. As the wild melee involving almost fifteen hundred prisoners threatened to spread to the other enclosures near by, the troops opened fire and seventy-seven POWs died, either right away or later from their wounds. One American was killed and thirty-eight were wounded. Instead of ending the POW protests, the fight simply riled the inmates in most of the compounds and caused the explosive potential to spread.

As might have been expected, the killing of the POWs was exploited for propaganda purposes by the Communists, both in Korea and around the world. Peace talks were in progress at Panmunjom and U.N. negotiators there found that the Koje situation made a difficult job even more onerous.

But while the extreme overcrowding on the prison island would likely have led to problems in any event, a far more sinister state of affairs existed. A hard-core group of Communist agitators was locked up on Koje. No matter what measures were taken to ameliorate matters, these men were determined to be trouble-makers. They were also there as intelligence operatives, supplying information to their Communist superiors in the north. Often these men, who had been trained in guerrilla and intelligence tactics, had allowed themselves to be taken prisoner, to become planted operatives within the POW compound. By extension, the compounds, and the men in them, were regarded as a new battlefield where the troops who fought happened to be incarcerated.

The protracted wrangle over what prisoners should be repatriated continued to cause headaches at Panmunjom. At the same time, because of the Koje riot in mid-February, the situation there remained explosive. Towards the end of April, U.N. intelligence reported a Communist plot to kidnap Brigadier General F. T. Dodd, the newly appointed Commandant at Koje. The rumour was that Dodd would be held hostage, and would only be released if the prisoners were granted a long list of concessions concerning food, living conditions, and so on. As well, the Red negotiators at the peace talks knew that if they could take a prisoner, and a senior officer in particular, the chances of exploiting the matter as propaganda would be almost limitless. The fact that in spite of these warnings Dodd actually allowed himself to be captured stands out as one of the more incredible incidents of the entire war.

Early in May, prisoner agitation increased. In Compound 76 the situation became particularly acute, with Communist flags, propaganda scrolls, and weapons reported and seen in the camp. Prisoners who had somehow managed to escape to seek asylum outside told of beatings, kangaroo courts, mutilation, intimidation, and murder of persons who did not wholeheartedly support the Communist line. There were reports that men who were killed either were buried in shallow graves, or were cut up into small pieces and removed from the compound inside the latrine buckets which certain prisoners carried out of the camp each day for disposal elsewhere. The latrine removal system was never proven completely, but later on, several half-buried cadavers were unearthed within the camp confines.

As the problems grew steadily worse, General Dodd took it upon himself to solve them. On May 7 he went to Compound 76, ordered the front gate opened, and stood in front of it, discussing prisoner complaints with the camp spokesmen. As this was going on, eighteen POWs who had been out dumping latrine buckets returned, moved up silently behind him, and rushed him inside the camp. The gates swung shut.

Almost immediately the propaganda machine lurched into life. Dodd was presented with a series of demands, among them a request by the prisoners for their own telephone. He and his successor outside the wire, Brigadier General Charles F. Colson, agreed to many of the demands, and Dodd was freed four days after he had been captured. The concessions made by Dodd and Colson soon reached the world press and their "admission" of brutal tactics by Americans at Koje was exploited to the fullest by the Reds.

While all of this was going on, General Mark Clark took over from Matt Ridgway as head of the United Nations Forces in the Far East.

One of Clark's first moves after assuming command involved cleaning up the mess on Koje. His first reaction was to "let them [the Communists] keep that dumb son of a bitch Dodd, and then go in and level the place." This outburst was understandable, but Dodd was freed before any such action came about. Later on, however, Clark's anger was no doubt ameliorated when the Department of the Army approved the demotion of Generals Dodd and Colson to the rank of colonel.

Clark then sent a man by the name of Boatner to Koje. Brigadier General Haydon L. Boatner was, in the opinion of many, the right man for the job. "Boatner wanted order at any cost," says Bill Boss, who was there with Canadian Press. "He was thorough — and he was a good soldier. His attitude towards the prisoners was, in effect, 'I don't care what you guys are about, but there's going to be order on this island. If obtaining order involves bashing, then we'll do some bashing; then we will talk.'

"While I was there," continues Boss, "I saw prisoners who were crazed, insane, beside themselves in fits of shouting, shrieking, shedding their blood, gouging their flesh, impaling themselves on obstructions in the wire, doing things that would boggle the mind. I never actually saw prisoners killing other prisoners, but I saw several after they had been killed by their comrades. It was obvious they weren't all of the same persuasion on the island."

At 10 a.m., Sunday, March 25, Baker Company, 1st RCR, arrived at Koje to help maintain order. "There were about a hundred of us," recalls Tom McKay, "and we were there for about seven weeks. I really enjoyed it, particularly because I was glad to get out of the line for a while.

"Shortly after we got there, this guy Boatner addressed us. He was one tough sonofagun and I'll never forget him. He told us what he expected from us: 'If you see somebody escaping and you're going to shoot, then make goddamned sure you kill him because the hospital's full right now. You would also be wise not to shoot the guy who is almost over the fence. Shoot the one who's trying to stop him. The first one may want to come over to our side.'

"Major E. L. Cohen was our C.O. We went in and lived in tents and made our whole area spick and span. We had our own flag-pole, all the stones around the place whitewashed, parade square, gates, and so forth. The place looked great. The Americans gave us about one week of riot drill and then we took over the guarding of Compound 66. We shared the job with a British company — twenty-four hours on, twenty-four hours off. We had guys in guard towers and gun emplacements. There was an outer fence and an inner one, but we rarely went inside. On occasions when we did, we didn't stay long.

"The prisoners would sometimes run up a North Korean flag. Somebody would report it and we'd rouse a few of the guys who were off duty. They would fix bayonets; we'd lob a couple of tear-gas grenades over the fence, open the gate, rip down the flag, and get out. This happened several times. They would do it to taunt us. It became somewhat of a game."

Within days of their arrival at Koje, the Canadians were involved in helping to clear out the large compounds and move prisoners to newer, smaller ones. But shortly before they began the operation, Ottawa learned for the first time that there were Canadians on Koje.

The politicians were not pleased.

Brigadier M. P. Bogert had given the order for the company of RCRS to go to Koje, but only after he had been instructed to do so by his senior officers in the U.N. Command. General Mark Clark had given the order, and he seemed to be puzzled over the Canadian reaction. "I was surprised at the cricitism from Canada," he has written. "After all, it was a United Nations command and one of its important responsibilities was to control and guard the recalcitrant POWs, all of whom were U.N. POWs, and many of whom had been captured by the Canadians themselves."

What Clark did not say was that many Canadians were of the

opinion that the U.S. guards, and in particular their leader, General Dodd, had botched the job on Koje and now wanted to spread the blame. By getting Canadian and British troops to the island, the Americans hoped they could polish their tarnished image. "The disturbances on Koje . . . had received a mixed reception in the Canadian press, [and] Mr. St. Laurent felt that the use of Canadians in guarding prisoners would have an unfortunate effect on public opinion," wrote Lieutenant-Colonel Herb Wood in *Strange Battleground*, the official history of the Canadian Army in Korea. Colonel Wood continues: "The Canadian determination . . . did not extend to the assumption of a portion of the blame for what appeared to be a very lax and inefficient prisoner of war operation." This view was shared by the British, and Clement Attlee no doubt rubbed salt in raw American wounds when he told the House of Commons in London that the problems in the camps at Koje "would not have happened if they had been under British control." Politicians in Canada might not have been as blunt in public, but Lester Pearson was probably reflecting the view of many when he wrote: "We did not want to be . . . associated with the . . . events on Koje." On May 26, Pearson told the House of Commons that the government was concerned because Canadian troops had been sent to Koje without prior authorization by Ottawa. He went on to say that it was the wish of the Government of Canada "that it may be possible to re-unite this Company with the rest of the Canadian brigade as soon as possible." For Tom McKay and the other RCRs on Koje, these words from Pearson would soon end their time in the south.

At 6:15 a.m. on June 10, General Boatner gave the order to clear the first compound. The Communists protested, and informed the American officer that they would not move voluntarily. He ignored their protests and sent tanks and troops to do the job. The *Globe and Mail* told the story on its front page: "The toughest Communist compound on this prison island fell today after a fanatic last-ditch stand against U.S. paratroopers who smashed their way with tanks and flamethrowers into Compound 76. Many of the Red captives clung to their trenches to the last, fighting with metal-tipped spears, some of them finally plunging their weapons into one another to keep from falling into Allied hands. After a 45 minute battle, casualties were 32 Communists killed and 136 wounded. Two U.S. soldiers were killed and 13 wounded. Within three hours the troops had emptied the enclosure and the 6,000 Communists in the compound were on their way to other camps."

The operation proved to the prisoners that the new C.O. was a far tougher man, and a more formidable foe, than General Dodd had been. A few days later, a prisoner spokesman who started screaming at the General for something or other soon found that he was getting nowhere. Boatner, who spoke fluent Chinese, calmly turned to the prisoner, and told him to "shut up". "He did not [said Boatner], so I ordered guards to take him to solitary confinement where he stayed for the remainder of his captivity."

Three days after the wild evacuation of Compound 76, the Commonwealth troops moved the prisoners from Compound 66 without bloodshed and without protest. The entire operation was both peaceful and orderly.

"The prisoners liked us," says Tom McKay, "possibly because our approach was so different from the Americans'. We had our red berets with our RCR badge which looks a bit like a star. We picked up one of the Communist songs and when we were being trucked down to the beach or somewhere, we'd bellow out this song at the top of our voices. The prisoners would look at us and cheer. Perhaps they thought we were Russians." (Years later, when I talked to Stu Meeks about his time on Koje, he not only recalled all the words of the song but gave me a hearty rendition of it.)

Tom McKay is still of the opinion that the prisoners enjoyed going to whatever lengths they could to taunt the Americans: "We were told by the U.S. intelligence people that if we picked up any notes or suspicious materials, these should be turned in for examination. So this day one of our guys found a roll of toilet paper with some Korean writing on it. He dropped it off at the intelligence tent. Well, the next thing we knew, the Americans moved in with this massive ditch-digger, because the notes on the toilet paper said a tunnel was being dug. They dug up around the whole damned camp; there wasn't any tunnel at all. But you know the Americans. The prisoners thought it was great."

The Canadians left Koje on July 10, but not before they had established a peaceful rapport with the prisoners and an excellent reputation with their American colleagues. In the meantime, the peace talks proceeded at Panmunjom.

The Korean peace talks had actually commenced at a place called Kaesong exactly one year to the day earlier. The U.N. delegation was headed by Vice Admiral C. Turner Joy of the United States Navy, along with one South Korean and four other U.S. officers. The Communist delegation was composed of two Chinese and two North Koreans. Canada did not participate at any time.

From the day the talks opened, until they finally ended some two years and two weeks later, they were never amicable, often bitter, and almost always interminably dull. For days — and occasionally weeks — at a time, the same arguments were tossed back and forth, neither side wanting to concede, particularly when concession was often viewed as weakness. And at a time when there were hundreds of matters that had to be agreed upon, the first concern centred on the location of the talks themselves.

In July 1951, as now, Kaesong was under Communist control. When a U.N. liaison party arrived there on July 8 to make preparations for the commencement of negotiations two days later, they were met by enemy soldiers brandishing guns and parading before cameramen who recorded the event for propaganda purposes. To the Communists, these U.N. representatives were depicted as coming to Kaesong to sue for peace.

The Communist strategy was given a temporary setback that day, however, when the U.N. party entered the negotiation room and by chance took seats along the north side of the conference table. As soon as they saw what had happened, the Red negotiators asked the U.N. people to move. They refused to do so, and learned later that according to Oriental custom in peace negotiations, the victor faces south while the defeated party looks north.

Two days later, when the formal peace talks began, the Communist representatives made sure they got into the conference room first and sat in the chairs on the north side of the table. Apparently this ploy was not enough to satisfy them, though. When Admiral Joy took his seat, he sank so low his head barely cleared the table. The chair he had been directed to use was a tiny one, with legs only a few inches high. When he sat in it, he found himself almost two feet lower than his counterpart across the table. The entry of the negotiators to the room had been filmed by Communist cameramen.

Negotiations droned on during the summer, only enlivened at times by some of the more ridiculous stratagems the Reds used for their own purposes. One day, for instance, Joy and his team spent considerable time listening to a fellow named Lee Sang Jo deliver a long, rambling, irrelevant dissertation on Communist dogma. As he did so, flies crawled across his face, and never once did he attempt to brush them off. In Admiral Joy's opinion, "apparently he thought this showed iron self-control. For my part, I concluded he was simply accustomed to having flies on his person."

In early October, the site for the talks was shifted to Panmunjom, midway between the front lines of the opposing armies in Korea. Deliberations continued for months — and as Canadians were not involved directly in them, the various measures agreed to will not be discussed here. There are several accounts available elsewhere, in particular Admiral Joy's book, *How Communists Negotiate*. Readers wishing to follow the step-by-step procedures at Panmunjom would be well advised to read what the American admiral has written.

In Canada as well the dragged-out negotiations were looked

upon as somewhat less than newsworthy. During the latter part of the Korean War, CBC television personality Roy Bonisteel was an announcer at radio station CJBQ in Belleville, Ontario. "I still remember reading the news and saying that there were no recent developments in the peace talks at Panmunjom," he told me recently. "The talks dragged on so long, it got to the point that our listeners didn't seem to care any more. But I know I hated repeating the same thing over and over again."

Stuart Keate, the former publisher of the *Vancouver Sun*, recalls an experiment carried out by the *Sun* during the peace negotiations: "Managing editor Hal Straight decided to test interest in the Korean story by running the same piece on page 1 for three days in succession. They had exactly three protests (or inquiries). Since the circulation of *The Sun* was then 250,000 daily, it means that 3 out of 750,000 noticed the reprint, or felt obliged to comment on it."

While the peace talks continued, there were periods of relative quiet in the line. However, some of the incidents that took place during these months would seem to indicate that just as many crazy things happened in Korea as had occurred in any war before or since. One night, for example, the Americans decided to try some rather unusual bombing techniques. They loaded one of the big transport planes with several thousand empty beer cans and dropped the entire load on sleeping Communist troops. Somewhat earlier, when the Canadians were just north of Uijongbu, a Korean truck pulled up loaded with bottles of what was known as "tiger whiskey". Brigadier John Rockingham saw them coming. "I had one of my medical officers with me at the time," he says, "and he did a quick analysis of the stuff. It turned out to be mainly urine and formaldehyde. We took the truck and dumped the whole thing off in a ditch and put a match to it and burned it. The Koreans started to raise hell but I told them if they brought any more loads like that near my soldiers I'd do the same thing."

Early one evening Stu Meeks and a buddy drove several Canadians to the Imjin River for a swim. "When we pulled up in our truck, there was a British truck already there, and a couple of Brits were swimming," says Meeks. "Then we noticed that the tires on their truck were flattened and so we knew it was loaded. For some reason or other, we thought it might be a load of food, so we stole it — and the guys' clothes.

"I can still see the two English chaps trying to run to shore, shouting at us to stop. I imagine they had some explaining to do. Then we forgot about our swim because by now we wanted to see what we had on the stolen truck. We found a fairly secluded place and off-loaded the cargo. It turned out to be batteries for radios and telephones. A few days later we had our bunkers electrified. There was a light beside each bed and all the guys were shaving with electric razors. One or two people even had electric fans.

"The night we took the truck, we started it up and drove with the lights off up onto a ridge called the saddle. Then we turned on the lights and ran like hell. The Chinese saw the lights, of course, and turned their guns on the truck. In about five minutes the truck was long gone. It was blasted all over the place."

Another Canadian who drove a truck in Korea recalls an incident that he set in motion. "I was a Service Corps driver with Number 56 Transport Company," says Frank Cassidy. "One night we were supposed to take four truckloads of ammunition up to the front. The only problem was that we got into some beer that day, so I guess we had a bit of liquid nerve. That was at a time when it was three beer per man, per day, perhaps. But we had a lot more than that.

"Around midnight, after we loaded the trucks, we started out. Now there were two bridges across the Imjin, and needless to say, we took the wrong one. I'm leading the parade, but we're not going to the Commonwealth front. As a matter of fact, we didn't know where the hell we were going. We had no maps. But we did know we were getting pretty close to something because there were a lot of fireworks just ahead of us — and it wasn't the first of July. But finally we came to the end of the road. There was just no place else to go. We're lost. So we turned the trucks around and everybody climbed out to relieve himself and have a smoke.

"Right out of nowhere, this jeep arrived with a big American officer. He was not pleased. He asked us who the hell we were and where did we think we were going. Then he pulled out his trusty 45 and threatened to put us all under arrest. Finally he told us we were in the 7th Division Front and that they were under attack. He then proceeded to tell us to put out the cigarettes, turn off our dim lights, put on our helmets, and get the hell out of there.

"So we scooted. We finally found the right bridge but our own artillery guys were not pleased. We were over an hour late getting the ammunition up to them."

Much of the area near the front was cleared of Korean civilians. However, the clearing process was never complete. There were always spies, some farmers and a few prostitutes in the nearby hills. From time to time, soldiers visited the women, and in general these liaisons were of little consequence. Sometimes, however, they took on an unfortunate cast.

Bud Scriver was back of the lines at the 40th Infantry workshop. He remembers one such incident. "One morning about nine o'clock a little Korean boy came running into our compound shouting 'Canada shot. Come quick! Canada shot. Come quick!' Our Sergeant-

Major listened to him and said, 'I want four volunteers — you, you, you, and you. Let's go.'

"We grabbed a stretcher and started following the kid. About five miles up into the mountains we found a Canadian who apparently received a 'Dear John' letter. He had been drinking and had shot this Korean girl, and then tried to shoot himself. She was dead when we got there but the guy was still alive. We radioed for help and a chopper came in for him. I heard later that he lived and was sent back to Canada to face a court martial. We carried the body of the girl out of the hills."

Another tragic incident occurred on July 1, 1952. Troops of the 1st Battalion, Royal 22nd Regiment, were in reserve several miles from the front. Late in the afternoon, twenty-year-old Joseph Sanscartier returned to the compound after attending an NCO course elsewhere. On the way back, he apparently bought one or more bottles of "Lucky Seven", a cheap Korean whiskey distilled from questionable ingredients. By 7 p.m., Sanscartier was not only roaring drunk, he was also angry at the world.

"I was in my tent some distance away," recalls Major Guy D'Artois, "and even though I'd heard the shots, I thought nothing of them. But then somebody came running and told me I was needed right away. I got in my jeep and went down to see what was happening. I found Sanscartier standing on a small hill, holding a 303 rifle and taking shots at the young Canadian soldiers who were near by. He had fired several rounds, and one nicked a chap in the ear. I doubt if Sanscartier even knew what he was doing."

Capitaine J. P. Savary watched what happened next. "The Major started to talk to the guy with the rifle, but he wouldn't drop it. He told Major D'Artois that if he came any nearer, he'd get it."

"I told Capitaine Savary to get a rifle," says D'Artois, "to get under a jeep and to keep me covered. Then I started to move closer to the guy with the gun. As I did so, I talked to him, told him to put the rifle down and we would talk about whatever his problem was. As I talked, I was slowly moving up the hill.

"Then, over to my left, some guy who had apparently been out running blundered onto the scene. He didn't know what was going on but picked one hell of a time to arrive. As he came closer, I noticed Sanscartier turn to get the runner in his sights. I knew Sanscartier was about to pull the trigger, so I took my pistol and shot him."

"Major D'Artois did what he had to do," states Savary. "He spent several minutes trying to talk the guy into dropping the gun, but he refused. The last shot came very quickly. The Major grabbed his gun and that was it. He didn't even seem to aim. Then it was all over. Sanscartier was gone."

"I hated to kill him," Guy D'Artois told me when I interviewed him about the incident. "But I wasn't given much choice. I hit him on the left side and the bullet came out the right. I took him in my arms and my Sergeant-Major took the rifle away. There was one shell in it. We called an ambulance but it was too late. Then I gave the men hell and told them that they had just seen what happens when you drink too much."

At a subsequent board of inquiry, D'Artois, a man who by any standards could be called a true Canadian hero, was acquitted of all blame in the shooting. However, even though he had won the DSO for resistance work in occupied France during the Second World War, and the George Medal for a rescue operation in the Canadian north, he was never promoted beyond the rank of major.

But there were other stories that ended on a pleasant note because somebody had some booze. "When I arrived in Tokyo, on my way to Korea," recalls Pierre Berton, "I went up to the Canadian Embassy and got thirteen bottles of Canadian Club for thirteen dollars. Then I chucked most of my gear except socks and a shaving kit and went on my way. I knew the whiskey would come in handy in Korea. And it did — several times, but none more so than one night after I had flown in a noisy old crate from Seoul to Pusan. I had a priority on the plane, but as it turned out, that didn't help.

"We landed at Taegu and I was bumped by some senior officers. Here I am, in what seemed to be nowhere, all by myself beside a crappy, pockmarked runway in the middle of the goddamned night. The airstrip was absolutely empty and I had no idea where in hell to go. The place was really gloomy. Then I noticed a tiny light in the distance, so I started walking in that direction. I finally got to this little building, nothing more than a shack really, where I'd seen the light. I knocked on the door. No answer. I knocked louder. Still no answer. Then after I'd pounded on the damned thing the third time, the door opened a crack and I could see an American soldier staring out at me. He took a long look and said, 'You can't come in.' 'Why in hell can't I come in?' 'Because this place is secret.' So I said, 'I have some Canadian Club whiskey.' The guy swung the door open and said, 'Why didn't you say so? Come on in.'

"It turned out that they were from the Central Intelligence Agency. They kept telling me not to say anything, to keep quiet about whatever it was they were doing. At that stage, I didn't give a good goddam what they were doing. We played cards and they drank my whiskey. I left the next day."

No matter how effective American or U.N. intelligence might have been in Korea, the Chinese and North Korean methods of learning what the U.N. armies were going to do next impressed many of the Canadians who fought in Korea.

"I remember one time when Charlie Company of the RCR were deeply involved in planning a raid across the Imjin into North Korea," says Ken McOrmond. "The planning went on for several days, and had been supposedly worked out to the last detail. The whole thing was very hush-hush as well, and was to be a co-ordinated effort with the engineers, who would take us across the river. The weather reports were checked, fresh ammo was issued; the whole thing was rehearsed so that nothing would go wrong and we would have the advantage of complete surprise when we landed.

"After it was dark, we got into our boats and the engineers ferried us across as quickly as possible. Then, when we were twenty feet from the shore, in the exact spot where we were to land, we saw a big sign — black letters on a white background — letters a half-foot high reading 'WELCOME CHARLIE COMPANY RCR TO NORTH KOREA'. So much for all the secrecy."

Several Canadian soldiers remember other kinds of signs. These would often appear in the early morning, just in front of the U.N. lines — even though sentries had been on duty all night and in many cases patrols had been coming and going. "We would be in our bunkers, believing we were one or two miles from the nearest Chinese," one man says, "but when it was dawn, these big signs would appear, sometimes a few feet from our positions. The Chinese would sneak in, put up the sign, and leave so quietly we'd never hear them. Yet, first thing in the morning — there's the sign. It was eerie, and at times really scary. They could have slit our throats just as easily." The signs said such things as "COME BACK SOON, I NEED YOU BADLY", "WHY ARE YOU HERE?", "YOUR DEAR MOTHER MISSES YOU", or simply, "PLEASE COME HOME". There would often be smaller propaganda messages left with the signs. A favourite of many soldiers was a photo of U.N. troops on a daylight patrol during the Korean winter. Above and below the photo was the caption: "Mr. Moneybags is in Florida this Christmas. Where are you? In Korea! You risk your life, Big Business rakes in the dough."

But on at least one occasion, Communist delivery of the propaganda leaflets was far from quiet. "One day we found this pumpkin that must have weighed a hundred pounds," says Ed Haslip. "We cut the heart out of it, then we filled it with explosives and put in on a forward slope in front of our positions. Even our officers were afraid to go anywhere *near* it. We had trip-wires all the way from the pumpkin back to our bunkers.

"We went to all this trouble — but it was fun too — because the North Koreans and Chinese had been coming over and leaving all these propaganda leaflets around, and we'd got tired of reading the things. But one morning we saw three Koreans coming with three donkeys loaded down with this junk. When they spotted our pumpkin, they dropped the bags of propaganda leaflets and started looking at our pumpkin. There was one great blue flash and the mines and grenades we had hooked up all blew at once and killed the Koreans, the donkeys, and scattered the leaflets. We never found *any* of the pumpkin.''

On another occasion, just before Christmas 1951, there was a lull in the fighting along the front. Peace talks seemed to be going well at Panmunjom and army headquarters had placed a moratorium on aggressive action by U.N. troops.

''We resented this,'' recalls Stu Meeks. ''The Chinese were apparently able to shoot any time they wanted and we couldn't do a goddamned thing. But that Christmas Eve we had all our ration tins, our empty beer cans and bottles, all over the front slopes of the hill we were on. We had trip flares set up and anti-personnel mines all over the hill, as well as 45-gallon drums of gas wired with charges so that we could turn the time on, four seconds would elapse, and then there would be an explosion. The whole business would roll down on the Chinese. There was also barbed wire strung across the entire hill.

''Anyway, during the morning we heard this horrible goddamned noise down in the tin cans. We looked, and here's this little Chinaman crawling up. It sounded like a herd of elephants coming. He sure wasn't being subtle.

''We had our weapons trained on him but he just kept coming. He had wire-cutters and he cut a path through the wire as he climbed — right to the front of our trenches. We couldn't believe what we were seeing. He didn't seem to have a care in the world.

''When he got to where he saw us, he just kept walking and bowing, and bowing and walking closer. He was grinning from ear to ear and was carrying this flashlight with a little cloth sling on it. Finally, right in front of us, he bowed for about the hundredth time, took the flashlight, and hung it on the barbed wire. Then he grinned again and said, 'Presento, presento.' He left the flashlight there and began backing down the hill. He kept backing down, backing down slowly, watching us.

''We waited until he got some distance away and then we threw these phosphorus grenades at him. Every time I see one of those cartoons of the Road Runner disappearing over the hill I think of that little guy. That's what the guy looked like because the white phosphorus went all over him.

''I also remember that we thought the flashlight was booby-trapped. We got it and gingerly tied it to a stake. Then we took a machete tied to a long piece of wood and cut the sling off. We also used a long stick and eventually turned the light on. It worked! This was from behind sandbags. Finally one of the guys figured that when the light went off, perhaps the thing would blow up. We waited and waited and the light got dimmer and dimmer and finally went out. When there was still no explosion we took two boards and some wet cloth and managed to unscrew the bottom. It took hours to do this. Finally the batteries popped out and lay on the ground. They had Chinese markings. We then went forward and examined the thing. It was just a flashlight. The guy had given us a present and we had burned him to death."

Stu Meeks was also involved in another rather unorthodox endeavour during the war. He and a buddy named Karl Fowler came upon some dead Chinese near an outpost in front of the main trench lines. Meeks, whom Fowler promptly named "Mingo Meeks", brought some of the heads closer to the outpost and propped them up on stakes or on one of the larger leg or arm bones. Ken McOrmond and Tom McKay also recall the heads, and McKay remembers the decomposed skin, like leather, which covered the skulls.

"We only wanted the skulls," says Stu Meeks, "and once the head had deteriorated a lot, we would skin the hide off it. One day I was sitting in my bunker and the company commander looked in and asked me what I was doing. Just for laughs I said, 'Skinning heads, sir.' Well, all hell broke loose. We had to take all those heads and bury the goddamned things. It was strictly an innocent thing. We were putting the heads around our outpost on the assumption that the Chinese would stay the hell away from us. It didn't work."

From time to time, celebrities from Canada, the United States, Britain, and elsewhere arrived in Korea and spent anywhere from a day or so to a couple of weeks visiting the troops. Bob Hope was there; so were Johnny Wayne and Frank Shuster; so was Arthur Menzies, the then Canadian Ambassador in Japan; so were a team of Canadian newspaper sportswriters who told the soldiers what was happening in the world of sports in this country. But the visit by hockey star Red Kelly was a particular hit. Kelly was in the prime of his playing career, and he easily related to the young soldiers who asked for his autograph wherever he went. He was the same age as the men he saw, and he was a link with home — a home they missed with ever-increasing intensity.

Finally the day came when they would miss it no more. After all the patrols, the bloodshed, the fear, and the instant death, the fight finally came to an end. Now Kapyong, Chail-li, Hill 355, and all the rest would slip into history. The seemingly endless peace negotiations at Panmunjom concluded on July 27, 1953 — three years and one month after the war began. The war that began in the Sunday morning rain ended at 10 a.m. on a sunny Monday morning.

15

THE GUNS
FALL SILENT

As soon as the guns fell silent across the tortured hills of central
Korea, the job of building the peace began. Troops who faced
each other at the front pulled back, vacating a 4 km-wide strip of
land that stretched north and east from the Imjin estuary to the Sea
of Japan. This strip of land was called the Demilitarized Zone, and it
in turn was divided by the Military Demarcation Line. The same line
divides Korea today.

According to the terms of the armistice, opposing sides in the
conflict were given seventy-two hours to remove all their supplies,
ammunition, and equipment from the Demilitarized Zone. They were
also directed to dismantle the bunkers, communication facilities,
storage areas, and so on. As it turned out, the removal of bunkers
was a far greater job than the truce negotiators apparently realized.
Both sides had to be given extra time to complete the task. But as they
set about the job on the day after the hostilities ended, the Canadians
along the front noticed a phenomenon that to them was as chilling
as it was unexpected.

Out of the bunkers immediately opposite them there appeared
not just a few score, or even a few hundred, Chinese troops, but
thousands and thousands of them, swarming through no-man's-land,
across the trenches on the Chinese side, and up and over the scrub
hills leading back from the front. These thousands of men moved,
shifted, spread in waves across the terrain, like wind-blown wheat
on the Saskatchewan prairie. To the astonished young men from
Canso, Chicoutimi, and Brandon, there were "what looked like
millions of Chinese opposing them." Captain C. A. Kemsley, who
was there that morning with 3rd PPCLI, adds: "No one will ever forget the psychological impact of seeing for the first time the 'human
sea'." And no one who saw the legions of Chinese carpeting the
land was inclined to believe that the West could ever win a land war
in Asia.

But the war that Brigadier and later General J. V. Allard would describe to me as "not resembling the First World War or the Second World War, but resembling only the Korean War — in that we couldn't fight the thing without asking permission of almost God," had faded into history. The armistice worked out across the green baize table at Panmunjom would herald the end of the destruction, maiming, and death that the North Koreans had brought upon so many thousands of men, women, and children because of their decision to attack the south thirty-seven months before. Now the ordinary people of Korea, the innocent victims of war — at least those that survived — would begin to put their lives back together, while the armies that fought on their land would begin to go home at last.

Many of the sick and wounded had already gone, among them prisoners taken earlier by the Communists. The first Canadian who was released from a POW camp was twenty-year-old Paul Dugal, whose paralysing wounds affected neither his powers of observation nor his fantastic memory. Lance-Corporal Dugal, of the 1st Royal 22nd Regiment, had been captured in June of 1952, and during his time as a prisoner of war had met or seen several other Canadian POWs. Many of these contacts had been fleeting, and in some instances very little, if any, conversation had taken place. For example, his association with Joe Liston, in the back of an army truck, had been brief. Not only that, but Dugal had been so unwell at the time that they had barely spoken. Yet, as Liston told me years later, he noticed Dugal "staring at my cowboy boots".

After his release in Operation "Little Switch", Dugal was able to identify fifteen Canadians held by the Chinese. He didn't know Liston's name, but "he said he had studied pictures of my husband and recognized him as a fellow prisoner," Mrs. Liston told the *Ottawa Journal* on September 3, 1953. "He mentioned . . . a pair of cowboy boots [and] I knew it was Joe. He had bought the boots at a Kenora shoe store."

Dugal's widowed mother, Yvonne, had actually planned a funeral for her son but could not go through with the service because she refused to believe he was dead. "I never despaired of seeing him again," said Mrs. Dugal in a Toronto *Telegram* story on April 20, 1953. "I took steps to have a funeral service for him. At the last minute I decided to wait, convinced that he was still alive. . . . Many people told me not to think of him any more and to pray for the repose of his soul. I knew inside me that my Paulo was still alive." Later on, Paul Dugal was awarded the British Empire Medal for bringing back the names of those who were still in POW camps, and information about them.

Gradually the Canadians departed the front, Korea, and, finally, the Far East.

Most went by truck to the nearest rail head. From there they travelled in dusty, slow, terribly uncomfortable old rail cars with wooden seats to the port of embarkation. While each man's story may be unique in some ways, the return from the line rarely differed in its generalities. Whether he was an officer or a private, whether he left during the war, immediately after it, or not for several weeks or months, the soldier welcomed his departure from Korea with relief. One man celebrated before he even left.

"Long before I was to leave, my boss promised me a bottle of liquor for my last night there," recalls Don Randall. "So when I was told I was going home, I told him to pay up. 'Well, you caught me at a very bad time,' he said. 'All I have is a bottle of Benedictine liqueur. That's all I've got but you're welcome to it.' I took it and I must have drank almost all of it. It was sweet. Sickeningly sweet. For about five years afterwards I couldn't touch *any* liqueur. I was never so sick in my life. It almost killed me. But it was relief that made me drink it. I just wanted to get out of there so badly.

"I then went by truck to Seoul. By train to Pusan and by ship, the *Joe P. Martinez*, to Sasebo, Japan. At Sasebo they gave us medical checks, blood tests, and so on, then put us on a train for Yokohama where we boarded a ship for home."

It was the start of John McIntyre's journey home that he remembers most. "The Queen's Own Rifles came in to replace us," he recalls. "So we had to double-bunk on our last night there. We slept on the floor because the new guys had our bunks. Anyway, at half past *two* they got us up, sent us over to the mess tent for some breakfast. Then, after breakfast, still in the dead of night, they lined us up and called the roll. Then they came along and gave everybody a sandwich — two little slices of bread with jam in between, wrapped in waxed paper. As soon as we had our sandwich, they told us to sit on the ground and wait. So we did. We waited until *four* o'clock when some trucks came in. We climbed on the trucks and they took us no more than two and a half miles to a parade square that we had built earlier.

"And there we sat, and sat, and sat — until *one* o'clock that afternoon. While we were there, I bet you, without a word of a lie, they called the roll at least seven times. Now, I ask you: Who's going to go away? We wanted to leave all right, but not on our own. Finally, in came some more trucks and this time they took us to the railroad, put us on old coaches that looked like cattle cars, and that was the way we went to Inchon.

"Waiting for us at the rail terminus there were five tractor trailers with racks on the back. They packed us into these. As we were getting on I remember one officer asking where the jeeps were for the officers. A big American sergeant looked at him and said: 'If you want to ride, fine. If you don't, then walk!' The officer got onto the truck with the rest of us.

"Near the docks they herded us into these barracks and told us to shower, eat, and go to sleep. No one could leave the building for any reason. Guards were posted. Then the next morning they got us up at six, fed us, put us back on the same trucks, and drove down the pier to where there were several barges. Then they towed the barges out to a ship called the *Marine Lynx*. There were rope ladders over the side of her, and we had to climb the rope to get on board. This was with all our gear. If you couldn't get up that way, too bad — you fell in the drink. Finally, we're all aboard and we leave."

After their departure from Korea, many Canadians spent time in Japan, receiving medicals, sightseeing, and souvenir-shopping prior to leaving for home. After the turmoil and deprivations they had experienced in Korea, Japan was a welcome change. When asked today about their memories of the Korean War, they cite, along with the jumble of bittersweet recollections of battles, sights, smells, and fears, the time in Japan as a pleasant experience. That nation was not at war, and the goods or amenities that were scarce or non-existent in Korea could be found in abundance in Tokyo, Kure, Sasebo, and elsewhere.

"The big problem was trying to carry enough money to buy the stuff," recalls Lorne Barton. "When I was there first we were getting about 360 yen [Japanese currency] to the dollar and the biggest bill they had was only 100 yen or something. I know that one time I went to buy a camera and I had to take a tote bag crammed full of money. But I only had $150–$175 or so; 360 yen to the dollar was quite bulky when you were wearing a navy uniform. You only have two pockets, and if you smoked, your cigarettes were in one pocket, your wallet in the other. That was why you had to take the suitcase for the money. Half the time you looked like Rockefeller on the way to the bank."

Clarence Fisher of London, Ontario, was a sergeant at the Canadian Quartermaster stores in Tokyo. "We looked after our troops who were coming through on R and R," he says today. "And because I was there for several months, I met a lot of our men and I also saw a lot of Japan. And I loved it. Getting the posting there was one of the best things that ever happened to me. Because I was working in Japan, as opposed to just passing through, I was able to meet more of the Japanese and see more of their country than the fellows who were there for only a few days.

"I love the Japanese and I grew to love their country. I wandered the streets, down to the old Imperial Palace, to the Ginza, everywhere.

I climbed Mount Fuji and travelled around the country. I smelled the beautiful odour of Tokyo in the spring when the blossoms came out, and I was invited to Japanese homes once or twice a month. As far as our soldiers who passed through Japan were concerned, I don't care if they live to be a hundred, when they speak of Japan their eyes light up. They will always remember Japan as a different happening.

"Japanese food was strange at first, but I tried it all — raw fish, octopus, the biggest prawns I ever saw, soups, rice dishes, even fish eyes. But fortunately no one told me what they were until I got them down. No, I'll never forget Japan."

But whether they were in Seoul, Pusan, Tokyo, or Kure, to the young military people from Canada, only one country was home. And whether he or she was in the Far East for two months or two years, there came a time when the adventure was over, when it was time to go home. When the ships for Canada were ready to leave port, their young passengers, who had often been on board for some time, lined the rail chanting "Let's go! Let's go! Let's go!"

"The ship I was on, the *General Funston*, burned out a bearing after we were some distance out," says Don Randall. "We were told afterward that if we had been the only ones on board, they might have kept going and repaired or packed it at sea. However, because the passenger list was mixed: two hundred Canadian soldiers, about four hundred American sailors, and a couple of hundred other Americans with their wives and children, we came back for repairs, but they wouldn't let us off the ship.

"I recall that one of our fellows had venereal disease, but he had concealed it when he went through the FFI, or Free from Infection, check. Then when he was on board and the ship was under way, he thought he was home free, so he turned himself in for treatment. However, when we turned back, they took him off and we didn't see him again. In general, when you were picked up at a time like that with the disease, you got yourself in a lot of trouble. At one point they were sending fellows like that back to Korea to serve thirty more days. I don't know what happened to this guy. He should have kept quiet about his problem for a bit longer."

As the Canadians continued their voyage towards home, the country they were returning to had grown increasingly tired of the war on the other side of the world. While it was being fought, newspaper men and women from many of the nation's largest papers, wire services, and radio stations described the hostilities, the land known as Korea, the plight of the refugees, and, most often, the day-to-day routine of the ordinary soldier — generally naming his home town, his unit, his buddies, and his particular location when the item was filed.

Often the stories were stories of heroism — courage under fire, woundings, selfless risk-taking — but just as often they were stories of death. Instant, tragic, sometimes needless, but always terribly, terribly cruel. For example, when the *Toronto Star* ran a piece on Wednesday, October 29, 1952, mentioning the death of Robbie Arding, the story began: "Five days after Robert Francis Arding . . . celebrated his 18th birthday, he died on a Korean battlefield. He joined the army to send some money every month to his mother. . . . He wrote just one letter home. It came a few hours before the telegram announcing his death."

No wonder the people at home began to hate the war.

"The job of a reporter in Korea was recognizing that you were doing the job of the country weekly for the people back home," recalls Bill Boss, the Canadian Press correspondent who was in Korea longer than any other reporter from this country. "Everything was fair game, everything was part of the report. It had to be. It was the big picture and the small picture. The training picture from the point of view of the Colonel. The social picture from the point of view of the Corporal. I had to try to make that adjustment and provide coverage that was fair."

Pierre Berton wrote several stories about the war, but some of his fondest memories are of Japan. "It was a marvellous place for war correspondents," he says today. "First of all, it was cheap as dirt and it was very exciting. War correspondents could go off limits to places where the troops couldn't go — or at least couldn't go with the kind of freedom we had — to the Ginza, to night-clubs, places like that. It was marvellous."

Several of Canada's best-known reporters filed stories from Korea, and some, such as Ross Munro of Southam News Services, discussed the plight of the correspondent in the war zone. In a *Globe and Mail* article on August 11, 1950, Munro wrote: "This is a war in which correspondents have no standard uniform and everything from civilian clothes to bits and pieces of last war equipment are worn. Many do not even have tin hats. They wear no identification disks. Nobody knows their blood type if they are hit.

"This Korean affair will probably go down in newspaper history as one of the more costly in reporters. At time of writing, there are 10 killed or missing."

Blair Fraser mentioned the reporter's best friend in a story published in *Maclean's* on January 1, 1951: "At Kimpo, the airport for Seoul, I went over to the cargo tent to see about hitching a ride. . . . The major was unenthusiastic. 'We're not supposed to carry you fellows,' he said.

"Then after a short pause, he added, 'The trouble with you correspondents, you never bring over any whiskey.'

"'I've got some Canadian rye,' I said.

"The major beamed. 'Well now, that's different. I can send you out on the next plane — she'll be loaded in about ten minutes.'

"And he did. He didn't even bother weighing my kitbag, which was 26 ounces lighter."

Larry Henderson, the man who would go on to become the first CBC national television news announcer, covered the war for a group of twenty-two Canadian radio stations. "I was doing a daily local-colour newscast," he told me. "But it was really pioneering work in radio in those days. There were no international networks set up and I was unable to use satellite or anything like that. It didn't exist. So what I was sending back was simply tape, and in those days tape hadn't been reduced to the small recording machine. I had heavy equipment with me and I had to get it up to the front lines to inter-view men there. Every day or two I would take my tapes to the nearest American air base and get the pilot, in exchange for a bottle of hooch or something, to take the tape for me to the Pan Am office in Tokyo. Somebody there would put it on a plane to Vancouver.

"Of course, then I felt I needed to do the story with some local colour, and so, thirty years or so later, I'm ready to admit that I used to set the stage a bit. I would get my interviewees all lined up and we would wait until a barrage came in so there would be a back-ground of bombs exploding and so on, and I would conduct my interview against that background.

"I was young then and I guess I didn't stop to think that all my broadcasts were conducted against a barrage of incoming shells. Gordon Sinclair, who picked this up in Toronto, wrote in his column at the time that he thought that Larry Henderson was holed up in some geisha establishment in Tokyo and was adding the sound ef-fects in the background."

A number of other reporters were in Korea for varying lengths of time, and some simply passed through on the way to somewhere else. Some saw Korea and retreated to the relative safety of Tokyo to do their work from there. Evelyn Caldwell of the *Vancouver Sun* was one who did not. She was with the troops and her dispatches showed it. René Lévesque reported from the war theatre for CBC Radio. Another would-be politician was also in Korea, but as a soldier, not a writer. Tory hopeful Peter Worthington would later go on to a journalism career with the Toronto *Telegram* and later the *Toronto Sun*.

Jock Carroll reported on the war for the *Telegram* and for *Weekend Magazine*. He also wrote an excellent children's novel about what he saw in Korea. However, one of his best pieces was a front-page *Telegram* article published on August 2, 1951.

Carroll had just returned to Canada after four months in the Far

East when he was sent to cover a "Peace Rally" at Queen's Park in Toronto. One of the speakers at the rally was Nora Rodd, a Canadian Communist who reported on her trip to North Korea. In her speech she described atrocities in North Korea, and implied that U.N. soldiers were bayoneting Korean babies and committing other despicable crimes against humanity. Carroll quoted her as saying: "Pregnant women were cut open and hung from trees. Husbands and wives had their heads cut off in front of their children. Prisoners had cartridges exploded inside their mouths. We were told again and again who did these things because we asked again and again. We know who did it. There were British troops there, and Canadian troops, and Turkish troops but we know who most of the troops were." Jock Carroll responded: "Americans, Mrs. Rodd. Most of the United Nations soldiers were Americans. You implied that American soldiers were doing these things." But then Carroll added: *"Whoever told you that is a liar, Mrs. Rodd."*

The article continued in much the same vein, with each of Mrs. Rodd's charges refuted and contrary arguments presented by Carroll. When I was researching this book I interviewed Mrs. Rodd, and after all these years she has not deviated in her views. "I remember one time there were probably two hundred mothers gathered together in an area in an old building," says Mrs. Rodd. "Some of them had little babies on their laps and they said: 'What have we done to your country that it's helping the United States with this war?' We could only weep. We saw people crawling out of holes in the ground. We saw mothers who had lost their children. We saw many sad people."

Later, on her way back from North Korea, Mrs. Rodd did at least one broadcast on Moscow Radio. On the program she described what she had seen in Korea. When I asked her what she said, she told me: "I said what Kim Il Sung [the North Korean Communist leader] told me to say." When she returned home she mentioned that she spoke in several cities, but then added: "One of the places that I would have liked to have spoken was Ottawa, but they said no."

Several times during my interview with her, Mrs. Rodd referred to James Endicott, the United Church minister who, like her, was less than enthusiastic about Canada's involvement in the Korean War. Several newspapers, probably most members of Parliament, and certainly the RCMP were worried about what Endicott was saying in his criticism of the war effort and of the U.S. motives in it. For a more detailed account of Endicott's views, and reasons why they got him into difficulties with Ottawa, the reader is advised to see the biography written by his son Stephen, *James G. Endicott: Rebel Out of China*. Perhaps the fact that Endicott Senior was awarded the Stalin Peace Prize in 1952 should give the reader some indication of the man's political leanings. Much more recently, however, Val Sears reported in the *Toronto Star* on January 6, 1983, that "Prime Minister Louis St. Laurent and the federal cabinet of 1952 agonized over Canada's role in the Korean War that year and considered prosecuting a United Church missionary for treason, according to Cabinet minutes released after a 30-year secrecy period. . . . The Cabinet decided not to charge Rev. James Endicott, who had accused the United States of waging germ warfare in Korea, because if he had been convicted the punishment was death." Lester Pearson called the germ-warfare charge a "clumsy hoax" and "Soviet communist propaganda".

Finally the troops came home.

For the most part, they came quietly. The ships that carried them slid alongside quays in Seattle generally, and the Canadians on board went by train to Vancouver, for transfer across the country. Occasionally a band played or there were a few "welcome home" speeches, but just as often there was nothing. The happiness the soldiers felt on returning to Canada was tinged with sadness as they saw their buddies leave the train as it travelled eastward. Their exultation turned to disappointment as they saw how little their country seemed to care about where they had been or what they had done while they were away.

"There were no parades or big welcome parties for anyone," recalls one soldier. "It was sure different than it had been when the Second World War ended. Now, I am not saying we had to have big celebrations, but in my case at least, no one seemed to even *notice* that I was home."

"My wife met me at the station," says another man, "and before we were back to the house, she told me I'd have to fix the toilet. It didn't flush properly. Here I was, away for fifteen months and she's worried about a toilet."

"Dad and Mom drove all the way to Regina to meet the train," remembers a young soldier from Saskatchewan. "We had a meal together in the city, but I wanted to see the farm so badly we left for home as soon as we could. I think Mom wanted to go shopping and now I wish I'd been a bit more patient and let her."

"By the time we got to New Brunswick, all the fellows I was close to had dropped off along the way," says a former corporal. "By the time I got home I was lonely. Isn't that weird?"

"A week later they had a dinner for me," recalls an Ontario man. "Somebody gave a speech and then they asked me to tell them about the war. I tried, but I found it hard to know where to start. There were so many things I thought of saying after I sat down."

And so it went. Happiness, sadness, regret, relief. The troops were home and the weary war they went away to fight was over. As a war, it may not have been as long, or as terrible, as the First World War, the Second World War, or Viet Nam. But it happened, and it is part of our history. To the men who came of age in Korea, however, it is the war that was their war. If we respect them, if we respect what they did for us as a nation, we cannot continue to regard Korea as simply Canada's forgotten war. It is too important for that.

EPILOGUE

A total of 516 Canadians died for the cause of peace in Korea. Of these, 312 were killed in action during the war itself. The others died from various causes in training, in transit, or in the war theatre, between 1950 and 1956. Over 25,000 Canadians fought in Korea during the war, while more than 7,000 others remained in that country to help preserve the peace after the armistice was signed. By comparison, more than 325,000 Republic of Korea soldiers were killed, along with 33,629 Americans and 935 British troops. No one knows how many civilians lost their lives.

The armistice that was signed on July 27, 1953, has been an uneasy one at the best of times. It has been marred by hundreds of "incidents" or border clashes that erupted within hours of the armistice-signing and have continued to the present day. Perhaps the best known of these was a dispute over tree-trimming at Panmunjom on August 18, 1976, when two American army officers were killed. As well, the North Koreans have been caught digging tunnels under the Demarcation Line. These tunnels have varied in length, with the longest being 3.5 km. While researching this book I went down in what is known as the third such excavation, some 73 m underground and large enough for a jeep to pass through. ROK soldiers in the area believe the tunnel could be used by the North Koreans to launch an invasion of the south, as up to 30,000 troops could pass through in one hour. The tunnel has been sealed to prevent such use.

Korea itself has changed markedly since the war. Where shacks and blasted buildings once stood, modern high-rises, expressways, and boulevards now exist. Today Seoul is a city of over eight million people, and is growing each day. When I was there, a modern subway system was being expanded, but it is already in operation from downtown Seoul to the port of Inchon. National and multinational corporations flourish in the country, but most seem to have a flavour that is distinctly Korean. For example, I cashed travellers' cheques at a Bank of Montreal in Seoul, but apart from the name and the familiar counter slips and so on, the bank seemed to be as Korean as the currency I purchased.

Since the war, the Korean Veterans Association has become well established and has within the past eight or nine years moved towards greater contact with the Canadian organization of the same name. The Koreans are interested in their Canadian counterparts, and in recent years have sponsored revisits to Korea by Canadians who fought there. The feeling among Canadians who have "gone back" seems to be positive, although several told me they couldn't believe they were in the same country they lived in thirty years ago. On the other hand, the fact that Korea *has* changed so much is perhaps the best kind of proof that fighting there may have been worth while.

APPENDIX A

THE HONOUR ROLL OF THE KOREA SPECIAL FORCE
THOSE WHO MADE THE SUPREME SACRIFICE IN KOREA

*Denotes KILLED IN ACTION

RANK	NAME	DATE OF DEATH	UNIT
Pte.	ALFORD, C. M.	27 Sept. 51	PPCLI
Pte.	ALLEN, J. R.*	23 Oct. 52	RCR
Pte.	ALTHOUSE, H.	1 May 53	PPCLI
Pte.	ANAKA, G.*	23 Oct. 52	RCR
Pte.	ANDERSEN, F.*	23 Feb. 51	PPCLI
Lieut.	ANDERSON, N. M.	25 Aug. 54	QOR
Pte.	ANDREWS, F. A.	4 June 56	RCOC
Pte.	ANDREWS, L. F.*	22 July 51	RCR
Pte.	ARD, H.	14 May 53	RCR
Pte.	ARDING, R. F.*	23 Oct. 52	RCASC
Pte.	ARNOTT, R. V.*	23 Oct. 51	PPCLI
A.B.	BAIKIE, E. A.*	2 Oct. 52	HMCS *Iroquois*
Lieut.	BANTON, D. W.*	3 May 53	RCR
Pte.	BATSCH, J. W.*	30 Nov. 52	PPCLI
L/Cpl.	BAWDEN, C. F.*	23 Oct. 52	RCR
Pte.	BEAR, M.	3 May 53	RCR
Pte.	BEARDMORE, J. G. S.*	11 Oct. 51	RCR
Pte.	BEAUDRY, J. G.*	25 May 51	RCR
Pte.	BELAND, M.*	19 Aug. 52	R 22 R
Tpr.	BELL, J. R.	6 June 53	RCD
Pte.	BERGERON, E.*	10 Aug. 52	R 22 R
Pte.	BETTS, W. M.	28 July 53	RCR
Cpl.	BIGNUCOLO, C. E.	17 Oct. 52	RCR
Pte.	BILYK, F.*	20 Oct. 52	RCR
Pte.	BISHOP, J. J.*	9 Jan. 53	RCR
Cpl.	BLACK, W. A.	14 Nov. 51	PPCLI

RANK	NAME	DATE OF DEATH	UNIT
Pte.	BLANCHARD, J. R.*	1 Sept. 52	R 22 R
Cpl.	BOATH, D. H.*	23 Oct. 52	RCR
Pte.	BOLDUC, M. A.*	24 Nov. 51	R 22 R
Cpl.	BOLTON, R. W.*	5 Sept. 52	RCR
L/Cpl.	BOSSE, C.*	24 Nov. 51	R 22 R
Pte.	BOSSE, G. H.*	28 May 53	R 22 R
Pte.	BOUDREAU, J. V.*	24 Nov. 51	R 22 R
Pte.	BOUDREAULT, P.-E.	17 Dec. 53	R 22 R
Pte.	BOURDEAU, J. L.*	6 Sept. 52	R 22 R
Pte.	BOUTIN, B.	4 Nov. 53	R 22 R
Pte.	BRADSHAW, E. F.*	23 Oct. 51	PPCLI
Pte.	BRAYLEY, J. S.	31 Aug. 50	RCR
Pte.	BRODEN, E. P.	6 Nov. 51	PPCLI
Pte.	BROOKS, K. S.*	29 May 52	RCR
Pte.	BROWN, B. B.*	23 Feb. 51	PPCLI
Pte.	BROWNLOW, L. D.	23 July 52	RCR
Pte.	BRUCE, W. E.*	23 Oct. 52	RCR
Pte.	BRUNEAU, P.*	9 July 51	R 22 R
Pte.	BRYDON, H. B.	8 Oct. 51	PPCLI
Pte.	BUCHANAN, E. C.	30 June 51	PPCLI
Pte.	BURAK, J. N.	3 May 53	RCR
A.B.	BURDEN, W. M.	2 Oct. 52	HMCS *Iroquois*
L/Cpl.	BURGESS, T.*	17 Aug. 52	R 22 R
L/Cpl.	BUTKEVICH, B.	31 July 52	R 22 R
Cpl.	CALKINS, J. A.*	23 Feb. 51	PPCLI
Pte.	CAMPBELL, H. P.	18 Mar. 51	RCASC
Cpl.	CAMPBELL, R. D. M.	31 Oct. 52	PPCLI
Pte.	CAMPEAU, J. J. M. M.*	3 Nov. 51	RCR
Pte.	CANNING, L. A.	2 May 52	PPCLI
Lieut.	CARRIER, J. L. R.*	20 July 51	R 22 R
Pte.	CASEY, R. D.*	6 Dec. 51	RCR
Cfn.	CHAPMAN, E. A.	8 Jan. 54	RCEME
Cpl.	CHARPENTIER, M.*	24 Nov. 51	R 22 R
Cpl.	CHARTIER, M. E. H.*	12 Sept. 51	R 22 R
Pte.	CHATIGNY, D.*	6 Sept. 52	R 22 R
Pte.	CHIASSON, M. P.	3 May 53	RCR
Pte.	CHIASSON, O.	17 Apr. 53	R 22 R
Pte.	CHOUINARD, V.	21 May 51	R 22 R
Pte.	CHRISTIE, R. A.	15 Feb. 54	RHR
Pte.	CHRISTOFF, J. J.*	3 May 53	RCR
Cpl.	CLARK, P. A.	5 July 54	R 22 R
Pte.	CLARK, R.*	3 May 53	RCR

RANK	NAME	DATE OF DEATH	UNIT
Pte.	CLEMENTS, B.	15 Dec. 53	PPCLI
Lieut.	CLEVELAND, H. R.	15 May 51	PPCLI
Pte.	COLBOURNE, T. H.*	23 Feb. 51	PPCLI
Pte.	COLLINS, J. L. M.*	9 July 51	R 22 R
Pte.	COPAGE, W. A.	31 Jan. 53	RCR
Pte.	COPINACE, R.*	3 May 53	PPCLI
Pte.	CORBEIL, G.*	23 Sept. 51	R 22 R
Pte.	CORMIER, G. M.*	1 Oct. 52	RCR
Sgt.	CORNISH, V. K.*	20 Nov. 51	RCA
Pte.	COTA, D. E.	4 Aug. 51	RCASC
Pte.	COTE, J. R. I.*	25 Mar. 52	PPCLI
Pte.	COUNTRYMAN, L. G.*	23 Oct. 52	RCR
Pte.	COURCHAINE, L. J.	4 Aug. 56	RCASC
Sgt.	COWAN, S. F.	17 Nov. 52	RCASC
Pte.	CROMPTON, K.*	3 May 53	PPCLI
L/Cpl.	CROWELL, R. W.	8 Sept. 51	RCASC
Sgt.	CUMBERBATCH, A. E. W.	4 July 54	RCASC
Sgt.	CURRIE, C. J.*	23 Oct. 51	PPCLI
Pte.	CUSSON, F. W. A.	20 May 53	R 22 R
Pte.	DALLAIRE, R.*	23 Nov. 51	R 22 R
Pte.	DANEAU, J. F. L.	18 May 53	R 22 R
Pte.	DARRAH, H. C.*	1 Oct. 52	RCR
Pte.	DAVID, J. A. L.*	19 Oct. 52	R 22 R
Spr.	DAVIS, H. G.	7 Nov. 51	RCE
Pte.	DAWSON, W.*	23 Oct. 52	RCR
Pte.	DeBECK, M.*	21 June 52	PPCLI
Pte.	DESCHENES, J. R. R.	24 Oct. 51	R 22 R
Pte.	DESCHESNES, J. A. A. F.	9 Jan. 53	R 22 R
Pte.	DESILETS, G.*	10 Aug. 52	R 22 R
Sgt.	DESJARDINS, J. A. G.*	20 May 53	R 22 R
Pte.	DesROCHERS, J. R. A. R.	10 Jan. 52	R 22 R
Pte.	DIEHL, F. A.*	3 May 53	RCR
Pte.	DIONNE, P.-E.*	24 Nov. 51	R 22 R
Pte.	DISTEFANO, G.*	23 Oct. 51	R 22 R
Cpl.	DOHERTY, G. E.*	12 July 53	RCR
Major	DUBE, J. L. Y.	16 July 51	R 22 R
Spr.	DUCASSE, G.	11 Aug. 52	RCE
Pte.	DUCHARME, G.	12 Jan. 52	PPCLI
Pte.	DUGUAY, L. J.*	19 Oct. 52	R 22 R
S/Sgt.	DUHAIME, J. J., CD	13 July 55	RCASC
Pte.	DUMAS, J. B.*	2 Oct. 51	R 22 R
Pte.	DUNPHY, M. A.*	11 July 51	PPCLI

RANK	NAME	DATE OF DEATH	UNIT
Pte.	DUPUIS, J. E. A.*	6 May 52	R 22 R
Pte.	DUROCHER, Y. V. J.	5 Sept. 52	R 22 R
Pte.	DURY, G. H.*	4 Oct. 51	RCR
Pte.	EARHART, A. C.	15 Feb. 54	RHR
L/Cpl.	EDGLEY, H. V.*	6 June 51	PPCLI
Cpl.	EDMUNDS, R. A.*	30 May 51	RCR
L/Cpl.	ELLIOTT, R. D.	17 Apr. 53	PPCLI
Pte.	ELLIOTT, W. H.*	1 Oct. 52	RCR
Pte.	EMARD, M.*	24 Nov. 51	R 22 R
L/Cpl.	EMERSON, L. A.*	22 Oct. 52	RCR
L/Cpl.	EMERY, R. E.	18 Sept. 52	C Pro C
Pte.	ENOS, R. C.	25 Nov. 51	PPCLI
Pte.	ERB, K. I.*	26 Mar. 52	RCR
Cpl.	EVANS, G. R.*	25 Apr. 51	PPCLI
Cpl.	EVANS, J. K.	23 Oct. 51	RCR
Pte.	EVERINGHAM, D. W.*	3 May 53	RCR
Pte.	FAIRFIELD, B. P. J.*	13 Sept. 52	R 22 R
L/Cpl.	FAIRMAN, J. H.	13 Oct. 52	RCR
Pte.	FAIRSERVICE, R. B.	9 Apr. 51	PPCLI
Pte.	FANCY, C. R. E.	5 June 51	RCR
Pte.	FARAND, A. J.*	19 Nov. 52	PPCLI
Rfn.	FERLAND, N. P.	31 Mar. 54	QOR
Cpl.	FERLATTE, J. A.*	21 July 53	RCR
Pte.	FERRON, H. A.*	4 Sept. 52	R 22 R
Pte.	FIELDING, L. T.*	25 Apr. 51	PPCLI
Pte.	FONG, W.*	23 June 52	R 22 R
Spr.	FORTIER, A.	22 Feb. 53	RCE
Pte.	FOWLER, W. J.*	26 Mar. 52	PPCLI
L/Cpl.	FRANCOEUR, G.*	19 Aug. 52	R 22 R
Pte.	GAGNIER, J. L. R.	30 Sept. 53	RCR
Pte.	GAGNON, J. O.	7 June 52	RCASC
L/Cpl.	GALLANT, J. M.	16 July 53	R 22 R
Pte.	GALLINGER, P. H.*	3 May 53	RCR
Pte.	GARAND, J. E. H.*	19 Nov. 51	PPCLI
Pte.	GARDINER, R. L.*	3 May 53	RCR
OS	GAUTHIER, L. A.	11 Jan. 51	HMCS *Nootka*, RCN
Pte.	GENDRON, R.	6 May 52	R 22 R
Pte.	GIGUERE, R.	8 Sept. 51	R 22 R
Cpl.	GILL, J. F.*	1 Jan. 53	RCR
Pte.	GILLAN, J. R. Q.	20 Mar. 51	PPCLI
Cpl.	GILMORE, J. F.*	26 Mar. 52	RCR
Pte.	GIRARD, H.*	20 May 53	R 22 R

RANK	NAME	DATE OF DEATH	UNIT
Pte.	GIRARD, J.*	24 Nov. 51	R 22 R
Pte.	GIRARD, J. A. F.*	28 Sept. 51	R 22 R
Pte.	GIRARD, R. F. T.*	3 May 53	RCR
Pte.	GLADU, L. P.	3 Apr. 51	PPCLI
Pte.	GOODWIN, E. H.*	4 Oct. 51	PPCLI
Major	GOSSELIN, J. P. L., ED*	9 July 51	R 22 R
Pte.	GOSSELIN, L. J.*	22 June 52	RCR
Major	GOWER, P. E., MC	9 Dec. 56	QOR
Pte.	GRAY, A. L.*	16 Apr. 53	PPCLI
Tpr.	GRAY, K. A.	14 June 52	LSH
Pte.	GRENIER, H.-L., CD	8 Nov. 55	RCASC
Pte.	GRENNAN, R. J.*	3 May 53	RCR
Pte.	GUY, A. S.*	2 July 51	RCR
Pte.	HACKETT, J. C.*	21 Oct. 52	RCR
Pte.	HALL, R. A.*	4 Jan. 52	RCAMC
Lieut.	HAMILTON, J. D.*	12 Apr. 52	PPCLI
Pte.	HANSEN, A. E. R.*	25 Feb. 51	PPCLI
Pte.	HANSPIKER, E. J.	23 Nov. 51	PPCLI
Pte.	HARALSON, R. O.*	16 Dec. 52	PPCLI
Pte.	HARMON, J. F.*	21 June 52	PPCLI
Lieut.	HARRIOTT, C.	5 Sept. 52	RCR
Pte.	HARRISON, H. C.	3 Feb. 52	RCIC
Pte.	HARRISON, R.	15 Feb. 52	PPCLI
Cpl.	HASTINGS, D. P.	15 Oct. 52	PPCLI
Pte.	HAYES, C. A.*	25 Apr. 51	PPCLI
Pte.	HEARSEY, J. W.*	13 Oct. 51	PPCLI
Capt.	HEATH, J. K.	4 Sept. 51	RCA
Pte.	HEDDERSON, T. J.*	3 May 53	RCR
L/Bdr.	HELMAN, A. J.	25 Apr. 53	RCA
Lieut.	HERMAN, A. G.*	19 Aug. 52	R 22 R
Spr.	HIEBERT, H. B.	22 Mar. 52	RCE
L/Cpl.	HIGGINS, H. E.	21 June 52	PPCLI
Pte.	HILTON, J. W.	24 Oct. 52	RCR
Pte.	HOWARTH, W. R.*	30 May 51	RCR
Cpl.	HUGHES, E. J.*	2 Oct. 52	RCE
Sgt.	HUOT, J. W. A.	14 May 51	R 22 R
Pte.	ISABELLE, J. L. P.*	23 Nov. 51	R 22 R
L/Cpl.	JOHNSTONE, W. E.	15 Oct. 52	PPCLI
Pte.	JONES, D. R.*	19 Nov. 52	PPCLI
Pte.	JONES, K. B.	8 Jan. 52	RCASC
Pte.	JONES, R. J.	11 Oct. 51	RCR
Pte.	JORDAN, J. A.	24 Nov. 51	PPCLI

RANK	NAME	DATE OF DEATH	UNIT
Lieut.	KAIN, E. G.	20 Jan. 55	R 22 R
Pte.	KEATING, J. P.	3 May 53	RCR
Pte.	KEMP, J. F.*	30 May 51	RCR
L/Cpl.	KENNEDY, J. W.*	5 Nov. 51	PPCLI
Pte.	KILPATRICK, J. E.	13 Oct. 52	RCR
Pte.	KING, A. A.	24 Dec. 52	RCR
Pte.	KING, R. F.*	19 Nov. 52	PPCLI
Cpl.	KINROSS, G. E.	9 Mar. 52	RCR
Pte.	KNIGHT, E. J. M.*	23 Oct. 52	RCR
Pte.	KNORR, G. G.	31 Mar. 52	PPCLI
Pte.	KNOTT, G. C.	27 Apr. 52	RCR
Sgt.	KOCH, G. W.	4 Aug. 54	QOR
Pte.	KOSTIUK, W.*	1 July 53	PPCLI
Pte.	LABRECQUE, J. O. G.*	13 Nov. 51	RCAMC
Pte.	LACHANCE, H.*	25 Nov. 51	R 22 R
Cpl.	LADOUCEUR, J. G. M.	6 Sept. 52	R 22 R
Pte.	LADOUCEUR, L.	3 July 53	R 22 R
Pte.	LAFLAMME, J. L. L.*	24 Nov. 51	R 22 R
Pte.	LAFRAMBOISE, C. J.	14 June 54	RHR
Pte.	LAFRANCHISE, J. P. C. R.*	13 Aug. 52	R 22 R
Pte.	LANDRY, R. E.*	11 Jan. 52	R 22 R
Pte.	LANGLOIS, F.*	17 May 51	R 22 R
Pte.	LAPKA, W.	8 Mar. 51	PPCLI
Pte.	LARSON, B. W.	1 Dec. 52	C Pro C
Pte.	LATHAM, M. E.*	13 Oct. 52	RCR
Pte.	LAUZIER, A.*	10 Aug. 52	RCASC
Pte.	LAVALLEE, H. J.*	19 July 53	PPCLI
Pte.	LAVENE, W. H.	5 Sept. 52	RCR
Pte.	LAWLOR, L. J.	26 May 51	RCASC
Pte.	LEACH, R. C.*	9 Dec. 52	PPCLI
Pte.	Le BEAU, H. J. G.*	24 Nov. 51	R 22 R
L/Cpl.	LEBLANC, J. G. A.*	6 May 52	R 22 R
Pte.	LECLERC, J. A. J. M.	10 Oct. 52	R 22 R
Pte.	LEGGE, H. D.*	8 Nov. 51	PPCLI
Pte.	LEONARD, J.-M.	5 July 52	R 22 R
Sgt.	LEONARD, M. C.	16 June 54	RCASC
L/Cpl.	LEROUX, J.-C.*	19 Jan. 53	R 22 R
Pte.	LESSARD, J. M. L.*	25 Apr. 51	PPCLI
Sgt.	LETENDRE, J. L.	5 July 54	R 22 R
L/Cpl.	LETKEMAN, T. N.*	7 Mar. 51	PPCLI
Lieut.	LEVISON, J. Y.*	26 May 51	PPCLI
Pte.	LEWIS, A. C.	26 Feb. 51	PPCLI

RANK	NAME	DATE OF DEATH	UNIT
Pte.	LINDEN, W. J.	13 July 51	RCR
A.B.	LISKA, V.	4 Dec. 50	HMCS *Cayuga*
Pte.	LOCKHART, W. J.	19 June 53	RCR
Pte.	LUCAS, G. L.*	21 June 52	PPCLI
Pte.	LUCAS, W. F.*	2 May 53	RCR
H/Maj.	LUPIEN, J. A. R.	8 Feb. 52	RCAChC
Pte.	LUXTON, W. A.*	22 June 52	RCR
Cpl.	MacASKILL, E.	3 Apr. 51	PPCLI
Cpl.	MacCORMACK, J. D.*	31 Dec. 51	RCR
Pte.	MacDONALD, B. A.*	8 Jan. 53	RCR
Pte.	MacDONALD, B. M.*	25 Apr. 51	PPCLI
Pte.	MacDONALD, E. W.	14 Oct. 53	PPCLI
Pte.	MacDONALD, R.*	19 Nov. 52	PPCLI
F/Sgt.	MacDONELL, H. T., CD	6 Sept. 53	426 Sqn.
Pte.	MacDOUGALL, L. F.*	4 Oct. 51	RCR
Pte.	MacKAY, E. G.	23 Feb. 51	PPCLI
Cpl.	MacLEAN, D. H. R.*	3 May 53	RCR
Pte.	MacLEOD, N. T.	8 May 52	RCR
Pte.	MacMILLAN, M. R.	22 June 54	RCR
Pte.	MacPHEE, S. H.*	24 Mar. 52	RCR
Pte.	MacPHERSON, D. W.	18 Jan. 53	RCR
Sgmn.	MADDISON, W. B.	29 Nov. 52	RC Sigs
L/Cpl.	MADORE, J. N. J. C.	4 Sept. 51	R 22 R
Pte.	MAISONNEUVE, J.-P.*	6 Jan. 53	R 22 R
Pte.	MAJOR, J. W.*	19 Aug. 52	R 22 R
Pte.	MARSHALL, W. J.*	25 Apr. 51	PPCLI
Pte.	MARTIN, J. R.*	27 Nov. 51	R 22 R
Pte.	MATHIEU, O.*	4 Sept. 52	R 22 R
Pte.	MAURER, D. P.	29 Aug. 52	RCR
L/Cpl.	MAXWELL, J. N. J.*	25 Feb. 51	PPCLI
Lieut.	MAYNELL, G. B.*	3 May 53	RCR
Pte.	McHUGH, J.*	20 Dec. 51	RCR
Pte.	McINNES, G. D.	23 Aug. 55	PPCLI
Pte.	McINNIS, A. W.*	23 Oct. 52	RCR
Pte.	McINTYRE, E. A.*	15 Jan. 52	PPCLI
Pte.	McKINNON, H. I.*	1 Oct. 52	RCR
Spr.	McNEIL, A.	21 May 54	RCE
Pte.	McNEIL, N. G.	6 Jan. 52	RCR
Pte.	McPHAIL, W. C.	19 Mar. 51	PPCLI
Pte.	McPHEE, R. F.*	15 Jan. 52	PPCLI
Pte.	McVICAR, R. P.	18 July 52	RCR
Pte.	MEHAN, J. C.*	3 May 53	RCR

RANK	NAME	DATE OF DEATH	UNIT
Pte.	MERCIER, J. A.*	17 Aug. 52	R 22 R
Pte.	MERCIER, J. R.*	25 Nov. 51	R 22 R
Pte.	MICHAUD, J. N.	4 Dec. 51	R 22 R
Cpl.	MICHAUD, M. H.	8 Oct. 53	R 22 R
L/Cpl.	MICHAUD, R.*	24 June 53	PPCLI
Pte.	MILLAR, R. E.	24 Oct. 52	RCR
Gnr.	MILLER, E.	10 Aug. 52	RCA
Pte.	MILMORE, W. E.*	16 Sept. 51	RCR
Pte.	MITCHELL, A. G.*	26 Mar. 52	RCR
Pte.	MONAGUE, K. R.	21 Mar. 52	PPCLI
Pte.	MONETTE, J.-P.*	22 June 53	R 22 R
Pte.	MOREAU, H. J.*	20 May 53	R 22 R
Pte.	MOREAU, M. J.*	2 Oct. 51	PPCLI
Pte.	MORFORD, J. H.*	7 Mar. 51	PPCLI
Pte.	MORIN, C. J.	6 Aug. 52	R 22 R
Cpl.	MORIN, J. A.*	10 Apr. 53	R 22 R
Pte.	MORNINGSTAR, C.	10 May 53	RCR
Spr.	MORRIS, F.	12 June 52	RCE
Pte.	MORRISON, C. J.*	23 Oct. 52	RCR
Pte.	MORRISON, W. E.	25 Apr. 53	RCASC
Pte.	MUDD, S. R.*	6 Dec. 52	PPCLI
Cpl.	MULLIN, F. A.*	30 Nov. 52	PPCLI
Pte.	MURCAR, J. R.*	14 June 53	PPCLI
Gnr.	MURPHY, R. R.*	13 Sept. 52	RCA
Pte.	MURRAY, L. L.*	26 Mar. 52	PPCLI
L/Cpl.	NANKERVIS, R. A.	9 May 53	RCR
Tpr.	NEUFIELD, L. G.*	20 Aug. 52	LSH
Cpl.	NEWELL, D. L.*	3 May 53	RCR
Cfn.	NICHOLSON, N. D.	21 Jan. 52	RCEME
Cpl.	NOLAN, P. J.*	22 June 52	RCR
Pte.	NORMAND, E.*	5 Nov. 51	PPCLI
Pte.	NORTON, K. W.*	5 Nov. 51	PPCLI
Pte.	NYSTEDT, R. S.*	1 Oct. 52	RCR
Pte.	O'BRIEN, K. D.	23 Feb. 51	PPCLI
Pte.	O'CONNOR, P. W.*	30 May 51	RCR
Pte.	O'DONNELL, L. J.	4 Nov. 53	RCASC
Pte.	OLIVER, L. H.*	7 Mar. 51	PPCLI
Cpl.	OUELLETTE, J. N. N.	15 Aug. 52	R 22 R
Pte.	OUELLETTE, J. O.*	21 May 52	PPCLI
Lieut.	PAILLE, A. E.*	21 Oct. 51	R 22 R
Pte.	PAQUETTE, J. A. J.*	24 Nov. 51	R 22 R
Sgt.	PARENT, C. A. D.	1 Jan. 52	R 22 R

RANK	NAME	DATE OF DEATH	UNIT
Pte.	PATRICK, R. R.	9 Apr. 52	PPCLI
Pte.	PATTERSON, E. E.*	26 Mar. 52	PPCLI
Pte.	PATTERSON, G. L.*	2 Oct. 51	PPCLI
Pte.	PAYTON, G.*	25 July 51	RCR
Pte.	PEARSON, R. B.*	7 Mar. 51	PPCLI
Pte.	PELLETIER, A.	10 Oct. 52	R 22 R
Pte.	PELLETIER, R.	13 Nov. 51	RCASC
Pte.	PENNEY, D. W.*	20 July 53	RCR
Pte.	PERRY, T. E.*	15 Aug. 52	R 22 R
Pte.	PETERS, L. E.	27 Feb. 51	PPCLI
Pte.	PICHE, J. S.*	28 Sept. 51	R 22 R
Pte.	PILOTE, R. J.	9 Apr. 53	R 22 R
L/Cpl.	POIRIER, J. H. B.*	20 July 51	R 22 R
Pte.	POIRIER, J. H. M.*	10 Nov. 51	R 22 R
Pte.	POLNUK, A. E.	31 Aug. 51	PPCLI
Pte.	POOLE, J. D.*	23 Oct. 52	RCR
Pte.	POTTER, T. V.	6 July 52	RCASC
Pte.	POUPART, A. G.	23 Feb. 52	PPCLI
Pte.	POWER, E. J.*	24 Dec. 52	PPCLI
Cpl.	PRESLEY, W. L.*	26 June 52	RCR
L/Cpl.	PRIEUR, J. A. M. P.*	27 Aug. 52	R 22 R
Pte.	PROULX, A. F.	16 July 53	R 22 R
Sgt.	PROVOST, J. R. R.	6 Dec. 56	R 22 R
Pte.	PRUD'HOMME, J. H. N.	18 Sept. 52	R 22 R
Lt.-Cdr.	QUINN, J. L.*	2 Oct. 52	HMCS *Iroquois*
Pte.	RACINE, R.	23 Oct. 53	R 22 R
Pte.	RAEBURN, I. N.*	3 May 53	RCR
Pte.	RAMAGE, E. J. J. C.	5 Jan. 53	R 22 R
L/Cpl.	REDMOND, P. G., CD*	22 Apr. 53	RCASC
Pte.	REGAN, W. P.	17 July 53	RCR
Pte.	REGIMBALD, A. A.*	5 Sept. 52	R 22 R
Rfn.	REID, G. P.	11 June 55	QOR
L/Cpl.	RICE, B. G. D.*	13 Oct. 52	RCR
Pte.	RICE, I. L.*	3 May 53	RCR
L/Bdr.	RICHARDS, C. W.	11 Mar. 53	RCA
Sgt.	RICHARDS, R. H.	27 Sept. 52	RCR
Gnr.	RIDDLE, J. F.	5 Oct. 51	RCA
Pte.	ROACH, L. S.*	3 May 53	RCR
Pte.	ROBBINS, L. M.	2 Nov. 52	RCASC
Pte.	ROBERTS, L. C.*	30 May 51	RCR
Pte.	ROBERTS, R. C.	25 Feb. 52	RCASC
Pte.	ROBINSON, G. E.*	13 Oct. 51	PPCLI

RANK	NAME	DATE OF DEATH	UNIT
Pte.	ROCHON, A. R.*	24 Nov. 51	R 22 R
Gnr.	ROSS, B.	9 May 53	RCA
Pte.	ROWBOTHAM, A.*	23 Oct. 52	RCR
Pte.	ROY, B.	8 Oct. 52	R 22 R
Pte.	RYAN, R. A.*	19 Feb. 52	RCR
Pte.	RYAN, W. C.	17 Oct. 52	RCR
Cpl.	RYAN, W. J.*	23 Oct. 52	RCR
Pte.	SABEAN, E. S.	26 Dec. 54	RHR
Pte.	ST-GERMAIN, J. V. F.	8 Oct. 52	R 22 R
Pte.	SANSCARTIER, J. E. H.	1 July 52	R 22 R
Lt.-Col.	SARE, P. F. L., OBE	31 Oct. 52	RCD
Pte.	SAUVE, J.	16 Jan. 53	PPCLI
Cpl.	SCHOULTZ, R. B.*	3 May 53	RCR
Cpl.	SCHWENNEKER, M. H. E.*	21 June 52	PPCLI
L/Cpl.	SCOTT, A. E.	20 May 51	PPCLI
Sgt.	SENECHAL, C. E.	23 Apr. 52	R 22 R
Spr.	SHAW, B. F.	16 Nov. 52	RCE
Sgt.	SHORE, H. J. D.*	2 Oct. 52	RCR
Pte.	SHORTREED, V. K.*	17 Oct. 52	RCR
Pte.	SIHA, T.	20 Mar. 51	PPCLI
A.B.	SKAVBERG, R. J.	27 Nov. 51	HMCS *Athabaskan*
Lt.-Col.	SLACK, W. R. I., CD	4 Feb. 56	RCAMC
Cfn.	SLATER, F.	25 Jan. 52	RCEME
Pte.	SMALL, G. C.	14 July 53	PPCLI
L/Cpl.	SMART, H.*	11 July 51	PPCLI
Tpr.	SMILLIE, J. F.	17 Dec. 51	LSH
Pte.	SPENCE, D. E.*	7 Mar. 51	PPCLI
Pte.	SPENCLEY, P. C.*	3 May 53	RCR
Tpr.	SQUIRES, S. J.	10 June 52	LSH
Pte.	STAINSBY, R.*	27 Oct. 52	RCR
Pte.	STANLEY, D. L.*	21 June 52	PPCLI
L/Cpl.	STEER, D. H.*	31 Dec. 51	RCR
Pte.	STENSETH, R. M.*	21 June 52	PPCLI
Pte.	STEWART, L. A.*	9 Dec. 52	PPCLI
Lieut.	STILWELL, F. S.	25 Jan. 54	RCD
Pte.	STONE, W. A.	23 May 52	RCR
Pte.	STOREY, A. E.	14 July 53	RCR
Pte.	STOREY, A. W.	22 Dec. 51	PPCLI
Pte.	STOWE, C. L.*	13 Oct. 52	RCR
Pte.	STRACHAN, W. L.*	30 May 51	RCR
Pte.	STROUD, R. D.*	16 Sept. 51	RCR
Spr.	SUTTON, T. P.	24 July 52	RCE

RANK	NAME	DATE OF DEATH	UNIT
Pte.	SWEENEY, R. R.	25 Mar. 52	PPCLI
Cpl.	SZLAHETKA, H. A.*	29 June 51	PPCLI
Gnr.	TAKEUCHI, T.	13 Nov. 51	RCA
Cfn.	TAYLOR, R. H.	19 Apr. 54	RCEME
Pte.	TELLIER, L. J.	16 May 53	PPCLI
Cpl.	THEOBALD, E. E.*	26 Mar. 52	PPCLI
Gnr.	THOMPSON, D. E.*	16 June 52	RCA
Pte.	THOMSON, A. F.	14 Nov. 51	RCR
W.O.I	THOMSON, J. R., CD	5 Oct. 56	RCASC
Pte.	THOVESON, T. H.*	4 Oct. 52	PPCLI
Pte.	TOLVER, R. H. G.*	25 Apr. 51	PPCLI
Cpl.	TOOLE, J. R.	11 Oct. 51	PPCLI
Cpl.	TOPPING, W. J. L.	16 Sept. 53	RCR
A.B.	TORRAVILLE, I. T. L.	5 Aug. 52	HMCS *Iroquois*
Pte.	TREMBLAY, G.	25 Dec. 51	PPCLI
Pte.	TREMBLAY, J. G.	23 June 52	R 22 R
L/Cpl.	TREMBLAY, M.*	23 Oct. 51	RCASC
Pte.	TREMBLAY, P. E.	17 Dec. 52	R 22 R
Pte.	TREMBLAY, P.-E.*	6 Sept. 52	R 22 R
W.O.II	TRENTER, G. S.*	11 Oct. 51	PPCLI
Pte.	TRUDEAU, D. J.	12 Jan. 53	RCR
Gnr.	TRUTHWAITE, M. A.*	3 May 53	RCA
Pte.	TURNBULL, R. E.	1 Jan. 54	RHR
Pte.	VAILLANT, J. L. F. P.*	7 Oct. 52	R 22 R
Lieut.	VIPOND, M. C.	18 Mar. 55	QOR
Pte.	WALCH, W. J.	6 Sept. 53	PPCLI
Tpr.	WALDNER, G. H.*	2 Oct. 52	LSH
Pte.	WALKER, D. E.	22 May 51	PPCLI
Sgt.	WALKER, G. W. M.	12 July 53	RCR
Pte.	WALKER, R. L.*	25 Apr. 51	PPCLI
Pte.	WARD, S. A.*	23 Oct. 51	RCR
Pte.	WARREN, J. R.*	7 Mar. 51	PPCLI
Gnr.	WATSON, J. E. M.*	20 Nov. 51	RCA
Spr.	WATSON, L. A.	23 Nov. 51	RCE
Pte.	WEATHERBEE, V. R.*	13 Oct. 51	PPCLI
Gnr.	WEBB, C. D.*	16 June 52	RCA
Gnr.	WEIR, C. D.*	3 May 53	RCA
Pte.	WELLINGTON, D. M.*	3 May 53	RCR
Pte.	WELLS, F. O.	8 Mar. 51	PPCLI
Gnr.	WHITE, J. J.	21 Nov. 50	RCA
Pte.	WHITE, R. O.*	1 Oct. 52	RCR
Pte.	WHITING, F. J.*	23 Oct. 52	RCR

RANK	NAME	DATE OF DEATH	UNIT
Pte.	WILLIAMS, B. E.*	2 July 51	RCR
Pte.	WILLIAMS, J. H.*	26 Mar. 52	RCR
Pte.	WILLIAMS, R. T.*	2 July 51	RCR
Pte.	WILSON, E. H.	27 June 53	RCR
Pte.	WOOD, F. R.*	10 Dec. 51	PPCLI
W.O.I	WOOD, J. D.	18 Jan. 51	PPCLI
Pte.	WOODBURY, T. R.*	3 May 53	RCR
Cpl.	WOODCOCK, N.*	2 Oct. 51	PPCLI
Sgmn.	WOODS, R. F.	26 Oct. 55	RCCS
Pte.	WORKS, F. G.	3 Apr. 51	PPCLI
Pte.	WOTTON, T. B.*	25 Apr. 51	PPCLI
Pte.	WRIGHT, D. E.*	15 Nov. 51	PPCLI
Spr.	WRIGHT, J. O.	25 Aug. 51	RCE
Pte.	WYLIE, L. K.*	7 Mar. 51	PPCLI
Pte.	ZANTOLAS, J. R.	6 Nov. 51	RCASC
Pte.	ZIEGLER, C. J.	13 May 55	RCAMC

APPENDIX B

THOSE WHO MADE THE SUPREME SACRIFICE WHILE SERVING
IN THE KOREA SPECIAL FORCE WITH NO FAR EAST SERVICE

RANK	NAME	DATE OF DEATH	UNIT
Sgmn.	AKINAM, W. J.	1 Sept. 50	RC Sigs.
Gnr.	ATCHISON, A. J.	21 Nov. 50	RCA
Pte.	AUSTIN, W. J. L.	20 Dec. 50	RCR
Pte.	BARKHOUSE, H. A.	13 Jan. 52	PPCLI
Gnr.	BARKHOUSE, W. E.	21 Nov. 50	RCA
Pte.	BARRIE, C.	14 July 52	RCR
Pte.	BEST, W. W. G.	29 Nov. 52	RCR
Pte.	BONNET, J. M. R.	2 June 51	R 22 R
Pte.	BRAYLEY, J. S.	31 Aug. 50	RCR
Pte.	BROWN, R. J.	28 Oct. 50	RCIC
Gnr.	CARROLL, N. W.	21 Nov. 50	RCA
Pte.	CLOONEY, W. D.	29 Sept. 50	RCR
Pte.	COLLINS, A. R.	24 May 52	RCR
Pte.	COLP, R. L.	15 Feb. 52	PPCLI
Gnr.	CONWAY, F. W.	21 Nov. 50	RCA
Gnr.	CRAIG, R. A.	21 Nov. 50	RCA
Pte.	GAGNON, J. G.	19 July 52	R 22 R
Gnr.	GEORGE, A. E.	21 Nov. 50	RCA
Cfn.	GOOD, D. C.	12 Nov. 51	RCEME
Pte.	HELM, C. C.	6 Dec. 51	PPCLI
Pte.	HOWSE, A. G.	7 July 52	LER
Pte.	HUGHES, N. E.	31 Aug. 50	RCR
Pte.	HULL, D. G.	10 July 51	PPCLI
Sgt.	JODRIE, R. A.	26 June 54	PPCLI
Sgmn.	JONES, E. J.	28 July 51	RC Sigs.

RANK	NAME	DATE OF DEATH	UNIT
A.B.	LAKER, F. R.	21 July 51	HMCS *Sioux*, RCN
Pte.	LAURIE, G. D.	28 Sept. 50	RCR
Lieut.	LECUYER, C. B.	15 Aug. 51	RCR
Gnr.	LEVESQUE, U. J.	21 Nov. 50	RCA
Pte.	LITTLE, T. E.	30 Aug. 51	C Pro C
Pte.	MacEACHRON, H. B.	30 June 51	PPCLI
Gnr.	MANLEY, R. W.	21 Nov. 50	RCA
Gnr.	McKEOWN, B. P.	21 Nov. 50	RCA
Pte.	McKINNON, D. A.	15 Feb. 52	PPCLI
Pte.	MICHAUD, F.	24 Sept. 50	R 22 R
Pte.	MONROE, J. A.	3 Oct. 50	RCAMC
Pte.	MOODY, J. L. A.	21 May 51	R 22 R
Gnr.	MOONEY, L. R.	6 Feb. 51	RCA
A.B.	MOORE, R. J.	21 July 51	HMCS *Sioux*, RCN
Spr.	MUIR, W.	5 Oct. 50	RCE
Pte.	MURPHY, D. J., MM	31 Aug. 50	RCR
Gnr.	ORR, A. W.	21 Nov. 50	RCA
Gnr.	OWENS, D.	9 Dec. 50	RCA
Pte.	PLUMB, R. A.	6 Dec. 51	PPCLI
S/Sgt.	RATHBUN, W. A.	18 Jan. 51	RCAC
Cpl.	RAY, K. R.	31 Aug. 50	RCR
Pte.	ROYLES, M. R.	28 Sept. 50	RCR
Pte.	ST-LAURENT, J. R.	2 Sept. 50	R 22 R
Pte.	SIMARD, A.	6 Oct. 51	R 22 R
Gnr.	SNOW, L. A.	21 Nov. 50	RCA
Gnr.	STROUD, A. G.	21 Nov. 50	RCA
Gnr.	THISTLE, J.	21 Nov. 50	RCA
Bdr.	WENKERT, J. M.	21 Nov. 50	RCA
Gnr.	WRIGHT, W. D.	21 Nov. 50	RCA

LEST WE FORGET

APPENDIX C

ROYAL CANADIAN NAVY HONOURS AND AWARDS KOREA

DISTINGUISHED SERVICE ORDER

Captain Jeffry Vanstone Brock, D.S.O., D.S.C., C.D., RCN — HMCS *Cayuga*

THE MOST EXCELLENT ORDER OF THE BRITISH EMPIRE

Captain William Moss Landymore, O.B.E., C.D., RCN — HMCS *Iroquois*

Captain James Plomer, O.B.E., D.S.C. and Bar, C.D., RCN — HMCS *Cayuga*

Commander (Acting Captain) John Curwen Reed, O.B.E., D.S.C., C.D., RCN — HMCS *Athabaskan*

BAR TO THE DISTINGUISHED SERVICE CROSS

Commander Robert Phillip Welland, D.S.C. and Bar, C.D., RCN — HMCS *Athabaskan*

DISTINGUISHED SERVICE CROSS

Lieutenant-Commander John Henry Gordon Bovey, D.S.C., RCN — HMCS *Crusader*

Lieutenant Andrew Lawrence Collier, D.S.C., RCN — HMCS *Cayuga*

Captain Dudley Gawen King, D.S.C, C.D., RCN — HMCS *Athabaskan*

Commander Dunn Lantier, D.S.C., C.D., RCN — HMCS *Haida*

Commander Edward Thomas George Madgwick, D.S.C., C.D., RCN — HMCS *Huron*

Lieutenant-Commander Donald Roy Saxon, D.S.C, C.D., RCN — HMCS *Cayuga*

Commander Richard Miles Steele, D.S.C., RCN — HMCS *Nootka*

Captain Paul Dalrymple Taylor, D.S.C., C.D., RCN — HMCS *Sioux*

Lieutenant (G) Douglas Frederick Tutte, D.S.C., C.D., RCN — HMCS *Iroquois*

DISTINGUISHED SERVICE MEDAL

Chief Petty Officer Albert Leo Bonner, D.S.M., B.E.M., RCN — HMCS *Nootka*

Petty Officer Gerald Edwin Jamieson, D.S.M., RCN — HMCS *Iroquois*

BRITISH EMPIRE MEDAL

Chief Petty Officer Douglas James Pearson, B.E.M., RCN   HMCS *Cayuga*

Petty Officer Edward Hannford Randall, B.E.M., RCN   HMCS *Nootka*

Petty Officer Thomas Shields, B.E.M., RCN   HMCS *Athabaskan*

Chief Petty Officer George Charles Vander-Haegen,
D.S.M., B.E.M. RCN   HMCS *Athabaskan*

AMERICAN AWARDS

LEGION OF MERIT: DEGREE OF COMMANDER

Commander Edward Thomas George Madgwick,
D.S.C., C.D., RCN   HMCS *Huron*

LEGION OF MERIT: DEGREE OF OFFICER

Captain Jeffry Vanstone Brock, D.S.O., D.S.C., C.D., RCN   HMCS *Cayuga*

Commander James Plomer, O.B.E., D.S.C., C.D., RCN   HMCS *Cayuga*

Commander Paul Dalrymple Taylor, D.S.C., C.D., RCN   HMCS *Sioux*

Commander Robert Phillip Welland, D.S.C., C.D., RCN   HMCS *Athabaskan*

LEGION OF MERIT: DEGREE OF LEGIONNAIRE

Commander Alexander Beaufort Fraser-Harris, D.S.C.
and Bar, C.D., RCN   HMCS *Nootka*

Commander Dudley Gawen King, D.S.C., C.D., RCN   HMCS *Athabaskan*

DISTINGUISHED FLYING CROSS

Lieutenant Joseph J. MacBrien, RCN   Task Force 77

BRONZE STAR MEDAL

Commander John Henry Gordon Bovey, D.S.C.,
C.D., RCN   HMCS *Crusader*

APPENDIX D

ROYAL CANADIAN AIR FORCE HONOURS AND AWARDS KOREA

DISTINGUISHED FLYING CROSS

F/L	E. A.	GLOVER

AIR FORCE CROSS

S/L	J. D.	DICKSON
F/L	R. M.	EDWARDS
W/C	H. A.	MORRISON
F/O	D. M.	PAYNE

AMERICAN AWARDS

DISTINGUISHED FLYING CROSS

F/O	S. B.	FLEMING
F/L	E. A.	GLOVER
G/C	E. B.	HALE
F/L	J. C. A.	LaFRANCE
F/L	J. A. O.	LEVESQUE
S/L	J. D.	LINDSAY
F/L	L. E.	SPURR

U.S. AIR MEDAL

S/L	J.	MacKAY
F/L	G. H.	NICHOLS
F/O	G. W.	NIXON
S/L	E. G.	SMITH

APPENDIX E

CANADIAN ARMY
HONOURS AND AWARDS KOREA

COMPANION OF THE MOST HONOURABLE ORDER OF THE BATH

Brigadier	J. M.	Rockingham, CBE, DSO, ED

COMMANDER OF THE MOST EXCELLENT ORDER
OF THE BRITISH EMPIRE

Brigadier	M. P.	Bogert, DSO, OBE, CD
Brigadier	F. J.	Fleury, MBE, ED
Colonel	G. L. M.	Smith, OBE, CD

DISTINGUISHED SERVICE ORDER

Lieutenant-Colonel	P. R.	Bingham
Major	J. H. B.	George
Major	V. W.	Jewkes, MC
Lieutenant-Colonel	E. M. D.	Leslie
Major	R.	Liboiron
Lieutenant-Colonel	J. L. G.	Poulin, CD
Lieutenant-Colonel	H. W.	Sterne, MBE, CD
Lieutenant-Colonel	N. G.	Wilson-Smith, MBE

2nd BAR TO DISTINGUISHED SERVICE ORDER

Lieutenant-Colonel	J.R.	Stone, DSO, MC

OFFICER OF THE MOST EXCELLENT ORDER OF THE BRITISH EMPIRE

Lieutenant-Colonel	E. A. C.	Amy, DSO, MC
Lieutenant-Colonel	A. J. B.	Bailey, DSO, MBE, ED
Lieutenant-Colonel	E. G.	Brooks, DSO, CD

Lieutenant-Colonel	B. L. P.	Brosseau, MC
Lieutenant-Colonel	J. R.	Cameron
Lieutenant-Colonel	K. L.	Campbell, MBE, CD
Lieutenant-Colonel	C. B.	Caswell, MC
Lieutenant-Colonel	G. C.	Corbould, DSO, ED
Lieutenant-Colonel	E. D.	Danby, DSO
Lieutenant-Colonel	J. A.	Dextraze, DSO
Lieutenant-Colonel	J. D.	Galloway
Lieutenant-Colonel	R. A.	Keane, DSO
Lieutenant-Colonel	M. F.	MacLachlan, MC, CD
Major	D. H.	Rochester
Lieutenant-Colonel	P. F. L.	Sare
Lieutenant-Colonel	L. F.	Trudeau, DSO, CD
Lieutenant-Colonel	J. A. A. G.	Vallée, CD

MEMBER OF THE MOST EXCELLENT ORDER OF THE BRITISH EMPIRE

Major	A. J.	Abbott
Major	J. C.	Allan, DSO, CD
Major	A. J.	Baker, CD
Major	H. W.	Ball
Major	J. P.	Beer
Major	R. M.	Black
Captain	G. S.	Blake, CD
Major	H. B.	Brodie
Major	R. F.	Bruce, CD
Captain	S. L.	Campbell
Major	J. A.	Clancy, MC
Captain	J. R.	Connell, CD
Captain	D. R.	Copcutt
Major	R. A.	Couche, CD
Major	G. R.	Covey, CD
Major	J. L.	Dolan
Captain	A.	Dubois
Major	J. R.	Ferris
Captain	J. A.	Filshie
Captain	G. R.	Fortin
Major	E. T.	Galway, MC, GM
Major	D. H.	George, MC
Major	C. J. A.	Hamilton
Captain	R. J.	Hauser, CD
Major	E. G.	Hession
Major	J. S.	Hitsman
Major	B. D.	Jaffey
Captain	H. W.	Johnson

Major	F.	Klevanic
Major	R. C. D.	Laughton
Major	Q. E.	Lawson, CD
Major	J. E.	Leach, CD
Lieutenant	A. C.	Leonard
Major	T. M.	MacDonald, CD
Captain	J. H.	MacGregor
Major	C. E. C.	MacNeill, ED
Major	P. A.	Mayer, CD
Major	J. R.	McLarnon
Captain	H. E.	McLaughlin
Major	I. M.	McLaughlin
Major	J. S.	Orton, MC
Major	C. A.	Pilley, CD
Major	W. R.	Preston
Major	A.	Robinson, MC
Major	J. S.	Roxborough
Major	J. G.	Sévigny, DSO
Lieutenant-Colonel	R. A.	Smillie
Captain	H. C.	Stevenson
Captain	N. G.	Trower
Major	L. R. P. G.	Turcotte
Captain	W. E.	Wheeler, CD
Lieutenant	M. B.	Wood
Squadron Sergeant-Major	E. J.	Armer
Regimental Sergeant-Major	R. V.	Armishaw
Regimental Sergeant-Major	J. M.	Fernets
Regimental Sergeant-Major	P.	Hache, CD
Regimental Quartermaster Sergeant	W. H.	Hardon
Regimental Sergeant-Major	W. T.	Seed

ROYAL RED CROSS

Captain (Matron)	E. B.	Pense, ARRC, CD

MILITARY CROSS

Captain	E. W.	Berthiaume
Captain	D. S.	Caldwell, CD
Lieutenant	C. D.	Carter
Lieutenant	J.	Clark
Captain	H. G.	Cloutier, CD
Lieutenant	L. G.	Côté
Captain	J. E.	deHart
Major	W. H.	Ellis, CD

Lieutenant	F. R.	Freeborn
Lieutenant	H. R.	Gardner
2nd Lieutenant	E. H.	Hollyer
Captain	G. H.	Howitt
Captain	J. G.	Jenkins, CD
Lieutenant	A. M.	King
Captain	R.	Leclerc
Lieutenant	D. G.	Loomis
Lieutenant	E. J.	Mastronardi
Lieutenant	J. G. C.	McKinley
2nd Lieutenant	H. O.	Merrithew
Lieutenant	D. A.	Middleton, MM
Captain	J. G. W.	Mills
Lieutenant	M. T.	O'Brennan
Lieutenant	A. A. S.	Peterson
Lieutenant	H. C.	Pitts
Major	W. H.	Pope
2nd Lieutenant	J. B.	Riffou
2nd Lieutenant	W. C.	Robertson
Lieutenant	G. E. M.	Ruffee
Major	L. E. C.	Schmidlin, MBE, CD
2nd Lieutenant	C. B.	Snider
Major	G. G.	Taylor, ED
Lieutenant	J. P. A.	Therrien
Captain	J. P. R.	Tremblay

DISTINGUISHED FLYING CROSS

Captain	P. J. A.	Tees

ASSOCIATE OF THE ROYAL RED CROSS

Lieutenant (Nursing Sister)	J. I.	MacDonald

DISTINGUISHED CONDUCT MEDAL

Private	R. E.	Bauer
Sergeant	R. G.	Buxton
Lance-Corporal	J. P. A.	Harvey
Sergeant	D. A.	McCuish
Private	W. R.	Mitchell
Corporal	E. W.	Poole
Sergeant	J. H.	Richardson

BAR TO DISTINGUISHED CONDUCT MEDAL

Corporal	L.	Major, DCM

GEORGE MEDAL

Lance-Corporal	S. L.	Sinnott

MILITARY MEDAL

Sergeant	T.	Allen
Staff-Sergeant	P.	Anderson
Private	E.	Asselin
Private	L.	Barton
Private	K. F.	Barwise
Sergeant	A.	Beaudin
Private	C. O.	Bell
Sergeant	B.	Bergeron
Private	D. W.	Carley
Sergeant	J. R.	Champoux
Staff-Sergeant	V. D.	Cole
Corporal	D.	Cormier
Bombardier	T. E.	Dearden
Lance-Corporal	A.	Dion
Lance-Bombardier	F. M.	Dorman
Lance-Corporal	S.	Douglas
Corporal	J. G.	Dunbar
Sergeant	K.J.	Dunphy
Sergeant	G. E. P.	Enright
Corporal	V. L.	Fenton
Corporal	K. E.	Fowler
Company Sergeant-Major	G. M.	Fox
Private	R.	Gagnon
Gunner	A. M.	Garaughty
Lance-Corporal	J. R.	Gingras
Sergeant	W. G.	Graveline
Private	J. G.	Guay
Private	J. D.	Johnson
Company Sergeant-Major	L. A.	Johnson
Private	G. P.	Julien
Lance-Bombardier	A. O.	King
Corporal	D. G.	Lemoine
Corporal	G. A.	McKinney
Corporal	J. C.	McNeil
Corporal	K. V.	McOrmond

Corporal	J. G.	Ostiguy
Corporal	J. P. R.	Pearce
Corporal	C. W. H.	Pelley
Corporal	W. D.	Pero
Sergeant	R. A.	Prentice
Sergeant	M.	Prociuk
Private	W. D.	Pugh
Corporal	J. E.	Rimmer
Private	G. G.	Rowden
Private	J. A.	Sargent
Corporal	A. A.	Scott
Sergeant	S.	Sommerville
Sergeant	L.	Steadman
Trooper	R. C.	Stevenson
Corporal	A. I.	Stinson
Lance-Corporal	P. C.	Thompson
Private	O. M.	White
Gunner	K. W.	Wishart

BRITISH EMPIRE MEDAL

Sergeant	J.	Bourdeau
Sergeant	B. I.	Charland
Staff-Sergeant	B. C.	Clouston
Corporal	W. M.	Downs
Lance-Corporal	P.	Dugal
Sergeant	G. W.	Elliott
Staff-Sergeant	D. F.	Eveleigh
Sergeant	L. P.	Gardiner
Sergeant	M. S.	Haynes
Bombardier	H. E.	Long
Company Sergeant-Major	P. A.	Lynch
Lance-Corporal	H. J.	McCreary
Lance-Corporal	M. J.	Nixon
Sergeant	J. W.	Parker
Sergeant	R. L.	Ross
Sergeant	C. A.	Stewart
Sergeant	A. E.	Thompson
Sergeant	P. J.	Tomelin
Sergeant	K. G.	Tutte
Sergeant	W. E.	Walters
Trooper	H.	Wyatt

AMERICAN AWARDS

LEGION OF MERIT — DEGREE OF OFFICER

Brigadier	J. V.	Allard, CBE, DSO, ED
Brigadier	M. P.	Bogert, CBE, DSO, CD
Brigadier	F. J.	Fleury, CBE, ED
Brigadier	J. M.	Rockingham, CB, CBE, DSO, ED

LEGION OF MERIT — DEGREE OF LEGIONNAIRE

Colonel	G. L. M.	Smith, CBE, CD
Lieutenant-Colonel	E. D.	Danby, DSO, OBE

BRONZE STAR MEDAL WITH "V" DEVICE

Major	E. J.	Williams

BRONZE STAR MEDAL

Lieutenant-Colonel	E. A. C.	Amy, DSO, OBE, MC
Major	C. O.	Huggard
Major	R. D.	Medland, DSO
Captain	R. J.	Staples
Bombardier	G. I.	Reid

DISTINGUISHED FLYING CROSS

Lieutenant	A. G.	Magee
Lieutenant	J. F. O.	Plouffe
Lieutenant	W. E.	Ward
Captain	J. R. P. P.	Yelle

AIR MEDAL

Lieutenant	A. P.	Bull
Captain	L. R.	Drapeau, DCM
Captain	J. H.	Howard
Lieutenant	D. G.	MacLeod
2nd Lieutenant	W. C.	Robertson

BELGIAN AWARDS

OFFICIER DE L'ORDRE DE LÉOPOLD II AVEC PALME and LA CROIX DE GUERRE 1940 AVEC PALME

Captain	M. H.	Marchessault, CD
Major	J. C.	Stewart
Major	J. E. Y.	Theriault, MC

CHEVALIER DE L'ORDRE DE LÉOPOLD II AVEC PALME and LA CROIX DE GUERRE 1940 AVEC PALME

Lieutenant	J.	Gagne

CHEVALIER DE L'ORDRE DE LA COURONNE AVEC PALME and LA CROIX DE GUERRE 1940 AVEC PALME

Lieutenant	R. W.	Bull

DÉCORATION MILITAIRE 2e CLASSE AVEC PALME and LA CROIX DE GUERRE 1940 AVEC PALME

Corporal	R.	Portelance

AFTERWORD

On June 25 each year the Korean people commemorate the outbreak of the Korean War. The event, of course, is not a matter for celebration, but something which is painful to recollect.

They observe the occasion to remember and thank those who made extreme sacrifices — in lives, blood and comfort — so that the Republic of Korea could survive as a free nation, and also to renew their determination to defend themselves in case the tragedies of 1950 should be repeated.

The Korean War may be largely a forgotten affair in today's world, even in countries which participated in the multinational effort to repel the Communist aggressors. Many events of worldwide gravity have occurred since that time.

Yet the situation today remains one of profound concern to the Korean people. North Korea, across the Demilitarized Zone, under the rule of the same man who ordered the attack on the South more than three decades ago, has not changed its belligerent attitude. It has built up an alarming degree of military strength and the entire land has been turned into a military camp. The menace in the North is as real as ever.

It is gratifying, therefore, to find in this volume a dramatic narration of Canada's role in the Korean War. It sheds light on the heroic actions of Canadian fighting men in that faraway theatre. It also shows that the sacrifices in that war were not in vain, as the world marvels at the development the Republic of Korea has achieved in the years since hostilities were brought to a close.

I believe this book will provide us with many valuable lessons.

Kyoo Hyun Lee
Ambassador of the Republic of Korea
Ottawa
March 1983

PHOTO CREDITS

Public Archives Canada, Department of National Defence: photo no. 27, PA 128825; photo no. 31, TN 83-262-8.

Lorne Barton: photo no. 29.

Caza: photo no. 23, PA 128833.

Courtesy George Griffiths: photo no. 39.

Courtesy Ed Haslip: photo no. 35.

Courtesy Helene Liston: photo no. 36.

Maclean: photo no. 28, C 79010, Public Archives Canada.

Courtesy Hazel Mathieson: photo no. 40.

Courtesy Ken McOrmond: photo no. 18; photo nos. 33 and 34.

Mary Melady: photo no. 6.

Courtesy Mrs. Vera O'Connor: photo no. 37.

Sergeant W. H. Olson, Department of National Defence: photo no. 2, PA 128821; photo no. 9, PA 128864; photo no. 14, PA 128870; photo no. 16, PA 128817; photo no. PA 128866; photo no. 42, PA 128813.

Captain Phil Plastow, Department of National Defence: photo no. 1, PA 128822; photo no. 10, PA 128819; photo no. 25, PA 128879.

Courtesy James Plomer: photo no. 30.

Sailman, Department of National Defence: photo no. 41, PA 128831.

Stephens, Department of National Defence: photo no. 26, PA 128859.

Sergeant Paul Tomelin, Department of National Defence: photo no. 3, PA 128858; photo no. 4, PA 128810; photo no. 5, PA 128875; photo no. 7, PA 128847; photo no. 8, PA 128846; photo no. 11, PA 128802; photo no. 12, PA 128848; photo no. 15, PA 128839; photo no. 17, PA 128855; photo no. 20, PA 128806; photo no. 22, PA 128845; photo no. 24, PA 128851.

George Whittaker: photo no. 13, PA 128835.

United States Air Force; courtesy Mrs. E. Glover: photo no. 32.

NOTES

Page	Line	Prologue
3	10	Lieutenant-Colonel Herbert Fairlie Wood, *Strange Battleground: The Operations in Korea and Their Effects on the Defence Policy of Canada*, p. 235.

Chapter One

Page	Line	
8	13	H. Edward Kim, *Korea: Beyond the Hills*, p. 14.
8	27	*Facts About Korea*, p. 69
10	37	Joseph C. Goulden, *Korea: The Untold Story of the War*, p. 19.
12	26	Robert T. Oliver, *Why War Came in Korea*, pp. 5-6.
12	41	Robert Smith, *MacArthur in Korea*, p.15.
12	44	William Manchester, *American Caesar*, p. 639.
13	38	Robert Leckie, *Conflict: The History of the Korean War, 1950-53*, p. 27.
14	13	Goulden, *Korea: The Untold Story*, p. 25.

Chapter Two

Page	Line	
17	16	David Detzer, *Thunder of the Captains: The Short Summer in 1950*, p. 64.

Page	Line	
17	34	Merle Miller, *Plain Speaking: An Oral Biography of Harry S. Truman*, p. 289.
18	4	Margaret Truman, *Harry S. Truman*, p. 495.
19	9	*The History of the United Nations Forces in the Korean War*, Vol. II, p. 69.
19	10	Kim, Chum-kon, *The Korean War: 1950-53*, p. 222.
19	27	Ibid., p. 237.
21	13	Miller, *Plain Speaking*, p. 293.
21	31	Goulden, *Korea: The Untold Story*, p. 68.
21	40	Lester B. Pearson, *Mike: The Memoirs of the Right Honourable Lester B. Pearson*, Vol. 2: 1948-1957, p. 145.

Chapter Three

Page	Line	
25	31	Harry S. Truman, *Memoirs by Harry S. Truman*, Vol. 2: *Years of Trial and Hope*, p. 384.
27	28	Goulden, *Korea: The Untold Story*, p. 82.
28	19	J. W. Pickersgill, *My Years with Louis St. Laurent: A Political Memoir*, p.128.

Page	Line		Page	Line	
29	23	Jeffry V. Brock, *Memoirs of a Sailor: The Dark Broad Seas*, Vol. 1: *With Many Voices*, p. 203.			*Combat Correspondent*, p. 83.
			57	6	Goulden, *Korea: The Untold Story*, p. 111.
31	16	Ronald A. Keith, *Bush Pilot With a Briefcase: The Happy-go-lucky Story of Grant McConachie*, p. 265.	57	18	Leckie, *Conflict: The History of the Korean War*, p. 91.
			57	29	Higgins, *War in Korea*, p. 92.
31	22	Pearson, *Mike*, p. 145.			
31	25	Ibid., pp. 145-6.			**Chapter Six**
31	40	Brock, *The Dark Broad Seas*, p. 214.	60	9	Smith, *MacArthur In Korea*, p. 166.
32	43	Smith, *MacArthur in Korea*, p. 35.	60	26	Goulden, *Korea: The Untold Story*, p. 244.
			60	34	Harry S. Truman, *Memoirs*, p. 412.
		Chapter Four	60	42	Pearson, *Mike*, p. 159.
36	11	Wood, *Strange Battleground*, p. 20.	60	44	Lawrence Martin, *The Presidents and the Prime Ministers*, p. 163.
36	17	Ibid., p.21.			
36	38	Frank H. Underhill, "Korea," *The Canadian Forum*, August 1950, p.98.	67	42	Phillip Knightley, *The First Casualty*, p. 346.
			68	4	Pierre Berton, "Corporal Dunphy's War," *Maclean's*, June 1, 1951.
37	17	Pearson, *Mike*, p. 153.			
37	31	Blair Fraser, *The Search for Identity: Canada, Postwar to Present*, p. 99.	68	41	Eric M. Hammel, *Chosin: Heroic Ordeal of the Korean War*, p. 17.
40	17	Wood, *Strange Battleground*, pp. 29-30.	69	6	Edgar O'Ballance, *Korea: 1950-1953*, p. 121.
43	9	Ibid., p. 33.	70	42	G. R. Stevens, *Princess Patricia's Canadian Light Infantry*, Vol. 3: 1919-1957, p. 294.
44	36	*Regina Leader Post* November 22, 1950.			
45	32	John G. Diefenbaker, *One Canada: Memoirs of the Right Honourable John G. Diefenbaker*, Vol. 1: *The Crusading Years, 1895-1956*, p. 115-16.	71	24	Knightley, *The First Casualty*, p. 343.
					Chapter Seven
		Chapter Five	73	20	Captain Michael G. McKeown, "Kapyong Remembered: Anecdotes from Korea," p. 17. The author gratefully acknowledges the assistance of Captain McKeown in the preparation of
56	28	Goulden, *Korea: The Untold Story*, p. 141.			
56	40	Marguerite Higgins, *War in Korea: The Report of a Woman*			

Page	Line	
		this chapter. Some of the anecdotes about Kapyong which I have used were collected by him and included in the above unpublished paper. The paper itself was made available to veterans of Kapyong who attended the Kapyong 25th Anniversary reunion at Winnipeg in 1976.
75	18	Wood, *Strange Battleground*, p. 76.

Chapter Eight

Page	Line	
79	23	Pierre Berton, *Maclean's*, June 1, 1951.
82	11	Major-General John M. Rockingham, "Recollections of Korea," p. 11. The author gratefully acknowledges the assistance of General Rockingham in the preparation of this book. Quotations attributed to him are derived from the above unpublished manuscript, from several of his letters to me, and from telephone and personal interviews.
86	18	Smith, *MacArthur in Korea*, p. 156.
86	24	Ibid., p. 155.
86	31	Manchester, *American Caesar*, p. 761.
86	33	Harry S. Truman, *Memoirs*, p. 501.
87	11	Goulden, *Korea: The Untold Story*, p. 477.
88	17	*Time*, April 23, 1951.
88	22	Pearson, *Mike*, p. 182.

Page	Line	
88	27	Ibid., p. 180.
89	44	Miller, *Plain Speaking*, p. 308.
90	3	Jack Anderson with James Boyd, *Confessions of a Muckraker*, p. 161.

Chapter Nine

Page	Line	
92	3	James Cameron, "Cameron's Wars," *The Guardian*, November 7, 1982.
92	20	Ibid.

Chapter Ten

Page	Line	
103	7	Brock, *The Dark Broad Seas*, p. 219.
103	19	Ibid., pp. 219-20.
104	40	Ibid., p. 239.
105	4	Thor Thorgrimsson and E. C. Russell, *Canadian Naval Operations in Korean Waters, 1950-1955*, p. 32.
105	20	Ibid., p. 35.
105	31	Ibid., p. 41.
107	31	Thorgrimsson and Russell, *Canadian Naval Operations*, p. 111.
108	32	*Life*, January 28, 1952.
108	41	Robert Crichton, *The Great Impostor*, p. 125.
110	17	Thorgrimsson and Russell, *Canadian Naval Operations*, p. 64.
111	12	Ibid., p. 69.
111	43	Public Archives Canada, RG 24, Vol. 8292.

Chapter Eleven

Page	Line	
114	19	*The Roundel*, December 1954.

Page	Line	
115	35	Samuel Kostenuk and John Griffin, *RCAF: Squadron Histories and Aircraft, 1924-1968*, p. 232.
116	16	Goulden, *Korea: The Untold Story*, p. 303.
120	2	Brian Nolan, *Hero: The Buzz Beurling Story*, p. 99.

Chapter Twelve

| 128 | 27 | *Weekend Magazine*, Vol. 5, No. 8, 1955. |
| 128 | 43 | *Weekend Magazine*, Vol. 5. No. 9, 1955. |

Chapter Thirteen

148	11	James Michener, *The Bridges at Toko-ri*, p. 3.
148	16	René Cutforth, *Korean Reporter*, pp. 4-5.
148	27	W. L. White, *Back Down the Ridge*, pp. 93-4.
149	30	Ibid., p. 95.
150	9	Ibid., p. 93.

Chapter Fourteen

156	23	Goulden, *Korea: The Untold Story*, p. 596.
157	39	Mark W. Clark, *From the Danube to the Yalu*, pp. 226-7.
158	4	Wood, *Strange Battleground*, p. 193.
158	15	Ibid., p. 195.
158	18	Pearson, *Mike*, p. 157.
158	23	Ibid.
159	3	Goulden, *Korea: The Untold Story*, p. 599.
160	33	Admiral C. Turner Joy, *How Communists Negotiate*, p. 14.
161	11	Letter to the author, Sept. 22, 1981.

Chapter Fifteen

| 168 | 27 | Wood, *Strange Battleground*, p. 243. |
| 176 | 10 | Stephen Endicott, *James G. Endicott: Rebel Out of China*, p. 298. |

BIBLIOGRAPHY

Anderson, Jack, and Boyd, James. *Confessions of a Muckraker.* New York: Random House, 1979.

Brock, Jeffry V. *Memoirs of a Sailor: The Dark Broad Seas.* Vol. 1: *With Many Voices.* Toronto: McClelland and Stewart, 1981.

Clark, Mark W. *From the Danube to the Yalu.* New York: Harper and Brothers, 1954.

Condon, Richard. *The Manchurian Candidate.* New York: Dell, 1959.

Creighton, Donald. *The Forked Road: Canada 1939-1957.* Toronto: McClelland and Stewart, 1976.

Crichton, Robert. *The Great Impostor.* New York: Random House, 1959.

Cutforth, René. *Korean Reporter.* London: Allan Wingate, 1952.

Detzer, David. *Thunder of the Captains: The Short Summer in 1950.* New York: Thomas Y. Crowell, 1977.

Diefenbaker, John G. *One Canada: Memoirs of the Right Honourable John G. Diefenbaker.* Vol. 1: *The Crusading Years, 1895-1956.* Toronto: Macmillan of Canada, 1975.

Eayrs, James. *In Defence of Canada: Peacemaking and Deterrence.* Toronto: University of Toronto Press, 1972.

Eden, Sir Anthony. *The Memoirs of Sir Anthony Eden: Full Circle.* London: Cassell, 1960.

Endicott, Stephen. *James G. Endicott: Rebel Out of China.* Toronto: University of Toronto Press, 1980.

Facts About Korea. Seoul: Korean Overseas Information Service, 1981.

Fraser, Blair. *The Search for Identity: Canada: Postwar to Present.* Toronto: Doubleday, 1967.

Goulden, Joseph C. *Korea: The Untold Story of the War.* New York: Times Books, 1982.

Granatstein, J. L., and Hitsman, J. M. *Broken Promises: A History of Conscription in Canada.* Toronto: Oxford University Press, 1977.

Guttmann, Allen, ed. *Korea and the Theory of Limited War.* Lexington, Massachusetts: D. C. Heath, 1967.

Hammel, Eric M. *Chosin: Heroic Ordeal of the Korean War.* New York: The Vanguard Press, 1981.

Handbook of Korea, A. Seoul: Korean Overseas Information Service, 1981.

Higgins, Marguerite. *War in Korea: The Report of a Woman Combat Correspondent.* New York: Doubleday, 1951.

Historical Section; General Staff. *Canada's Army in Korea: The United Nations Operations, 1950-53, and Their Aftermath.* Ottawa: Queen's Printer, 1956.

Jackson, Robert. *Air War Over Korea.* London: Ian Allan, 1973.

Johnson, Air Vice-Marshal J. E. *Full Circle: The Story of Air Fighting.* London: Chatto and Windus, 1964.

Joy, Admiral C. Turner. *How Communists Negotiate.* New York: Macmillan, 1955.

Keith, Ronald A. *Bush Pilot With a Briefcase: The Happy-go-lucky Story of Grant McConachie.* Don Mills: Paperjacks, 1972.

Kim, H. Edward. *Korea: Beyond the Hills.* New York: Kodansha International, 1980.

Kim, Chum-kon. *The Korean War, 1950-53.* Seoul: Kwangmyong, 1973.

Kim Il Sung. *Selected Works.* Pyongyang: Foreign Languages Publishing House, 1971.

King, O. H. P. *Tail of the Paper Tiger.* Caldwell, Ohio: The Caxton Printers, 1961.

Knightley, Phillip. *The First Casualty: From the Crimea to Vietnam: The War Correspondent as Hero, Propagandist, and Myth Maker.* New York: Harcourt Brace Jovanovich, 1975.

Kostenuk, Samuel, and Griffin, John. *RCAF: Squadron Histories and Aircraft, 1924-1968.* Toronto: Samuel Stevens Hakkert, 1977.

Leckie, Robert. *Conflict: The History of the Korean War, 1950-53.* New York: G. P. Putnam's Sons, 1962.

MacKay, R. A., ed. *Canadian Foreign Policy 1945-54: Selected Speeches and Documents.* Toronto: McClelland and Stewart, 1970.

McKeown, Captain Michael G. "Kapyong Remembered: Anecdotes from Korea." Paper prepared for Kapyong 25th Anniversary reunion at Winnipeg, 1976.

Manchester, William. *American Caesar: Douglas MacArthur 1880-1964.* New York: Dell, 1978.

Martin, Lawrence. *The Presidents and the Prime Ministers.* Toronto: Doubleday, 1982.

Michener, James A. *The Bridges at Toko-ri.* New York: Bantam, 1953.

Miller, Merle. *Plain Speaking: An Oral Biography of Harry S. Truman.* New York: Berkeley, 1973.

Nicholson, Colonel G. W. L. *The Gunners of Canada: The History of the Royal Regiment of Canadian Artillery.* Vol. II: 1919-1967. Toronto: McClelland and Stewart, 1972.

Nolan, Brian. *Hero: The Buzz Beurling Story.* Markham: Penguin, 1982.

O'Ballance, Edgar. *Korea: 1950-1953.* London: Faber and Faber, 1969.

Oliver, Robert T. *Why War Came in Korea.* New York: Fordham University Press, 1950.

Pearson, Lester B. *Mike: The Memoirs of the Right Honourable Lester B. Pearson.* Vol. 2: 1948-1957. Toronto: University of Toronto Press, 1973.

Pickersgill, J. W. *My Years with Louis St. Laurent: A Political Memoir.* Toronto: University of Toronto Press, 1975.

Rees, David. *Korea: The Limited War.* London: Macmillan, 1964.

Ridgway, Matthew B. *The Korean War.* New York: Doubleday, 1967.

Robbins, Charles. *Last of His Kind: An Informal Portrait of Harry S. Truman.* New York: William Morrow, 1979.

Rockingham, Major-General John M. "Recollections of Korea," Mimeographed, 1975.

Schurmann, Franz, and Schell, Orville, eds. *Communist China: Revolutionary Reconstruction and International Confrontation, 1949 to the Present.* New York: Vintage, 1967.

Sealey, D. Bruce, and Van de Vyvere, Peter. *Thomas George Prince*. Winnipeg: Peguis, 1981.

Smith, Robert. *MacArthur in Korea: The Naked Emperor*. New York: Simon and Schuster, 1982.

Stanley, George F. G. *Canada's Soldiers: The Military History of an Unmilitary People*. Rev. ed. Toronto: Macmillan of Canada, 1960.

Stevens, G. R. *Princess Patricia's Canadian Light Infantry: 1919-1957*. Vol. 3. Griesbach, Alberta: Historical Committee of the Regiment. n.d.

————. *The Royal Canadian Regiment*. London, Ontario: London Printing and Lithographing, 1967.

Thorgrimsson, Thor, and Russell, E. C. *Canadian Naval Operations in Korean Waters, 1950-1955*. Ottawa: The Naval Historical Section, 1965.

Truman, Harry S. *Memoirs by Harry S. Truman*. Vol. 2: *Years of Trial and Hope*. New York: Signet, 1965.

Truman, Margaret. *Harry S. Truman*. New York: Pocket Books, 1974.

Underwood, Horace H. *Tragedy and Faith in Korea*. New York: Friendship Press, 1951.

War History Compilation Committee. *The History of the United Nations Forces in the Korean War*. Seoul: The Ministry of National Defence, the Republic of Korea, 1973.

White, Theodore H. *In Search of History*. New York: Warner Books, 1978.

White, W. L. *Back Down the Ridge*. New York: Harcourt, Brace, 1953.

Wood, Lieutenant-Colonel Herbert Fairlie. *Strange Battleground: The Operations in Korea and Their Effects on the Defence Policy of Canada*. Ottawa: Queen's Printer, 1966.

INDEX